WITHDRAWN
UTSA LIBRARIES

Reprints of Economic Classics

GENERAL REPORT
ON
ENCLOSURES

Also in

REPRINTS OF ECONOMIC CLASSICS

By ARTHUR YOUNG

The Autobiography of Arthur Young [1898]

The Farmer's Tour Through the East of England [1771]

General View of the Agriculture of the County of Norfolk [1804]

Political Arithmetic [1771]

Political Essays Concerning the Present State of the British Empire [1772]

A Six Months Tour Through the North of England [1771]

A Tour in Ireland [1892]

[ARTHUR YOUNG]

GENERAL REPORT

ON

ENCLOSURES

DRAWN UP BY ORDER OF

THE BOARD OF AGRICULTURE

WITH AN INTRODUCTION BY

SIR JOHN SINCLAIR

[1808]

REPRINTS OF ECONOMIC CLASSICS

AUGUSTUS M. KELLEY · PUBLISHERS

NEW YORK 1971

First Edition 1808

(London: *Printed by* B. Macmillan, *Bow Street, Covent Garden*, 1808)

Reprinted 1971 by
AUGUSTUS M. KELLEY · PUBLISHERS
REPRINTS OF ECONOMIC CLASSICS
New York   New York   10001

I S B N   0 678 00702 0
L C N   72 120417

PRINTED IN THE UNITED STATES OF AMERICA
by SENTRY PRESS, NEW YORK, N. Y. 10019

GENERAL REPORT

ON

ENCLOSURES.

DRAWN UP BY ORDER OF
THE BOARD OF AGRICULTURE.

LONDON:

PRINTED BY B. McMILLAN, BOW STREET, COVENT GARDEN,
PRINTER TO HIS ROYAL HIGHNESS THE PRINCE OF WALES.

1808.

INTRODUCTORY OBSERVATIONS,

POINTING OUT SOME ADDITIONAL MEASURES, SUBMITTED TO THE CONSIDERATION OF THE BOARD OF AGRICULTURE.

BY SIR JOHN SINCLAIR, BART.

PRESIDENT OF THE BOARD.

NUMEROUS are the institutions, which, in this, and in many other countries, have been constituted, *for the purpose of collecting information*, regarding various branches of human knowledge; but the BOARD of AGRICULTURE, it is believed, is the first, either established by private individuals, or sanctioned by public authority, with a view, not only of collecting, *but of digesting the knowledge it has collected,* and of forming it into a regular system for the general benefit of the public.

It is not to be wondered at, that such an attempt should not hitherto have been made, considering the great time, labour, and expense, which such an undertaking requires, if it is intended to be executed in a proper manner. For instance, before it was possible to give a just view of the agricultural state of Great Britain, it was necessary to have repeated Surveys of the different Counties,

INTRODUCTORY OBSERVATIONS.

Counties, with funds very inadequate to such an attempt. From these Surveys, which are at last on the eve of being completed, it is now proposed to draw up, under distinct heads, as Enclosures, Implements, Management of Grass Lands, Cattle, Sheep, &c. the result of the whole inquiry. Nay, after a report on any given subject, is prepared by some individual conversant in that particular department, it is indispensably necessary, to submit his observations, in a printed state, to the examination of as many intelligent persons as possible, before a paper can ultimately be drawn up, in as complete a shape, and in every respect as perfect, as may be expected, if such a plan is judiciously carried into effect.

The BOARD of AGRICULTURE having now carried on its inquiries for several years, it seemed to be full time, that a specimen should be prepared of *condensed information*, regarding some important branch of Agriculture; and the subject of Enclosures was proposed, as one of peculiar importance, to which the attention of the public had been often directed; respecting the advantage of which, a variety of opinions had been entertained; and a subject which, if the BOARD could fully elucidate, would alone amply repay all the expenses which have been bestowed upon it. These sentiments having been approved of by the BOARD, the following Paper was prepared by a very intelligent Agriculturist, who seems to have done

done ample justice to the plan above suggested. What then may not be expected, when such a work undergoes the critical examination of a number of able men, who will be rewarded*, in proportion to the value of the additional information transmitted by them. In the course of next year, it is to be hoped, that the result of the whole, will be laid before His Majesty, and both Houses of Parliament, and communicated to the public at large. Such a paper, formed with so much care and attention, ought to be considered as a species of Code, or Standard, regarding all points connected with Enclosure; and indeed must set almost every question regarding it at rest. When one subject is thus gone through, other branches connected with Agriculture, will, from time to time, be explained, in a similar manner, and with equal care.

It will then appear, how essential it is for the public prosperity, to have all the information which a great nation can furnish, regarding any branch of useful inquiry, first collected, and then digested into a regular system, so as to be easily accessible to all those, to whom the acquisition of such knowledge may be desirable.

Is it possible for the public money to be better bestowed, than in promoting such institutions,

---

* For the Premiums offered, see the Paper annexed to this Introduction.

and

and effecting objects so essential for the general interest? The foundation of national prosperity must rest, *on the knowledge possessed by individuals, of Agriculture, and all the other useful arts;* and where, by public encouragement, that knowledge is in a double ratio extensively spread, a country must be doubly prosperous. Much, for that purpose, has been already effected by the exertions of the BOARD of AGRICULTURE, in the great department over which it presides; but if the measures above recommended, were completed; if the principles of every branch connected with Husbandry, were thoroughly explained, and digested; and if, by judicious laws, all the most material obstacles to the improvement of the country, were removed; and if, in particular cases, even encouragement were given to promote great and useful exertions; THE PROSPERITY OF THE BRITISH EMPIRE, WOULD INCREASE WITH A RAPIDITY, BEYOND ALL FORMER EXAMPLE, AND EVEN OUR PRESENT HEAVY BURDENS, WOULD SCARCELY BE FELT.

JOHN SINCLAIR.

Board of Agriculture,
1st August, 1807.

PREMIUMS.

PREMIUMS.

AS it is conceived by the Board, that a general knowledge of the advantages which have attended Enclosures, and of the means by which those benefits have accrued to the Public, will be found conducive to produce a continuance and enlargement of such operations; and as the Board circulates this Report merely for the acquisition of further information, it will give—

To the person who shall transmit to the President, the most valuable Additions, Explanations, and Illustrations, to this Memoir, founded on his own experience—*A piece of Plate, value Fifty Pounds, with a suitable Inscription.*

To the person who shall transmit the Additions, &c. next in value—*A piece of Plate, value Thirty Pounds.*

The Board does not limit the rewards to these cases, but will vote some remuneration to Correspondents who transmit information really valuable.

N. B. The Board, in all cases, reserves to itself, the power of withholding the whole or any part of their Premiums, if the Communications are not of merit to deserve them.

The Reports to be returned to the Board on or before the 1st of January, 1809; and it is essentially necessary that the Claimants should observe, that they do not sign their Names, but that they put a private mark, or motto, on their Reports, with a letter sealed, containing their Names enclosed.

CONTENTS.

Chap. I. Of the Lands which are the Objects of the Measure.

PAGE

Sect. I. Of Waste Lands, ... 1
 § I. Extent of the Waste Lands, ... 2
 § II. The present State and Value of the Waste Lands, 3
 § III. The Benefits that result from Enclosing Waste Lands, } 8
 § IV. The Progress that has been made under the present System, } 22
 § V. Why do many Tracts remain Waste, after Acts have passed for their Enclosure? } 23

Sect. II. Of Open Field Arable, ... 25
 § I. Extent of the remaining Open Arable Fields, .. 29
 § II. Present State and Value of such Open Arable Fields, } 30
 § III. The Benefits that have resulted from Enclosing Open Arable Fields, } 30

Sect. III. General Result of the Acts which have hitherto passed, } 46

Sect. IV. Of small Commons and old Enclosed Countries, 49

Sect. V. Of the Royal Forests, ... 50

Chap. II. Of the Legislative and Legal Means of Enclosing, } 52

Sect. I. By Act of Parliament, ... 55
 § I. Of the Rights that must be commuted, ... 56
 § II. Power of Commissioners, ... 61

SECT.

CONTENTS.

	PAGE
SECT. II. By Agreement,	65
SECT. III. By Individuals,	71

CHAP. III. Execution of the Work, — 72

SECT. I. Of the Survey,	73
SECT. II. Of the Valuation,	76
SECT. III. Allotments,	79
SECT. IV. Award,	80
SECT. V. Fences,	81
§ I. Arrangement of the Fields according to Soil,	81
§ II. Of the Size of Fields,	82
§ III. Of Enclosing without Subdivisions,	85
§ IV. Position of the Fences,	88
§ V. Of the sort of Fence,	89
SECT. VI. Roads, Bridges, &c.	90
SECT. VII. Drainage and Irrigation,	92
SECT. VIII. Expenses,	97

CHAP. IV. Produce of the Kingdom insufficient for its Consumption, — 100

CHAP. V. Necessity of a General Enclosure, 111

§ I. Of the Progress that has hitherto been made towards attaining a General Enclosure Act, — 112

APPENDIX.

No. I. From the Report of the Committee of the Board of Agriculture, — 137

General View of the Amount of Waste Lands in the Kingdom of Great Britain, — 139

No. II. Acres in the Counties of England, as detailed in the Returns to Parliament of the Poor-Rates, drawn up under the inspection of the Right Hon. George Rose, — 142

No. III.

CONTENTS.

			PAGE
No. III.	Wastes,		144
No. IV.	Effect on the Poor, of the Enclosures which took place during the first forty years of His present Majesty,		150
No. V.	Cottagers' Land,		164
No. VI.	Commons Enclosed,		171
No. VII.	Wastes Enclosed, in the first forty years of His present Majesty,		184
No. VIII.	Extent of the remaining Open Arable Fields,		210
No. IX.	Advantage to Landlords by Enclosing,		211
No. X.	Tithe,		223
No. XI.	Culture of Wheat,		229
No. XII.	Barley, Oats, Pulse, &c.		253
No. XIII.	Calculation of Benefit by Enclosing,		286
No. XIV.	Enclosing Acts,		290
No. XV.	Enclosure of small Commons,		300
No. XVI.	Fences,		308
No. XVII.	Expenses of Enclosures,		321
No. XVIII.	Corn,		335
No. XIX.	General Enclosure,		378

GENERAL REPORT

ON

ENCLOSURES.

CHAP. I.

OF THE LANDS WHICH ARE THE OBJECTS OF THE MEASURE.

THESE may be arranged in the following manner:

I. Of Waste Lands.
II. Of Open-field Arable.
III. Of small Commons in Enclosed Countries.
IV. Of Royal Forests.

SECTION I.

OF WASTE LANDS.

In order that the Board may the better comprehend, without the trouble of searching, the various documents which

which their attention has accumulated, it will be proper to distribute this subject under the following heads:

I. The Extent of the Wastes.

II. Their present State and Value.

III. The Benefits that will result from enclosing them.

IV. The progress that has been made under the present System.

§ I.—*Extent of the Waste Lands.*

It cannot be asserted that the documents collected by the Board, are sufficient to ascertain this with accuracy; but they certainly approach nearer to it, than any authorities that were in the possession of the public before the establishment of that Institution. Actual Surveys can alone yield complete satisfaction. As such have never been made, nor any probability of being ordered, the approximations to truth which have been effected, derive a value which, in more favourable circumstances, would not attach to them.

Considerable attention was paid to this subject by the Committee to whom the Board referred it in 1795. By examining the County Reports, from general information, and from the measurement in certain maps, they drew up an account, which is preserved in the Appendix (No. I.) By this it appears, that the number of acres were then,

In England,	6,259,470
Wales,	1,629,307
Scotland,	14,218,224
Total,	22,107,001

In order to examine how far these quantities are consistent with the late estimates of the general contents of the kingdom, compared with the former supposed total, the contents of the counties must be compared. This comparison is detailed in the Appendix (No. II.); and thence it appears, that by the late accounts depended on by Mr. ROSE, the total acres are, 37,334,400; and by the Reports returned to the Board, the amount was 37,909,455.

§ II.—*The present State and Value of the Waste Lands.*

It is not an easy undertaking, to endeavour to ascertain the value of an object which in some cases has no value at all, and in others, must be arranged as minus, in inquiries relating to profit. Authorities that pronounce common pastures to be of a value too contemptible for estimate, are numerous; and although this assertion, like many general ones on such subjects, is in some cases certainly carried too far, yet all who have attended to the stock and feeding of commons, must well know, that where advantage is most likely to accrue, the circumstances are so unfavourable, as much to lessen those benefits which would otherwise result. Where sheep are the stock, and the soil liable to rot, the loss by them has, in many cases, been felt severely. Still however, on the whole, they have certainly produced something.

" From the Westmoreland Report it appears, on the most unquestionable authority, that the liberty of keeping ten sheep for a whole year, may be hired for sixpence;

and

and as it is supposed to require six acres to maintain that number of sheep, the rent of such land, therefore, is only one penny per acre, and the price of the fee-simple of it, at twenty-four years purchase, two shillings. In Wales, where the commons are probably better, fourpence per head, per ann. is the rate of keeping a sheep on such ground, and other cattle in proportion. In many parts of the kingdom, however, it would appear, from several of the Reports transmitted to the Board, that many decline availing themselves of such a privilege, finding that it does not, on a fair calculation, pay even common interest for the capital employed.

" The following case (asserted by the late Mr. BAKEWELL), puts in the strongest point of view, that even a loss may be sustained by commonage. Let one man put a cow of any value upon a common, who has a right to do so for nothing, any time in spring, and let another give a farmer 1s. 6d. a week for the keep of his cow in an enclosure, both being of the same value when first turned out; if both are driven to market at Michaelmas, the difference of price will do more than repay the expence of the keep, without making any allowance for the additional quantity of milk which the cow kept in an enclosure must yield. In regard to sheep, if they are of a valuable sort, the profit of hiring land almost at any rent, instead of putting them on a common for nothing, is still greater. And the enormous losses sustained by that species of stock, when the rot, or any infectious disorder get into a neglected flock, can hardly be calculated. Can there then be stronger arguments in favour of giving every possible assistance and facility to the improvement of our waste lands? which at present are, in many cases, a real loss to the community, and a prejudice to those who might be supposed to derive some benefit from them, but which,

which, if improved, might add millions to the national wealth, and furnish the means of occupation and subsistence to millions of additional subjects*."

Are commons, then, in their present situation, of any value; or rather, are not they, in general, hurtful to the nation, and also to most part of their proprietors?—This question naturally arises out of the following observation.

Where an enclosure of the wastes has taken place, it is found that the old enclosures, or the ancient estates in the lordship or parish, do not diminish in value; but rather increase after the commons are severed from them; and that districts which have no common lands, lett higher, are better cultivated, and the people more industrious. Should this be found to be the case in general, is it not a very strong and convincing argument for a general enclosure†?

Even to cottagers who have been supposed to reap much benefit, Mr. BILLINGSLEY contends that commons are useless.

" Upland commons are principally depastured in the summer with sheep; and if a cottager were able to stock ever so largely, the winter keeping, and his total inability to furnish them with food between the 5th of April and 12th of May (before which times the commons ought not to be stocked), would be such a drawback, as effectually to exclude every idea of profit.

" On the moors, cottagers within a moderate distance from the common generally turn out a cow or two, perhaps a few geese, and I believe the latter are the only profitable stock. Not one in ten rent land to raise winter subsistence. In summer, the moor commons are fre-

---

* Report on Waste Lands, p. 8.
† Annals, vol. vi. p. 284.

quently inundated; the cattle must be removed, and temporary pasture hired on extravagant terms. On the other hand, should the season be favourable, the redundancy of stock, from an unlimited right of feeding, by reducing the produce of the cottager's cow so much below what it ought to be, deprives him of every real advantage.

"Proprietors or occupiers of large estates, in the vicinity of a common, by turning out great quantities of stock by day, and taking them home to feed by night, have derived the only benefit which an over-fed common could afford.

"The cattle of the cottager, as well as of the distant commoner, under this competition, must unavoidably suffer. The latter may be recruited by occasional removal to better pasturage : the former, having none, must hire, or leave them on the common either in a stunted or starved condition. These are facts of general notoriety, on which it will not be easy to deduce *(communibus annis)* any material benefit to the cottager from stocking; but when the expense of winter support is added, the question is decided, and the presumed advantage is converted into a positive loss.

"For ten or twelve shillings per annum a common-right might be rented. Nothing gives, with greater accuracy, the value of a thing, than fair and unrestrained competition : if so, when the privilege of stocking a common for a year might be obtained for ten or twelve shillings, by a farmer possessed of means to accommodate stocking to every variety of season, what can the value be to a cottager deprived of these? Instead of ten or twelve shillings, the annual nett value of common-rights enclosed, have been from three pounds to twenty pounds per ann.; which, as an unquestionable fact, establishes, without
scruple

scruple or hesitation, the private as well as public importance of the enclosing system.

" Most of the stocking cottagers have rights appendant to the cottages without land, under the denomination of auster tenements. To these, allotments are made, equal in quantity and quality, as to farms of the greatest extent. Here the cottage claimant, by relinquishing a privilege injurious rather than lucrative, is placed in a better situation than the proprietor of an extensive farm, who surrenders every advantage of stocking which capital, situation, and convenience give him, for an equality of allotment with the former, who has no sacrifice to make, but ignorance and prejudice, and who derives from his allotment a clear undiminished profit.

" This description is by no means exaggerated. The parish of Wedmore, which abounded with cottage commons, and one of the largest and most opulent in Somersetshire, will illustrate the value of commons. Within twenty years there have been enclosed upwards of 3000 acres of rich moor land, heretofore, when in commons, rendered unproductive by inundations and their consequences, six or seven months in the year; and when pasturable for the remaining months, of little value, from being overstocked; which land is now set, with liberal allowance of profit to the occupier, from 30 to 60$s.$ per acre. These enclosures are made by ditches, which by annual cleansing, and spreading the contents over the surface, afford an excellent manure, with a new and extensive source of labour, of the most productive kind; whereby the poor's-rate has been reduced, or at least has not exceeded its former amount, before any enclosure had taken place."

That these are important facts cannot be denied; and they tend very strongly to prove, that the value derived

from

from feeding commons must be estimated at a very low rate.

What proportion of the twenty-two millions of waste acres is to be considered as impossible to cultivate, except by planting, there are no documents which will enable us to ascertain; and especially as planting, which is so generally applicable, must be considered as a very beneficial purpose to which to apply the greater part of such lands.

In the Appendix (No. III.) are some notes relative to certain wastes, which it is presumed will shew the importance of cultivating them.

§ III. — *The Benefits that result from Enclosing Waste Lands.*

This is a subject which can detain a reader but a short time. Where the value while in common is so low, that many good judges have questioned whether all the commons in the kingdom are worth a groat to the public, the enclosure, division, and cultivation of them in any degree, must be a great advantage indeed*. The Board possesses ample proofs of this fact, from which a very cursory selection will leave not the slightest doubt. As the subject, however, should be clearly understood in all its bearings, and the degree of the merit of these measures ascertained, even where most decisive, it will be necessary to examine this result in relation to,

---

* To the public: for it is of advantage to the public to vest money in bringing land to produce, which did not produce before; yet not of advantage to an individual, unless he gets a return of five per cent. on money laid out.—*G. O. P.*

1. The

1. The Farmer.
2. The Landlord.
3. The Poor.
4. The Church; and,
5. The Public.

All these are interested in the measure.

1.—THE FARMER*.

There have been cases in which one or two great farmers, whose lands were conveniently situated adjoining a large, dry, and valuable common, who might possibly make a greater profit by sweeping off the food, and starving all other stock, by flocks of folding wethers, than such few individuals could receive from the share afterwards allotted to their farms; but as such benefit was always gained by an equal degree of loss to every one beside, it in no case merited the smallest attention, however clamorous such individuals might be against the enclosures. These cases also are rare, and demand no more than admitting the possibility of their existence. In all others, the division is absolutely beneficial, and even singularly so; for the farmers who in consequence of an enclosure act, receive the addition of allotments, cultivate them without adding to their capitals, perhaps not to their teams, and scarcely to their trouble or attention; the benefit is pure, and unmixed with any drawback, giving them a larger profit than that proportion of advantage which they derived from their original farms. The benefit to this class, therefore, cannot admit of any doubt.

---

* The interest of a farmer sinks in that of the landlord; unless is meant the farmer on long lease, to whose case this argument is good. He has a substantive interest at the moment of enclosure.—G. O. P.

" The

"The advantages arising from enclosing of commons, in respect to the improvement of stock, is obvious: while in a state of common, every one turns on what he pleases, and there is generally double the quantity of stock that there ought to be. The consequence is, they make no improvement; they barely exist; the yearly profits how small! Should an enlightened breeder wish to improve his sheep, how is he to effect it, while his ewes mix promiscuously with his neighbours' flocks? If he had the best tup in the kingdom, can he be sure that one of his ewes would be tupped by him, while there are probably not less than half a score of his neighbours to contest the female with him? On the other hand, if the common were enclosed, every one would stint with that species of stock for which his allotment was best adapted, and in such numbers as would ensure profit. When he can confine his ewes within his own enclosure, he can make whatever experiments he pleases, by putting a few, or many ewes, to any particular tup, without any fear or apprehension of having a spurious breed, by the interference of his neighbours: he is also enabled to keep his flock from many disorders: few commons, but have some tracts of land liable to the rot: how are they to be prevented from depasturing upon it? or if the scab, or other infectious disorders, have taken place among any flock on the common, how is he to avoid it*?"

2.—*THE LANDLORD.*

The case of the landlord is dispatched in a moment; for in no case whatever can he be supposed to have derived one hundredth part of the benefit from commons,

---

* Cumberland Report, p. 186.

which their enclosure gives him, by subjecting his portion to a rent per acre, proportionably to the benefit derived by the farmer. If he received any thing from the common by means of plantations, it must have been by enclosure under certain acts, and therefore is excluded from this consideration.

I do not, however, mean to assert, that landlords have in all cases profited: exceptions there certainly are; and it has been very properly observed, that " cases may be shewn, where the landlords have not received five per cent. on the enclosure of the best land; from extreme cost of commission, solicitor, contest, and enclosure*."

The Bishop of LANDAFF calculates, that a barren estate consisting of one thousand acres, though placed in a high and bleak situation, may be improved by plantation from 4*l*. 3*s*. 4*d*. to 400*l*. per annum, or 8*s*. per acre, reckoning the value of a reversion at a present certainty, and stating the interest of money only at 4*l*. per cent. In other places, however, more favourable to the growth of trees, the profit is estimated much higher. In the Hampshire Report, in particular, p. 30, it is stated by two very experienced nurserymen, that even poor land, when planted, will produce at the end of twenty-five years, at least 100*l*. of value in timber and fire-wood. In Scotland, Dr. ROBERTSON states the profit at 6*s*. per acre. Perth Report, p. 107.—The Bishop seems to have hit on a just and proper medium, applicable as an average to the whole kingdom†.

It may be observed here, that landlords have not, in many cases of waste commons, profited by applications to parliament, possibly for want of knowing that acts have passed for the sale, or letting of waste commons, and for

---

* Sir G. O. Paul. † Report on Waste Lands, p. 17.

applying

applying the profits thereof in aid of the poor-rates, and this without the appointment or expense of commissioners; by vesting such commission in trustees, and selling enough of the land to pay for the act

See the printed act for Colton, in Staffordshire.

3.—THE POOR.

The benefit in this case is by no means unmixed, and therefore demands a more careful examination: general assertions are of very little value, and especially when they come from persons directly interested in the measure. Many arguments have been framed, as well as assertions advanced, to prove that enclosing commons has been *universally* beneficial to the poor; but as this is directly in the teeth of their own feelings and positive assertions, as well as of those of many other most respectable eye-witnesses;— as the amount of the evil, if it exists at all, can never prove a reason against enclosing, but at most, call merely for a more tender attention to their interest, these papers would be very incomplete, if the question was not fairly examined. The national benefits of enclosing are much too great and decided, to want the smallest concealment in any point.

In the year 1800 a journey was made of above 1600 miles, in which the effect of enclosing, on the spot where the enclosures had taken place, was examined, without trusting to the reports of the poor only, but of the clergy, farmers, and even commissioners who had been employed; and it appeared, that in many cases the poor had unquestionably been injured. In some cases, many cows had been kept without a legal right, and nothing given for the *practice*. In other cases, where allotments were assigned, the cottagers

tagers could not pay the expense of the measure, and were forced to sell their allotments*. In others, they kept cows by right of hiring their cottages, or common rights, and the land going of course to the proprietor, was added to the farms, and the poor sold their cows: this is a very common case. The causes were in this manner various, but the result the same. The Board will observe that these injuries, *in fact*, though not in *legal right*, are not mentioned to shew that such enclosures should not have taken place; nor to assert that an increase of regular employment by the cultivation of the farmers might not more than make amends for them, which is another question, but to state the facts really as they are. In the Appendix (No. IV.) the cases are detailed, and there are added counter instances of enclosures, which have *increased* the cows of the poor, and thereby added greatly to their well being, their comfort, their morals, and their industry. No reflection attaches to the general measure of enclosing, but a call is afforded to give that attention to the interests of the cottagers, which has been very successfully paid in various instances.

In December of the same year (1800), a Committee of the House of Commons sat on the high price of provisions; the Right Hon. DUDLEY RYDER in the chair. By their orders, letters were sent to the ministers of the 1845 parishes and places that had been enclosed during the first forty years of his present Majesty. The object was, to ascertain the increase or decrease of the culture of wheat; but the clergy, in their answers (1384 in number), adverted to various other circumstances; and a few of them to this point—of the effect of the

---

* The great loss of the poor is the loss of fuel, where long custom has prevailed. (Appendix, No. IV.)

enclosures on the interests of the poor. In twenty-nine cases out of thirty-one noted, the poor, in the opinion of the ministers, were sufferers by losing their cows, and other stock. (Appendix, No. IV.) There does not appear to be any thing done illegally in any of these cases: in some instances, the poor had no legal right to keep stock* on the commons; and in others, allotments were assigned them; but as they were unable to be at the expense of the enclosure, it forced them not only to sell their cows, but their houses also. This is a very *hard* case, though a legal one; and as instances are not wanting of a much more humane conduct, it is to be lamented that the same motives did not operate in all.

Relative to the interests of the poor, in enclosing commons and waste lands, it is scarcely possible to have the subject fully before the Board, without referring to a subject which early in the institution obtained much attention, first brought forward in a paper " On the Utility of Cottagers renting Grass Land, by the Earl of WINCHILSEA;" and since very satisfactorily examined and exemplified in the detail of various other cases that have at different times been brought before the Board. These are very numerous, under very different circumstances, distant from each other, and uniform in only one point,—that of the incomparable effects which have attended the system.

This consists in permitting the labouring poor to rent land enough for the due support in winter as well as in summer, of one or more cows, according as they are able to procure them. The humanity of such a measure is a very strong recommendation; but in a general system, such a motive must be sunk, as too weak to expect any

---

* These are all cases which the Lawyers term Usurpation.

general operation. The grand object is the reduction of poor-rates; a burden which has of late years proceeded with so rapid an increase, as to threaten very heavy evils to the landed interest. The effect of the poor possessing property in cattle, and occupying land to feed them, has been so powerful a spur to industry and sobriety, as to have taken them entirely from the parish; insomuch, that wherever the plan has been carried into execution, the poor-rates are as low as they can be, and exist chiefly for objects with which the poor have little concern; and what shews the power of this motive to carefulness in a manner which ought to leave no doubt on the mind of the reader, is the circumstance, that where the system was established, *there* poor rates did not rise on account of the scarcities; the poor thus favoured, receiving no more from the parish at those periods than in common times, that is to say, nothing! Strange it is, that this system has many enemies on the question of the theory; but that which has stood the test of practice, and through two severe scarcities, is no proper object for theory to work upon. Reasoning on such a point, is little better than impertinence. In the Appendix (No. V.) some facts are collected bearing on this point, and which will be sufficient to establish its wise and prudent policy.

The motive for my introducing the subject here, is the capital opportunity which is offered by bills for the enclosure of commons, to execute this measure to the greatest advantage; it demands no other attention than to preserve allotments which are made in consequence of cottage common-rights, inalienable from the cottages, and not to be occupied but with them. This has already been provided for in certain acts, particularly those of Northwold and Wilbraham (for fuel land), and provision might also be made against any persons born to such families ever becoming

coming chargeable to the parish. It is clear, that a proper attention to this system, when commons are enclosed, might be the means of doing away nineteen twentieths of those poor-rates so heavily complained of; and at the same time, prove the greatest blessing to the poor themselves, who are every where eagerly anxious to possess a cow.

Sir GEORGE O. PAUL, Bart. in a Letter to Sir JOHN SINCLAIR, printed but not published in 1796, has some observations on the interest of the poor in enclosures, so pointedly just, and so well and ably written, that it would be a deficiency in this inquiry not to quote the passage here.

" If the Bill, in treating of ' Wastes and Commons,' was understood exclusively to regard wastes whereon there were no other interests to be satisfied, but such as were represented by some *real* or *substantial* claim, whereby the extent of the pretension might be correctly measured and indemnified; no more would be requisite to justice, than to provide a mode for obtaining the positive valuation of the respective claims, and to determine on a common standard of relative valuation, whereby to proportion the correspondent allotment. From the title of the bill, I suppose wastes *under all possible circumstances* to be included; indeed, I do not conceive that any line *exclusive* and *inclusive* can be drawn: under its operation therefore (if it passes into law), numberless wastes will be brought into question, whereon a variety of popular usages have been immemorially exercised, which, if not regarded *in* the law, will remain to be hereafter encountered *by* it. By the printed Report of the Committee, and its Appendix, we are assured, ' That every possible attention to the rights of such commons would necessarily be paid;—that their rights *would be preserved*, or such ample compensation made, that their situation would, in every respect, be ameliorated.' Notwithstanding

withstanding this promising hope for such authority; notwithstanding the clauses of the bill designing to fulfil it; I am not yet convinced but that there exists a description of persons, who, in carrying this national benefit into execution, must be deprived of privileges and usages, which, with the best disposition of parliament, it will be found nearly impossible to satisfy in like kind. Although it should be proved by the correct calculator, that such privileges will not be intrinsically valuable in that improving state of society which we are supposing, yet they are dear to the feelings of the possessors, and so natural to their habits, that they will reluctantly commute them for greater benefits. Numerous are the people, who, generation after generation, pass their lives in the enjoyment of their privileges, and draw from them the whole of their miserable existence."

Again.—" Distress, in time of a high price of corn, and consequent dependence on parish relief and private bounty, will press on each individual poor man in proportion as he is more or less destitute of land to cultivate, to produce the food of his family.

" Without entering into the very doubtful question of the good or evil tendency of large farms, it may be admitted, without contest, that in proportion to the population, the number of those persons who cultivate at all for themselves is grievously diminished; of those who cultivate sufficient for the supply of their family, and *a little more*, the class is nearly annihilated.

" Insomuch as a man cultivates a portion of the earth for himself, he will be protected from the evil arising from the high price of its produce.—If he can produce at

---

* Observations on the General Enclosure Bill, by Sir G. O. PAUL, Bart. 1796, p. 21.

home

home a sufficiency in kind for his sustenance, it will be of no importance to him what may be the price required by those who cultivate for others. Including manufacturers, a general position might be excessive, but it is not so to say, that every *agricultural* labourer (having a family) ought to occupy, at least, a third of an acre of land to cultivate for *himself*, which, though not gratuitous, should be let to him at a rent at which the landlord should only not be a loser, he should be a gainer by the division; which is to say, that if land be worth a guinea per acre in a field of thirty acres, the cottager should pay seven shillings per acre for his third. This is not a new view of the law of England, though the statute which encouraged it is obsolete and repealed. It is time it should be revived, on a more enlightened principle than it was before imagined.

" An evil exists, and is, I believe, every year increasing in extent in every part of the kingdom, namely, the want of wholesome dwellings for the poor, at a rent within the reach of that portion of earnings, which the master of a family may be supposed to set aside for that purpose. There is little reason to expect that such buildings will ever again be provided, as heretofore, by the speculations of self-interest*."

The same able writer observes, " I do not think it necessary that a special allotment of land should be given in fee to a day-labourer, earning six shillings per week, who cannot pay for the common necessaries of life for a family. A man cannot look forward to future interests who is pressed by the calamity of the moment; the bur-

---

* " This may be considered as an instance in point, of the evil consequence to the day-labourer, of the general rise of wages of the body of artificers."

den of the gift to such a man, would be doubled to the grantors, because it must, of necessity, be enclosed at their expense, and the benefit would be reaped by the baker or the huckster of the village, who with a view to the acquisition, would encourage a credit which would devour the estate in a few months.

" The labouring or agricultural poor form a class of the community, which, in a political as well as moral view, peculiarly require the protection of the legislature. It is the class, the rate of whose wages must ultimately decide the commercial interest of the kingdom; it is the class by whose individual comforts the sum of the general comfort of the empire must be calculated. But, in regard to this useful and numerous part of the community, I maintain, that instead of giving bounties and benefactions which tend to make them idle and dependent, they should be enabled to supply their necessities, and derive their comforts, through the means of their own industry: I contend for them, that an equitable balance should be restored between the earnings of an industrious, sober, and willing labourer, and the cost of house rent and the necessary articles of sustenance and clothing for himself, and a family of average numbers. When the labourer has thus enabled himself by his earnings to pay money for the use of a house, I then look to the national polity to provide so that he may obtain a house for his money; such a house as shall screen him from the inclemency of the seasons, and enable him to arrange his family in some degree consistent with moral decency.

" I further should require, that appurtenant to the cottage so to be rented, he should occupy so much garden ground as should ease his expenditure in the immediate productions of the earth, and secure him from the severe

severe effects of an occasional high price of them. In this view the allotment of portions of land to cottages, where it can be done, though not an *immediate bounty* to the poor, is their *consequent benefit:* so considered, the utility is the same, whether the owner in fee be the lord of the village or the mason of it; but, in either case, whether you give a bounty or satisfy a claim, I submit to you the equity of correcting the proposed manner of discharging the cost of enclosing."—P. 49.

4.—*THE CHURCH.*

In the various publications which have appeared at different periods in defence of the rights of the church and in favour of tithes, I do not recollect one word tending to show that the enclosure of common pastures is, in any respect, against the interests of the clergy. The benefit is too palpable and decisive to bear a question. The only consideration which the topic affords, is how far such objects of enclosure should induce incumbents and others concerned for the interest of the church, in reason to mitigate those demands which have in various cases prevented enclosure taking place. Many are the instances in which all commutation for land has been rejected, and the proprietors forced to undertake the heavily expensive business without an exoneration from tithe: this has generally been the case in Norfolk, and to this circumstance is to be attributed the unenclosed state of the remaining numerous commons in that county. Such a conduct is decidedly against the interest of the church; for it prevents future enclosures, and all the benefit that would result from them.

Sir G. O. PAUL, Bart. has given some observations on this subject, which well deserve attention.

" In

" In regard to lands in common, which from their large extent, or intrinsic good quality, will offer sufficient advantages to the capitalist, if a general law should be complete to their purpose, the parties intending to enclose will undoubtedly proceed under it; but if the General Act be wanting in material powers, which by a special application to parliament may be obtained, they will not accept the saving you purpose to provide.

" Suppose, for instance, it is designed to enclose a common containing a thousand acres of land, worth 15*l.* per acre, will any body of men in their senses enter on the measure without making a previous agreement, and obtaining sufficient powers to commute the tithes, which may arise from it in consequence of cultivation; when by the additional expense of a few hundred pounds, they may establish such agreement before they embark their capital in the speculation*?"

Again—" I maintain that the property of tithe-owners of every description (whether present or expectant) ought to be guarded as fully as that of the owner of any other share of the land rent (perhaps there are some reasons why it should be more particularly guarded by law). I would not call on them for a sacrifice of any thing beyond a prejudice, and even that should be liberally compensated; but if there does exist a prejudice, and if the sacrifice of it be highly important to the national income; if the cause of the national church be interested in the good understanding between the pastor and his flock; at least, let the legislature help forward the complete reconciliation. You may be assured that, so far as the harmony of a parish is in question, if the one half of it be left open to the vexatious mode, whilst the other half is

---

* Observations, &c. by Sir G. O. PAUL, Bart. p. 13.

relieved,

relieved, the conciliatory intention will fail of effect; the irritation will not be corrected, but rather excited by the perpetual comparison."—P. 17.

5.—*THE PUBLIC.*

The objections which have hitherto been offered against the enclosure of commons, have been so weak and ill-founded, as not to merit any particular attention, when urged as motives to prevent the attempt. At all events, the public must be benefited; to convert tracts really or nearly waste, into profitable farms; to change ling for turnips; gorse for barley; and overstocked and rotting grass lands to wheat, and every other useful production, is a real acquisition of territory, pregnant with every advantage attending the husbandry of the kingdom; food, population, wealth and strength.

Clearly as the benefit of such exertions must appear, that the vast importance may be the more strongly impressed, some cases much deserving attention are added in the Appendix (No. VI.)

---

§ IV.—*The Progress that has been made under the present System.*

At the period when the Board prosecuted its inquiries relative to the wastes of the kingdom, as introductory to a General Enclosure Bill, an argument then used to show that such a measure was unnecessary, was the very rapid effect of the measure commonly had recourse to, that of separate acts for each enclosure. In order to ascertain the degree of reliance which could be placed on this old system,

system, I have examined the returns from the Ministers of 1384 places enclosed by acts of parliament, which passed in the first forty years of His present Majesty, and have extracted from such as gave the number of acres of waste and common, the amount, which proved to be, in England and Wales, 598,942 acres. The particulars are given in the Appendix (No. VII.)

So small a proportion of the great mass of the wastes in so long a period, during which the system was in its fullest vigour, gives the most complete answer possible to the suggestion alluded to; and proves that this method of proceeding is so slow, that were it to advance with undiminished speed (which however is not to be expected), it throws the attainment of the object to so remote a period, that scarcity may repeat her visitation many times before such measures can have the smallest influence to prevent it.

§ V.—*Why do many Tracts remain Waste after Acts have passed for their Enclosure?*

It appears by the returns of the Clergy of the parishes enclosed in the first forty years of His present Majesty, that large tracts in various parts of the kingdom, and especially in the north, included in the acts, remain in the same waste state in which they were found on passing the bills: this is so remarkable, that it merits a few observations.

In all the cases which have come to my knowledge, it has been occasioned by the failure of ill-judged attempts to form corn-farms, or gain corn crops in soils or climates

mates improper for that production. On mountains and moors, where the elevation is considerable, such waste tracts should be converted to grass without attempting corn, which is extremely liable to fail in product, or be lost in a late harvest; and when this ill-judged plan has been attempted, the bad success discourages others; and such tracts of land, which might be highly useful in the hands of those who know what to do with them, are abandoned as not worth cultivating. This is a common, and very mischievous error; nor is it easy to conceive how a whole neighbourhood is prejudiced by such ill-judged attempts. It may in certain cases be proper to sow some oats, wherewith to lay down to grass, but rarely advisable to let them stand for a crop: they should be mown for hay. These elevated tracts, which are so ungenial for corn, are very well adapted to grass; and when the preparation is by sufficient draining, paring and burning, and lime (if to be procured), they will yield good turnip, cabbage, and potatoe crops, for the utter destruction of the ling, and then be in excellent order for laying down to grass to great profit. I have known draining, burning, and lime for grass-seeds, succeed even without tillage, and very valuable sheep-pastures formed at a comparatively small expense. In some cases, a crop of corn is mischievous, and in many unprofitable. The right plans for improving such lands are known and published, from ample experience; and it can only be ignorance of what has been already done, that can now lead men into errors, which, causing failures and disappointment, become productive of foolish prejudices against such wastes, in the minds of men as ignorant as the foolish undertakers, who look for corn where Nature intended only green crops and grass.

SECT.

SECTION II.

OF OPEN-FIELD ARABLE.

The open-field arable system, which has taken near a century to lessen in a small degree in this kingdom, was the general system of Europe, and prevails at present in every part of the Continent. A traveller meets with it from Andalusia to Siberia; and it abounds in proportion to the backwardness of all the countries in which it is found. A village of farmers and labourers surrounding a church, and environed by three or four, and in a few cases, by five open and extended arable fields, form the spectacle of Cambridge, Huntingdon, and Northampton shires, as much as on the Loire, and on the plains of Moscow. Convenience was certainly found in the arrangement, or it would not have been universal; and the custom once established, would necessarily bring with it those rights of commonage which have proved such a stumbling block in the path of modern improvers. The division and change of properties in the lapse of many centuries, have frittered down to morsels the portions which once might have been of a more rational extent; and brought other inconveniences which have since been felt severely. For the last fifty years it has not required many arguments to convince well-informed persons of the advantage of a new division and arrangement of these properties; but the mass has not yet been sufficiently enlightened; or the necessity of the application for distinct acts of parliament for every attempt at improvement, could not have been stuck to with such tenacious jealousy.

" A cer-

"A certain portion of each manor, under the name of demesne lands, was in general occupied by the proprietor, or lord, and was cultivated for his behoof, by his slaves or servants, assisted by the personal services of the neighbouring tenants; a second portion, under the name of common fields and meadows, was occupied by the tenants of the manor, who kept part of it in hay for the winter provision of their cattle, and who cultivated the rest for grain: the remainder was called the lord's waste, and being considered of little value, was appropriated for supplying the inhabitants of the manor with wood (for the purpose of building or repairing their houses, constructing implements of husbandry, fuel, &c.) also with turf and with herbage; where, in tolerable seasons, the cattle, sheep, and horses of the lord and his tenants, found the means of subsistence. The first portion was held in severalty; and even at an early period was often enclosed, to prevent the encroachments of the tenants in the neighbourhood. The second, whilst the crop was upon the ground, whether meadow grass or grain, belonged exclusively to the persons by whom it was respectively occupied; but no sooner was the crop secure, than it reverted into a state of commonage. The third division always remained in common, subject to a variety of regulations according to the customs established in the different manors, according as the common was stinted or unstinted, or whether more than one manor or township happened to be interested in the same waste*."

"The introduction of the common field husbandry seems to have been very slow and progressive. The dispersed situation and smallness of the pieces of common field lands now in cultivation, evidently show, that the occupiers began with tilling a single acre (viz. one day's

---

* Report on Waste Lands, p. 3.

work

work for a plough), or perhaps only half an acre each; and that, as a want of corn increased, they gradually increased their cultivation, until they had cultivated all that was most proper for that purpose; still leaving those parts which were less fit for the plough, or more distant from home, in a constant state of commonage; but, by mutual agreement, keeping the cattle out of cultivated parts till after harvest.

"This was the origin of common fields.

"By the same kind of mutual agreement they shut up, and in some cases enclosed, such parts of their common pastures which were most proper to mow for hay, dividing them into certain specific quantities, either by land-marks, or by lot, for mowing, and suffering the common herd of cattle to feed them again as soon as the hay was carried off, till it was time to lay them up for a new crop.

"This was the origin of common meadows.

"And these mutual agreements, originally founded in necessity, became, when approved by the lords, and observed for a length of time by the tenants, what are called "Custom of Manors," constituting the very essence of the Court Baron, or Manorial Court; by which, both lord and tenants were, and are still bound; and of which, though the lord or his steward is the judge, the tenants are the jury; the Custom of the Manor equally binding both*."

"The regular division of the manors in this district, shows that a great number of them were originally in one hand, and that their disposition was a matter of choice, and not of necessity or accident. The vallies of this district are (almost without an exception) intersected

---

* Agriculture of Wilts, p. 13, quarto edit.

longi-

longitudinally by rivulets. The sides of these rivulets, being the most eligible situation for building, became of course crowded with houses as much as possible. These vallies, with their accompanying rivulets (provincially called bourns), are frequently from three to five miles apart, and hills intervene between bourn and bourn. The shape of manors, therefore, necessarily became a narrow oblong. It was necessary that each manor should have water, should have meadow ground, and should have wood for fuel; (pit coal being very little, if at all in use at that time). The proper situation of the meadow ground was always near the river; for the wood, usually on the summit of the hills, the greatest part of them being evidently once covered with it, and many of them are still so.

"The natural division of the manors of this district was, therefore, into long narrow strips from river to wood, with a right to the use of both; and, as the disposition of much the greatest part of the district is in this way, it shows that such disposition was the work of accommodation, given by the original grantors or superior lords, to the grantees or inferior holders; and as a farther proof that it was so, there are numerous instances in this district, where a want of meadow, or of wood, was supplied by a grant of those necessary articles, taken out of other manors, at the distance of several miles from the manor to which they were annexed*."

"It is probable, that the open fields were formerly woodlands, and that the lords or chieftains suffered their vassals or dependents to obtain property therein, under certain services or quit-rents, by stocking and clearing them from rubbish, so as to become fit for tillage or

---

* Agriculture of Wilts, p. 14, quarto edit.

pasture;

pasture; that the method of their proceeding was, to confine themselves to small parcels at a time, or as much only as they could clear in one year; and that each person, or family, had separate undertakings, but all acted in the same tract. By this means the increase of property would be gradual, and also promiscuous. As to the rights of pasture, they seem to have been at first settled among themselves by private agreement, according to the quantity of cultivated land which each person or family became possessed of. The shifting of property, or the alternate possession of meadow or grass ground, which happens frequently in open fields, the right of pasturage on the unknown land, and the inter-commoning of different parishes, are circumstances which, at this time of day, we can hardly account for, otherwise than by supposing that such parcels were cleared jointly, and that the method of enjoyment was also settled by the private agreement of the several parties concerned, in the manner we now find it*."

§ I.—*Extent of the remaining Open Arable Fields.*

This is a desideratum for the future attention of some Committee of the House of Commons, or of the Board, if enabled by Parliament to effect it. At present it is to be regretted, that the documents in the possession of that body do not afford any means of calculating this space. It is well known, however, that much remains to do in most districts of the kingdom.

A few scattered notes are collected in the Appendix, (No. VIII.)

---

* Essay, p. 2.

§. II.

§ II.—*The present State and Value of such Open Fields.*

These lands, in every circumstance, resemble those which have been already enclosed; except, perhaps, that those open fields which promised the greatest profit by conversion to grazing pastures, would naturally sooner be had recourse to than others not promising an equal return for the great and heavy expense of the measure. But as the obstinacy of individuals may be effective in preventing the measure; as the great charge of separate acts, and the equally expensive proceedings of commissioners, in certain cases, deter many, the quantity remaining is very considerable: not to speak of a multitude of small fields which would not bear the expense under the present system.

---

§ III.—*The Benefits that have resulted from enclosing Open Arable Fields.*

This subject will be best explained by referring to the classes already detailed, viz.

1. The Farmer.
2. The Landlord.
3. The Poor.
4. The Church.
5. The Public.

1.—*THE FARMER.*

It is not uncommon to hear of the obstinacy and folly of farmers in opposing enclosures; and such general condemnation is too often listened to, and acquiesced in: but if the subject be more nearly examined, it will be found that many of those who have been inimical to the measure, have had very good reasons for their own personal conduct. In many instances they have suffered considerably for four, five, or six years. From the first starting the project of an enclosure act to the final award, has, in numerous cases, taken two, three, four, and even five or six years; their management is deranged; not knowing where their future lands will be allotted, they save all their dung till much of it is good for little; they perform all the operations of tillage with inferior attention; perhaps the fields are cross cropped and exhausted, and not well recovered under a course of years. Rents are greatly raised, and *too soon;* so that if they do not absolutely lose five years, they at least suffer a great check. In point of *profit,* comparing the old with the new system, attention must be paid to their capitals: open field land is managed (notwithstanding the inconvenience of its pieces) usually with a less capital than enclosures; and though the *general* profit of the latter much exceeds that of the former, yet this will entirely depend on the capital being adequate. In cases where the new enclosures are laid down to grass, all this becomes of tenfold force: to stock rich grass lands demands a far greater sum than open-field arable; the farmer may not possess it; this has often happened, and drove them to seek other investments, giving way to new comers more able to undertake the new system introduced; and if profit be measured by a per centage on the capital employed,

ployed, the old system might, at the old rents, exceed the profits of the new; and this is certainly the farmer's view of the comparison. He also who had given the attention of a life to the regular routine of open arable, without ten acres of grass ever having been in his occupation, may find himself much at a loss in the regular purchase and sale of live stock, the profit of which depends so much on habitual skill. Add to all this the previous circumstance of laying down to grass; the business, of all others, of which farmers know the least; of which I have many times seen in new enclosures striking instances; and if all these points be duly considered, we shall not find much reason to be surprized at the repugnance shown by many farmers at the idea of enclosing: but where minds of more than usual pliability are found amongst them, united with capitals sufficient for the new arrangement, we see a very different spectacle; the spirit of exertion animates them, and their profit becomes more considerable than ever.

As a general question, there can be no doubt of the superior profit to the farmer by cultivating enclosures, rather than open-field arable. In one case he is in chains—he can make no variations according to soil, or circumstances, or times. He is bound down to the production of corn only, in the sale of which he is rivalled by an ill-judged and never-ceasing import; sometimes by a forced one. Whatever may be the advantage of varying the crops, it cannot operate to his benefit—a mere horse in a team, he must jog on with the rest:

There is, however, one class of farmers which have undoubtedly suffered by enclosures; for they have been greatly lessened in number: these are the *little farmers;* and the diminution of them which have in many cases taken place, caused great complaints by many of the

Clergy

Clergy who made the returns from enclosed parishes. That it is a great hardship, suddenly to turn several, perhaps many of these poor men, out of their business, and reduce them to be day-labourers, would be idle to deny; it is an evil to them, which is to be regretted: but it is doing no more than the rise of the price of labour, tithe, rates, and taxes, would infallibly do, though more gradually, without any enclosure. These little arable occupiers must give way to the progressive improvement of the kingdom, and to the burthens which have accompanied it. The fact is, and must be so; but in cases where the land is laid down to grass, it is a great cruelty not to continue them, if they are able to stock the land; for they manage their little dairies just as well in many cases as their greater neighbours.

" The above state of the small farmer is founded on the strictest proofs. I have seen some small farmers in enclosed places, starving with their families, till necessity has forced them to quit their farms, and betake to labour, when they have afterwards earned a very comfortable living, and rejoiced in the necessity which compelled them to it.

" But in this place I must observe, that as I think it impossible for small farmers to exist as such in enclosed farms, so I would be understood to wish, that landlords would always endeavour to render the lot of labourers, or reduced farmers, as easy as possible, by laying to their cottage a sufficient proportion of land to enable them to keep a cow or two, which is also a great benefit to the landlord, as by such humanity, he ensures to the farmers the labour of these useful hands, and increases his own estate, by letting so much of his land to those who will pay an advanced rent for conveniency, more from the

the profit of their labour than the produce of the land*."

Upon the inconveniences of open fields it has been properly observed, " that almost innumerable inconveniences must attend the enjoyment of such property, of which the following are self-evident.

" 1st, The onus, or expense of cultivating known land promiscuously dispersed in fields, especially if they are of considerable extent, must be much greater than where lands are contiguous, and are laid convenient to the habitations, or out-buildings of the respective occupiers.

" 2nd, The attendance which is necessary upon all manner of cattle depastured in open fields, and the consequent expenses of it, are a great diminution of the value of such herbage.

" 3rd, The proprietors of open fields are liable to great trespasses and encroachments, both from their neighbours and each other.

" 4th, They are confined to a certain and expensive method of cultivation by tillage, although the nature of the land be such, as renders it convertible into good pasture, and capable of becoming equally advantageous to the proprietors, with a tenth part of the expense.

" 5th, The necessity of universal agreement among proprietors, especially where they are numerous, is an almost insurmountable obstruction to any improvements being made in lands during their open-field state.

" 6th, For want of such improvement and of shelter, the cattle depastured therein must be more exposed to hardships and inclemency of weather, and consequently are of less size and inferior value in all respects, to the proprietors, and the accidental losses much greater than

---

* The Advantages and Disadvantages of Enclosing Waste Lands, by a Country Gentleman, p. 30.

they would be in the same land, if it was several and enclosed*."

2.—*THE LANDLORD.*

The benefit of enclosures to the landlord is unquestionable. The measure can originate only with him, and if he were not well convinced that it was greatly to his advantage, none could take place. Opinions of speculation would be idle indeed, in a case decided by above 2000 experiments. Plain, however, as this position ought to be without investigation, some cases are collected in the Appendix (No. IX.)

3.—*THE POOR.*

So far as common pastures are in question, the subject has been already discussed: in relation to any change in the system of husbandry, the poor have no other concern with it than what results from a loss which in some places is sustained of the right of common shackage, or the feeding their geese and pigs in the stubbles after harvest. Compensation is usually given for this, in union with other common rights. For the rest, the question of the interests of the poor must be referred to the amount of labour before and after the enclosure. Where the open fields, on being enclosed, are laid down to grass for feeding and fattening live stock, the demand for labour must undoubtedly lessen; for after the fences are made, the reparation cannot amount to any thing like the work dependent on arable land. Some inconvenience may, and certainly has been found in certain cases, from this circumstance; but it is rarely to any great extent, and gradually wears away, by the demand, and the hands to an-

---

* Essay on the Nature and Method, &c. p. 6.

swer it, balancing each other. In numerous cases, the bringing into cultivation the commons and wastes which before yielded no employment, have more than answered the counter-loss of laying down portions to grass: and upon the whole account of enclosing, the increase in the acres of wheat, and the far greater augmentation in the culture of oats, prove decisively, that the poor must have received an augmentation in the amount of their labour.

4.—*THE CHURCH.*

That the interests of the church have been well attended to upon enclosing, is very generally known. They have in fact had such good care taken of them, that many are of opinion (and even some Commissioners are in the number) that it does not answer to commute the tithes; and accordingly many enclosure acts have passed without any application to rectors, &c. or where such has been made, the terms demanded have been rejected: a proof, that whoever may have lost by enclosures, the church has been sure to gain. This, however, has not been universal, for there are some complaints from the Clergy, in the parochial returns they made.

Of seventy-four enclosures examined by order of the Board in 1800,

  In 24, land was given;
   3, a corn rent;
   2, money per acre;
   2, a fixed money payment;
   1, free before;
   42 remain subject to tithe.
   ——
   74
   ——

(See Appendix No. X.)

Upon

Upon the peculiar weight of tithe upon arable land, Sir Geo. O. Paul, Bart. very well observes:

" The taking the tithe rent *in kind* from the produce, is not only a discouragement to agriculture in general, but is peculiarly so in regard to arable culture. Pasture land worth 40*s.* per acre, producing beef and mutton, will probably pay 3*s.* 6*d.* or 4*s.* for its tithe; whilst land worth 7*s.* bearing potatoes, may pay 20*s.*

" The taking the tithe of grass in kind is not very irksome to the occupant; the amount is not liable to any considerable variation in its relative proportion to the other parts of the rent; so that when taking a farm, the tenant can nearly calculate the amount of the tithe, considered as a fixed rent, for the whole term of his lease, and make a deduction accordingly from the landlord's rent. He does not meet the tithe-owner in his imagination on every speculation to improve, or vary his husbandry; nor does he, in this, as in the other case, feel the tithe as a tax on his skill and ingenuity*."

A case in which the commutation of tithe for a corn rent appears to have been satisfactory to all parties, is that of the parish of Corse. (See Appendix No X.)

5.—*THE PUBLIC.*

The advantages to the community at large from enclosures, are too well understood to demand a minute detail. That it must be highly beneficial to enable every land proprietor to apply the soil to the purpose for which it is best adapted, can scarcely be doubted. In fact, the great rise of rent which has taken place in nineteen cases in twenty, should alone be accepted as a sufficient proof

---

* Observations, &c. by Sir G. O. Paul, Bart. p. 58.

of this point; for what can be the inducement with a farmer to give double or treble his former rent, unless with a view to the profit of his business? And how is he to increase this profit without increasing the value of his produce? This must be admitted; but it has been contended by many, that enclosing has been injurious, by lessening the culture of corn (particularly that of wheat) by means of converting large tracts of land formerly arable into grass: and this is a great objection urged by many of the Clergy, in the returns already alluded to. That the fact is so, cannot, nor need it be denied. If the lands in question are much better adapted to grass than to corn, that is, will yield a greater neat profit, they certainly ought not to be under corn. The reason why they yield such profit, is clearly the price of the produce of grass-land being raised by the demand; and where is the writer who will contend that this demand should not be satisfied? If apprehensions of scarcity are the motives for urging the necessity of a greater production of wheat, surely a more enlarged enclosure of commons, and an increased cultivation of potatoes, are the more obvious means to prevent any such evils, than the absurd idea of counteracting the progress of direct prosperity, by preventing men from applying the soil to the products to which it is best adapted. Those two measures are absolutely in the power of the legislature; and they may be effected without absurdity, danger, or difficulty.

But relative to the effect of enclosures on the production of every sort of human food, we have documents which are far more satisfactory than any reasoning. The result of the inquiries in the parishes enclosed during the first forty years of His present Majesty, to which above 1300 replies were given, will state this matter in a clear light.

WHEAT.

WHEAT.

In 1,960,189 acres enclosed in 1213 parishes, the quantity of this grain was not returned for 192,528 acres. The number of acres of wheat in the rest since enclosing,
has been 165,837
Before enclosing they were 155,572

Increase 10,265

(Appendix No. XI.)

This is satisfactory; for we find that on an average of above 1200 enclosures, the number of acres sown with wheat, so far from having diminished, have on the contrary *increased*. The measure, therefore, *upon the whole*, cannot have had the effect which many have attributed to it.

If a discrimination be made, and we look only to the enclosure of open-field arable, here it is easy to suppose that wheat must of necessity be diminished. In the first place, very large tracts have been laid down to grass, and fed with bullocks, sheep, and dairy cows; here wheat is banished: next we may view the many open fields which were under the course of, 1. Fallow; 2. Wheat; 3. Spring-corn: these lands, on being enclosed, certainly would not generally be sown every third year; but probably only the fourth or fifth; and this change would lessen the acres of wheat, though not perhaps the quarters produced. These two circumstances must necessarily lessen the acres sown, considerably. Other circumstances, however, have tended to lessen this effect, and have in many cases increased the wheat culture. The returns were not so clear as could be wished, and in many cases it is difficult to ascertain whether the increase took place by reason of common pastures being ploughed, or merely by a change

in

in the open-field management. However, by a selection of parishes where the returns were least doubtful, it appears (Appendix No. XI.) that although in 407 enclosures the decrease of wheat amounted to 30,894 acres, yet that there were 239 in which an *increase* had taken place of 14,507 acres; consequently the balance or decrease on the whole amounted to no more than 16,387 acres. I believe, however, that had the returns been more explicit, this balance would have been larger. It might have been greatly more considerable, without affording any solid argument against enclosing open-field arable.

BARLEY.

The number of acres not having been demanded, the returns specify only whether increased in culture, decreased, or remaining as before; and the result was:

Enclosures	941
Increased in	506
Decreased in	256
As before in	179
	941

(Appendix No. XII.)

The culture of barley has therefore flourished greatly from enclosing, as far as this document will allow us to judge.

OATS.

With respect to oats, there can scarcely be a doubt. The following is the result:

Enclosures	963
Increased in	683
Decreased in	149
As before in	131
	963

PULSE.

PULSE.

Enclosures 779
Increased in 229
Decreased in 402
As before in 148

(Appendix No. XII.)
779

The Board will not be surprized at this great decrease in the culture of pease and beans. In very many open fields in the central counties, the regular course was: 1. Fallow; 2. Wheat; 3. Beans. This husbandry being changed by the introduction of clover, must necessarily lessen the quantity of beans. The crops, however, have probably been more productive, for the prices of these articles do not afford sufficient reason to conclude that the general production has suffered.

Hence then we are enabled to ascertain, that enclosing has not lessened the production of corn in England, but that, on the contrary, it has been increased by this measure. That it has increased equally with population during the same forty years, cannot be ascertained. There is considerable reason to suppose that it has not; and the reason is evident: the products of grass lands have risen greatly throughout nearly the whole of that period, whereas the price of corn from 1760 to 1794 was almost stationary, and at too low a price to induce any increase farther than the course of husbandry absolutely demanded. The price was kept down by a stream of importation. The nation has twice experienced severely the consequence of keeping the price of corn too low; and if it be persisted in with so increasing a population, the evil may occur again and again.

The

The question of corn being settled, it will next be satisfactory to the Board to examine what has been the effect of enclosures on the products of grass land.

CATTLE.

Enclosures	571
Increased in	354
Decreased in	106
As before in	111
	571

The full increase of produce does not appear in these numbers, for the difference in the size and value of the cattle is exceedingly great: it has been a change from poor half starved breeding stocks, to the best breeds for beef.

DAIRIES.

Enclosures	511
Increased in	255
Decreased in	143
As before in	113
	511

I examined this point in a different view, endeavouring to ascertain as nearly as might be, the degree of increase. If the number before enclosing be called twenty, the increase has raised it to twenty-four and a half. (Appendix No. XII.)

SHEEP.

Enclosures	721
Increased in	467
Decreased in	157
As before in	97
	721

The remark I made on cattle is equally applicable to sheep: these numbers, great as the increase is, do not mark the whole; for before, they were poor, lean, hungry, half starved *common* fed flocks for folding; but since, are become far superior in breed, value, and food. Before, they deeply suffered, and periodically, by the rot; but this is banished by effective draining: and in many cases, the new lands support great numbers of fatting sheep. In fact, the production of mutton and beef has increased enormously, beyond credibility to those who look only to the price they pay, notwithstanding the vast increase of produce. Beef and mutton cannot be imported, hence they have risen in price proportionally to the demand: but corn can be imported, and therefore the price is depressed below the proportion which the increase of population would otherwise have secured to the farmer, whose exertions have consequently been directed to those objects which bear a fair price; unaffected by the competition of countries where rent, labour, and all other expences are far below our own. There remain still some other articles.

HOGS.

Decreased in 26
No note of increase.

TURNIPS.

Increased in 80
No note of decrease.

CLOVER, &c.

Increased in 59
No note of decrease.
(Appendix No. XII.)

POTATOES.

Increased in 193
Decreased in 2

This article was examined in another light. Supposing 20 to mark the cultivation before enclosing, the present quantity amounts to 50.

The general result of the inquiry is just such as might have been expected from the measure. An Act of Enclosure frees the cultivator from the shackles in which he was before manacled. It enables him to apply the soil to the uses to which it is best adapted. He is no longer restricted from sowing turnips or clover. He is no longer forced to keep fields in tillage that will fatten a bullock. He is permitted, and even assisted in draining wet lands. Contiguity is given to occupations; he can, with a proper capital, pay double, and even treble his former rent; assuredly he does this by INCREASE of PRODUCE.

It is well observed by a late writer, " While in common (Wedmore, Blackford, Cross, Huntspill, Glastonbury, Westhay, Mark, Wookey), were they not, by the estimation of the most skilful farmers, of comparatively very little value? But now, in consequence of being drained and properly managed, are they not let at 25*s*. an acre? The surrounding lands, meantime, instead of being diminished in value, are they not even improved, and rented considerably higher? Are not the sheep on most of these new enclosures more numerous, and in the room of being, as formerly, poor and miserable, and often dying with the rot, are they not, even during the winter months, fatted and made fit for the butcher? Are not the neat cattle of every kind more than doubled? Are not the milch cows in the parish of Wedmore increased upwards of 500? And are not these, on the most moderate allowance, equal to an additional rental of 2000*l*. a-year, exclusive of the number of persons maintained by the employment they afford? The horses too,

too, although not multiplied in number, are they not, from the improvement in the breed, greatly augmented in aggregate value? The poor at the same time have been constantly so much better employed, that the rates have continued nearly the same, and do not increase, though it is well known that in many other parts of the kingdom they have been nearly doubled within twelve years. Amidst this profusion of produce, these multiplied flocks of fattened sheep; these crouded droves of kine and oxen, where is the evidence that these enclosures have contributed to heighten the price of beef and mutton? Would they be sold the dearer because three times the quantity were sent to market? Where is the probability that they could not be afforded as cheap as before? or that the increased products were not more than equivalent to the increased expenses? The improved condition of every rank of people here speaks the contrary*."

(See Appendix, No. XIII.)

---

* Rev. J. Howlett, Great Dunmow, Essex, p. 84.

SECT.

SECTION III.

GENERAL RESULT OF THE ACTS WHICH HAVE HITHERTO PASSED.

It will not be unacceptable here to combine the two objects of Waste Land and Open-Field Arable, in order for something of an estimate of the advantages which have been the result of all the Enclosure Acts which have passed in this kingdom.

It appears then, that from the reign of Queen ANNE to 1805, there passed 2591 Acts of Enclosure.

That in the ten years from 1785 to 1796, the average number per annum sunk considerably; but in the nine years from 1796 to 1805, that average has risen again higher than ever.

That in 1213 enclosures whereof there are returns in the first forty years of his present Majesty, the number of acres were 1,960,189, consequently, the average enclosure was of 1616 acres.

(Appendix, No. XIV.)

At 1616 acres each, there have been enclosed by the 2591 Acts, 4,187,056 acres.

It is well observed by a late writer, " Is it not evident that the inhabitants of this kingdom are greatly increased ? Is it not equally evident that the consumption of all kinds of provision is increased still more than our people? Is not wheaten bread the universal food of the lowest order of men in counties where it used to be confined to the middle and higher ranks ? Is not that bread

made

made of the finest flour? Is not the consumption of cheese and butter, in many places, almost trebled? Are not beef and mutton now eaten almost daily in villages where formerly the use of them was hardly known, or not more than once a week? Do not the farmers in most parts of the nation allow their servants and workmen three times as much strong beer as heretofore? Must not this have vastly augmented the consumption of barley? At the same time are there not thousands of quarters both of that and of wheat, distilled more than used to be? How has this increased consumption been supplied but by an increase of produce? Whence has arisen this increase of produce, but from an increase in the extent and still more, amendment, in the mode of the cultivation of our lands? Is it not for the interest of the community that the greatest possible produce should be obtained from every acre of ground, and that each acre should be applied to the properest use for which Nature designed it?

"Have not the improvements of late years, by the use of lime, chalk, marl, &c. and by the culture of turnips, clover, sainfoin, & rendered those high and light lands abundantly productive, which before were of little or no value? And as to the low and heavy ones, has not the general introduction of draining been the means of converting cold wet arable, to dry healthy pasture, and of rendering many thousand acres of boggy unwholesome meadow, sound and proper for breeding and fattening cattle, on which it was before impossible they should either be fatted or bred? In these several cases, have not the rents been doubled, trebled, and even quadrupled? And must not the produce have been enlarged in full proportion to enable the farmers to pay such heightened rents?

"If I am answered in the affirmative, allow me to ask,

ask, how could these things have been acccomplished, unless the common fields and pastures had been divided and allotted, in specific shares to every proprietor, so that he might have it in his power to manage his land in that way which Nature intended, and in which his own experience taught him it would be most productive and profitable?

"If I am answered in the negative, then let all the ancient enclosures, as well as the new, be again thrown open. Let us no longer boast of our improvements, but let us return to our primitive barbarity, and let our flocks and herds resume the undisturbed possession of the forests. No longer let WILLIAM the Norman be branded in history, for throwing down the enclosures of a few villages to enlarge his forest. We are now told (in what we were foolish enough to think the enlightened age of GEORGE III.) that he stopt his hand too soon; for that it is by forests alone we can find subsistence, and that the destruction of them and the destruction of the kingdom are inseparable*."

---

* Rev. J. HOWLETT, Great Dunmow, Essex, p. 98.

SECTION IV.

OF SMALL COMMONS IN OLD ENCLOSED COUNTRIES.

I live in a district where three parishes in four possess small commons. I am fifty miles from the sea, and could reach it by riding from common to common, with interruptions of small extent; yet of these commons there are but few of a size that can ever be enclosed by separate acts of parliament. In the numerous journies I have taken through most of our counties, I have remarked similar cases every where. Many of these commons are too small to demand attention, amounting to but few acres; but in general they are more extensive, though still inadequate to the expense of an act of parliament. From inattention to draining; from the abuse of digging up the surface, and from over-stocking, the present value is very trifling: but enclosure would convert them into very productive fields. If the present system of conducting this business continue, these wastes are condemned to remain for ever in their present state. But a General Act might be easily framed, applicable to such cases only (for instance, to such commons as do not exceed 100 acres) which would speedily cover the whole with profitable cultivation*.

(Appendix, No. XV.)

---

* See the Act for Colton, in Staffordshire, by which trustees were enabled to sell and lett wastes in aid of the poor-rate.

SECTION V.

OF THE ROYAL FORESTS.

When it is considered that some of the Royal Forests are situated upon soils which would be productive in all the usual crops raised by the common agriculture of the kingdom, they will, without question, appear to be an object which merits no slight attention. It is well observed by the very able Commissioners of the Land Revenue, that " The public interest certainly requires that so extensive and so valuable a part of the landed property of the country should not be suffered longer to continue in its present unproductive state; and that either the plan of management which has been pursued ever since the beginning of the present century, and which has had such destructive effects, should be completely altered, and new regulations established, which may render those forests useful nurseries of timber for the Navy; or that they should be sold, and converted to tillage or pasture, so as to add to the produce and population of the kingdom*."

The following statement will shew the extent of the land in which the timber belongs to the Crown, in each of the Forests which were submitted to the inquiry of those Commissioners.

---

* Eleventh Report of Commissioners on Land Revenue, vol. ii. p. 3.

GENERAL REPORT ON ENCLOSURES.

	Acres.	P.	R.
In New Forest,	66,942	3	26
Dean Forest,	23,015	3	29
Aliceholt and Woolmer Forest,	8694	1	31
Whittlewood Forest,	4850	3	32
Salcey Forest,	1847	0	23
Whichwood Forest,	3709	3	5
Waltham Forest,	3278	3	2
Sherwood Forest,	1466	3	10
Bere Forest,	926	2	13
Sulehay Walk, in Rockingham Forest,	860	3	23
	115,594	0	34

" Although any computation which might be made, before an actual settlement has taken place with those who have claims on the Forests, must be liable to error, yet we are persuaded no extravagant expectation is held out, when we suppose, that in the whole of those forests the allotments to the Crown may, altogether, amount to 60 or 70,000 acres, fit for the growth of oak*."

---

* Eleventh Report of Commissioners on Land Revenue, vol. ii. p. 24.

CHAP.

CHAP. II.

OF THE LEGISLATIVE AND LEGAL MEANS OF ENCLOSING.

A COMMITTEE of the Board having examined this point with much attention, and reported the result of their inquiries, their useful labours will here furnish much of the necessary information.

" Your Committee thought it necessary, previous to their stating, for the consideration of the Board, any new regulations for the facilitating the division of commons, in the first place to inquire into the nature of any proceedings for that purpose that might already exist, whether founded on common or statute law, or in equity; since it would be extremely desirable, that any alteration should be made as nearly accordant to the laws in being as possible, varying perhaps in the mode, yet agreeing in principle, so as to be the more easy and effectually carried into execution.

" In regard to the common law, it appears that writs of partition and admeasurement, for the division of property, have existed at common law from the time of earliest memory and record; and such were the ideas which at all times were entertained of the advantages to be derived by the public for the enjoyment of property in severalty, that there have been cases, where such proceedings have taken place in very ancient periods, and enclo-

sures

sures been made and supported, in a manner the most favourable to promote such partitions, divisions, and enclosures.

" Of the statutes which have passed in aid of the common law, there are only two which require to be particularly noticed. The first is the statute of Merton*, which, according to Coke, was only an affirmance of the common law. By this statute, such lords of manors as reserved sufficient pasture to their tenants, were empowered to improve the residue. By another act†, all doubts were removed whether the lord of a waste could approve against his neighbours as well as tenants. These are the only statutes which have any important reference to the subject in question. Your Committee need hardly remark, how insufficient they were for bringing any considerable portion of waste lands into a state of cultivation. It was seldom that any common was sufficiently extensive, to afford a surplus of any moment, after the claims of those who had right of common on it were satisfied. It was hardly possible indeed, in many cases, to ascertain, what was a sufficiency of pasture; and where a common of turbary, or estovers existed, the lord could not improve any part of that waste. The more opulent and powerful also the commoners of the kingdom grew, the more opposition they made, and the greater difficulty there was found in carrying on this proceeding; insomuch, that in modern times there is scarcely an instance of an approvement, as it is technically called, having taken place.

" Besides these proceedings, founded on the common and statute law, various determinations appear heretofore

---

* 2 Stat. Merton. 20 Hen. III. cap. 4.
† Stat. West. 2, 13 Edw. I. cap. 4. 6.

to have been made in the Court of Chancery. But from the difficulties and expense attending such proceedings, they have been long disused; and no other means of obtaining a division of commons having been sanctioned by law, the parties have been compelled, where an unanimous consent could not be procured, and the common divided by arbitration, to apply to the legislature for special acts in order to divide, and to put in a state of severalty, lands that otherwise would have remained waste, common, and uncultivated.

" It is hardly necessary for your Committee to trouble the Board with any observations on the insurmountable bars which must lie in the way of improving by far the greater portion of such wastes as remain in common, if some less troublesome and some less expensive mode of procuring a division, is not established. The practice of applying to parliament is already decreasing, and must soon come to a stand, in consequence of the heavy charges attending such a mode of proceeding, which are particularly severe, when the common is of small extent*."

---

* Report on Waste Lands, p. 24.

SECTION I.

BY ACT OF PARLIAMENT.

It is remarkable, that after the necessity of applying to parliament for powers to enclose was recognized, the progress made in the business was so slow as hardly to be perceptible. An act passed in the 17 CHA. II. for Malvern Chace, but it was more an act of regulation than enclosure. The first act of real enclosure ever passed, was the 8 ANNE, cap. 20, which being very short, it is inserted in the Appendix. The next was the 12 ANNE, for Farmington in Gloucestershire. In the whole reign of GEO. I. only 18 acts passed. In that of GEO. II. but 231: it was not till the reign of His present Majesty that this singularly beneficial measure became an object of general attention; and for the four first years of it, the number rose no higher than from 16 to 37 in a year. In the year 1764 there were 63 acts; and from that time the progress was considerable till 1779; but the number sunk greatly in 1780, and did not rise again till 1793, when it started remarkably, and fell no more. It deserves notice, that the Board of Agriculture was that year established, which immediately excited a great attention to agriculture, and was without doubt one cause of the spirit which appeared in this business, and in so many others at the same time.

Above 2500 of these acts have passed, by which four millions of acres have been greatly improved; but at the same time it must be observed, that this progress has been so slow, when compared with the immense tracts remaining

in

in wastes and open fields, that it has borne no proportion to the increase of population: indeed it has at periods greatly declined: the average from 1765 to 1779 was 58 per annum; but from 1780 to 1792 it was only 19 per annum; and thence to 1800 it rose no higher than 86 in one year; a number exceeded so long ago as 1777. This detail must convince every considerate reader, that the policy of rendering separate acts necessary, will not in many centuries permit these works in the kingdom to be completed.

§ I.—*Of the Rights that must be Commuted.*

" It seems unnecessary to enter much at length into a definition of the different rights of common, at present known to, or acknowledged, by the laws of England; because we trust and hope, that by a division of all wastes and commons, every right of that description will be extinguished. At the same time it may not be improper, shortly to state the nature of such a right in general, and the various distinctions of which it has been found susceptible.

" It is found, that a right of common is, in general understood to be, a profit which one person hath in another's land, without having any property in the soil. It is an incorporeal right out of, or by some grant, as originally commencing in some real or supposed agreement between lords and tenants, or incident to some manor for valuable purposes.

" It is also found that this right of common is divided, according to the subject matter, as follows:

" 1. Int o

"1. Into common of pastures; which is a right of taking the produce of land by the mouths of the cattle.

"2. Common of turbary; or the right of cutting turves (turf) for fuel.

"3. Common of estovers; or the right of cutting wood for fuel, for the repairs of the house, implements of husbandry, or of hedges and fences, And,

"4. Common of piscary; or the liberty of fishing in another's water—the consideration of which any Committee would judge foreign to the object of their inquiries*.

"The material variation between the different rights above stated, consist in the subject matter—common of pasture, being a right of feeding on the verdure and herbage of the soil; but, common of turbary, conveys a right of carrying away the very soil, or the produce of the soil itself. In other respects they resemble each other, so that we find it necessary to be particular in these illustrations of the right of common of pasture only.

"Common of pasture, they find divided technically as follows.

"1. Common appendant.

"2. Common appurtenant.

"3. Common in gross. And,

"4. Common because of vicinage.

"Common appendant, is incident of common right to all who hold land parcel of a manor, and is a right to depasture their commonable cattle (such as horses, oxen, cows and sheep), which are necessary either for the culti-

---

* In some parts of England also, there is a common of fowling, or a privilege of killing wild fowl, and a right of fulcage, by which is meant the right of cutting hay in a common meadow, according to the custom of the manor.

vation

vation or manurance of their lands, and levant and couchant thereon, upon the wastes of the manor.

" It must have had its origin before the time of legal memory, for at this day no such right can be created: as where the lord of a manor, before the statute of *quia emptores*, enfeoffed another of lands, parcel of the manor, the feoffee become entitled to common for his commonable cattle, levant and couchant on the lands granted, within the wastes of the lord, as incident to the feoffment.

" The soil of the land subject to this species of right is in the lord of the manor, and thus the lord and his tenant have a mixed enjoyment of the property; and it is laid down to have originally belonged to arable land only, though now it may be claimed as belonging to meadow or pasture.

" Common appurtenant, is a right belonging and appertaining to land, but not incident to any tenure. It must have its commencement by grant, and therefore may be (though no modern instance has occurred to any Committee) erected at this day, as where a man bargains and sells land to another, and grants therewith a right of common over certain of the bargainer's lands, this right shall be held as appurtenant to the lands sold.

" From the nature of its origin it may extend to every species of cattle, such as swine and also to geese. It may be limited to a certain number of cattle; or it may extend to all cattle *sans nombre:* but it is apprehended, that such a right cannot be extended beyond that number which the land to which the common is appurtenant can maintain throughout the year; or, in other words, they must be levant and couchant thereon.

" Common in gross, is where common appurtenant to land has been alienated, and is held separate from the lands

lands to which the common was appurtenant, and differs not from common appurtenant in any other particular, than by what necessarily attend such disannexation, viz. in its descendible quality through the same invariable line of descent from ancestor to heir, and not as an accessary to land. And from hence arise the distinction in the mode of claiming common appurtenant or in gross; the former claimant, stating his title to arise from an immemorial usage by all antecedent owners and tenants of the land to which the common is appurtenant, and the latter claimant, in himself and his ancestors for time immemorial.

" Common because of vicinage, is not properly a right, but is an excuse for a trespass; and is where two or more towns have common in the fields within their townships, which are open to the fields of the neighbouring townships. The cattle put to use their common, have been immemorially used to escape into the fields of the neighbouring towns, and therefore by enclosure of the fields of one or more townships, the common because of vicinage may be extinguished. All these species of rights of common, except where a particular grant can be shewn, must be prescribed for and proved by long and immemorial usage, and uninterrupted enjoyment, and the mode of enjoyment must point out the nature of the prescription; for they must agree with each other: as, if the common has been used for other than commonable cattle, the claim must be of a common appurtenant; and so of the rest.

" Whatever difficulties may occur in considering these different rights, they evidently have arisen from the necessity of holding out an inducement to the cultivators of land in ancient times, before the use of artificial pasture was

was known; to continue their land in an arable state, by annexing to such land a sufficiency of common for the support of their cattle. For this purpose, the policy of the common law annexed this right to all grants of lands by a lord of a manor, as incident to such grant; and the same policy might have prevailed in the grants of private persons, as the most effectual security for the payment of the reserved rent, and due cultivation of their lands.

" The only distinction which it seems necessary for a Committee to take notice of, is, where the right of common is stinted, or where it is unlimited. In the one case, the right only extends to the power of putting certain numbers of horses and other commonable cattle, at certain fixed times of the year, into such common pasture, under the denomination of cattle-gaits; every cow or ox being held equal to one cattle-gait, every five sheep to one cattle-gait, and every horse to one cattle-gait and a half; the proportion however, sometimes varying according to the ancient usages of particular districts. In many of these stinted commons, the commoners are owners of the soil, which distinguishes their rights materially from those above mentioned.

" The foregoing distinctions appear all that are necessary for the purpose of elucidating the nature of the several rights of common now existing in the southern parts of the united kingdom; and, aided by the general history of the country, they lead to this probable conclusion, that those rights could only have arisen in the infancy of agriculture, and of the arts therewith connected, which might render the existence of such rights more necessary.

" But whatsoever circumstances might have occasioned in those days, when land was of little value, and, from the

the scantiness of population, little in demand, such tracts of valuable territory remaining unoccupied and in common; yet in this age of extended population, of increased wealth, and of diffused knowledge in agriculture and its attendant arts, any intermixture of property in the same land, as being a great, and in many cases an insurmountable bar to all improvement, is an evil of such magnitude, that it need only be pointed out to a legislature distinguished for its attention to promote the public interest, in order to have it remedied*."

The allotment to the lord for his rights, has varied from one-eighth to one-seventeenth of the common.

§ II.—*Power of Commissioners.*

The power granted by most of these acts to Commissioners, is an extraordinary circumstance in the History of Enclosing. They are a sort of despotic monarch, into whose hands the property of a parish is invested, to recast and distribute it at their pleasure among the proprietors; and in many cases without appeal. But this great confidence is necessary; for such is the complexity and variety of interests to be examined and estimated, that if more cautious methods were resorted to, it would be impossible to effect the purpose; and the work of an enclosure would be spun through half a century.

The income of the Commissioners depends on their integrity and reputation: if they award unjustly, they will not be employed; and if they run expenses too

---

* Report on Waste Lands, p. 20.

high,

high, they impede the progress of enclosing. It must be admitted, that in the latter case instances have occurred that tend strongly to check the spirit of enclosing; and it is much to be regretted. The solicitor of the bill, here shares the obloquy.

"Commissioners appointed by acts of parliament for dividing and allotting common fields, are directed to do it according to the respective interests of the proprietors therein, without giving undue preference to any; but paying due regard to situation, quality, and convenience. The method of ascertaining is left to the decision of the major part of them, in all cases which are not expressly provided for under the act; and this without any other fetter or check upon them, besides their own honour and conscience; of late, indeed, awed by the solemnity of an oath. By this unbounded confidence, they have an absolute power vested in them, not only to settle all disputes which arise between any of the parties concerned, whether about the quality, the survey, or the property; but also to determine by the measure of their own abilities and judgment, and the proportion of mounding which each proprietor shall make for his estate, under the single restriction before mentioned. This is, perhaps, for the extent of the object, one of the greatest trusts which is ever reposed in any set of men in the kingdom; and therefore merits all the return of caution, attention, and integrity, which can result from an honest, impartial, and ingenuous mind*."

"To make, or at least to examine the necessary calculations arising from their own determinations; to form a judgment of the execution of a survey; to range pro-

---

* Essay, p. 60.

perly,

perly, and comprehend the evidence of controversial matters which come before them, and to give every object its due consideration and attention, are articles of business which it requires a considerable extent of abilities to conduct properly. In things of this nature, it is no wonder if persons of little learning, and unaccustomed to habits of thinking, are sometimes defective.

" The constitutional method established among us of deciding disputes about property, is by an appeal to twelve men, empannelled to give sentence upon their oaths according to the best of their judgment, and the facts which are laid before them. The witnesses on both sides the question are examined in a very solemn manner in open court, in the hearing of the most learned of the law, the reverend the Judges, who are to instruct the jury in points of law, and in the degree of evidence and probability which accompanies the relations which are made to them. This ceremony takes place when the matter in dispute is even of less value than five pounds ; and after all, the determination is not final, if either the verdict appears to the Judge to be given contrary to evidence, or there is an equitable plea in the case which the deficiency of the law will not extend to. How different is the method of settling the rights of proprietors upon enclosures! on which occasion the adjusting of property of forty or fifty thousand pounds value, is left to the arbitration of a majority of five, often persons of mean education, without any guide to conduct them, and yet without any legal appeal against their decisions, even in cases of unjust judgment. Though it might be of dangerous consequence to subject these matters to the cognizance and discussion of courts of law, which might create disputes, and occasion a great deal of frivolous and

vexatious

vexatious expense, yet it is to be wished that the confidence reposed in Commissioners was more limited, and that their practice could be regulated by some certain data or principles*."

* Essay on the Nature and Method, &c. p. iv.

SECTION II.

BY AGREEMENT.

Some cases have occurred, in which enclosures have been undertaken and executed by a private agreement among the parties; but in such cases, they have found it necessary to apply to parliament, for acts to legalize the proceeding, and such a method must necessarily leave out all public rights, such as tithe, &c.

"There is every reason to believe, that there are many commons in England, particularly those of small extent (where in general the land is the most valuable, and the fittest for cultivation), which would be divided among the parties interested therein, by agreement among themselves, did not various legal disabilities stand in the way of such agreement.

"It is principally for the purpose of removing such legal disabilities, that Acts of Enclosure are often resorted to; and so naturally are persons who can judge properly of their own interests, inclined to enter into such agreements, that many Acts of Enclosures—for instance, Farmington Enclosure, 12 Anne (private acts) c. 17; Thurscoe Enclosure, 2 Geo. II. c. 4; and indeed a considerable proportion of the acts which passed some years ago, were merely for the purpose of legalizing private agreements, previously settled among the parties

"There are many individuals, however, who, though they might be willing to enter into such agreements, yet, living at a distance from the commons in which either they, or those for whom they act, are interested, can be no judge whether the proposal submitted to them is fair or not; and would therefore rather incline to refer the whole to persons on whose skill and integrity they can depend, than to weigh and determine the matter themselves.

" This is more particularly likely to be the opinion of guardians, trustees, the church, and other corporate bodies; and indeed, as in all such cases, not only the interest of those in possession, but of others possessed of contingent rights, are implicated; it has been thought most advisable, to restrict the effects of such agreement to the appointment of Commissioners, who shall pronounce under oath an award, the general nature and tendency of which may have been previously arranged among the parties, but which shall afterwards be sanctioned by sworn Commissioners, with an appeal from their decision.

" As various incidents may occur, which may prevent unanimity in such agreements, a circumstance for which provision must be made, hence it becomes necessary to submit to the consideration of the Legislature, the propriety of authorizing the appointment of Commissioners, where three-fifths of the parties interested approve of the same; for no just reason can be assigned, why a small but stubborn minority, either in number or value, should controul a majority of persons interested in the same property, and prevent them from improving their share of it.—When the great advantages, however, under which pers ns may have their property allotted to them under the proposed Act, are considered, there is every reason to hope, that it will rarely happen, unless in commons of great extent, and where the parties interested are extremely numerous, that any considerable minority will be found to obstruct the division.

" The

" The principal difficulties which occurred in drawing up the following sketch were, regarding the appointment of the Commissioners, the share of the lord of the manor, and of the lay impropriator, and the interests of the church.

" With regard to the appointment of the Commissioners, that point has been found less difficult than was originally imagined; for on examining the various Acts of Enclosure, particularly those of a more recent date, it appears, that in case the Commissioners therein nominated, either die, or refuse to act, there are uniformly provisions for the election of other persons in their room; and nothing more is necessary, than to give the parties interested, the same power of original appointment that they have by private acts, of re-election; and the matter is settled on principles sanctioned by long usage, and by innumerable acts of the legislature. The probable result will be, the appointment of one Commissioner by the lord of the manor, of another by the tithe-owner, and of a third by the major part in value of the proprietors; at the same time, there can be no objection to their nominating only one or two Commissioners, if they think that number sufficient.

" It appears upon examining various Bills of Enclosure, for instance, 12 GEO. I. (private acts) c. 5; Croston and Finny Enclosure; also c. 32, of the same year, West Haughton Enclosure, Sherston Magna Enclosure, an. 1742-3, &c. &c. that the division was sometimes referred to a numerous body of commissioners, peers, gentlemen, and sometimes clergymen, residing in the neighbourhood, who acted without fee or emolument: and it is to be hoped that many of that description will undertake so useful a duty under this Bill, if it has the good fortune of receiving the sanction of parliament.

" But

"But when commons are extensive, and the division likely to be attended with great trouble, it is probable that it would be more expedient, and that it has been found by experience the better way, to appoint persons of an inferior class, who are likely to take more pains, in consequence of their receiving a fair remuneration for their trouble. The option, however, should be left to the parties interested, to appoint Commissioners of either description.

"Where the parties are unanimous, there can be little difficulty in effecting a division; but where they disagree, a different system must be adopted. In that event, it is proposed that the Commissioners and surveyors, shall first divide the share of those who assent, from those who dissent, and that the allotment of those who dissent shall remain subject to the rights of the lord of the soil, and of the tithe-owner, so that the Commissioners of neither, can have any wish for, or interest in, diminishing that allotment.

"This is certainly indulging, to its utmost extent, the prejudices of those who are hostile to Enclosures. They are thus enabled to possess their property in their own way, but they are not on that account to prevent others, desirous of improving their share, from enjoying the same privileges.

"As to the other points difficult to decide on, namely, the interest of lords of manors, lay impropriators, and of the church, a very minute and laborious investigation is now carrying on, for the purpose of analyzing a great number of preceding Acts of Enclosure; the general result and deduction from which, at an average of at least 1000 cases, indiscriminately taken, will, it is presumed, satisfy every one, should it be even somewhat less than the ideas he may at present be led to entertain of the extent

extent and value of his rights: and here it is proper to remark, that in consequence of the expense of division being so much reduced, as it necessarily must be to those who divide under the proposed Act, a smaller proportion, will in fact be more valuable, than a greater one, under a private bill, with all the charges attending it.

"The proportion of the common for tithes, will, it is believed, be thus ascertained on principles that cannot well be controverted; and where the tithes belong to a lay-impropriator, he will naturally be induced to improve and cultivate his allotment; but when the tithes are the property of a corporation, like the church, other regulations may be necessary; and in the following sketch, the expedient of a corn-rent is resorted to, as by far the most unexceptionable, and the happiest measure that perhaps the wisdom of man could have invented for consolidating the interest of the church and that of the public. In case, however, a corn-rent cannot be arranged to the satisfaction of the church, at the moment of division, power is given to the parson, with the consent of the bishop and patron, to grant leases, for the purpose of having the allotment of the church improved, and a revenue derived from it.

"It is one of the most important advantages resulting from diminishing the expense of enclosing and cultivating the wastes and commons, that it enables all other parties interested, to do the most ample justice to the cottagers and smaller commoners; and to effect so essential an object, there is a clause in the Bill, recommending it to the Commissioners, to annex plots of ground to the several cottages; and land sufficient for the pasture of a cow, to the smaller commoner entitled to that privilege. These and other regulations, as to fuel, &c. must

depend

depend much upon the custom of the common, its size, and a variety of other circumstances, and it is evident must be referred to the discretion and judgment of the Commissioners who may be appointed, but who will necessarily attend to any recommendation in an act of the legislature, under whose authority they are nominated*."

" *Enclosure by Private Commission.*—Some entire townships (except perhaps the unstinted commons), and many stinted pastures, have been laid out by Commissioners, chosen unanimously by the several interests concerned, without soliciting the assistance of parliament.

" By this means, the distinct properties are laid together, in well-sized and well-proportioned enclosures, with proper roads and drift-ways; and this without the expense, the inconveniency, or the hazard attending an application to parliament †."

---

* General Enclosure, p. 1.
† Marshall's York, v. i. p. 99.

SECTION III.

BY INDIVIDUALS.

Individual proprietors possessing considerable proportions or rights of open fields, or in common pastures; or having from property or character much weight and influence, have in various cases procured the necessary assents to the measure of enclosing, and effected it without any application to higher powers. In such cases, the expenses are small, and the benefit consequently great.

CHAP. III.

EXECUTION OF THE WORK.

HAVING passed through the consideration of those steps leading to Enclosure which depend on negotiations in the closet, or allegations at the bar of a House of Parliament, the legal processes necessary to prepare for field operations, it will now be requisite to follow the Commissioners in their execution of the works for which powers have thus been granted.

Here it will be necessary to touch on,

I. The Survey.
II. The Valuation.
III. The Allotments.
IV. The Award.
V. Fences.
VI. Roads, Bridges, &c.
VII. Drainage and Irrigation.

SECTION I.

OF THE SURVEY.

———

The modes of proceeding in which Commissioners execute the trusts reposed in them, have been not only different in different periods, but are at present, as I am informed, subject to a good deal of variation. In many cases the valuation of the lands preceded the survey; in some cases they have been carried on hand in hand; and in many the survey was the first step: these are variations, as well as many others, that must in every case be left entirely to their own judgment: they are alone the proper judges; and such heads of Sections as this and several which follow, find a place in these papers, more with a view to attract the attention of such gentlemen in or out of the profession, as may from their private experience have information to impart, than with the smallest idea of affording instruction to those who are alone capable of giving it.

It is remarked by a writer of experience, in whose contemplation and practice the valuation was the first step to be taken, that " The valuation of open fields succeed the survey; which cannot properly be begun till that is completed; because the surveyor is to measure every parcel, as it is separately valued, according to the descriptions and quality marks which those who value, have affixed to them. Partiality is much less to be apprehended in this article, than in the valuation; because the latter being merely arbitrary, it must be always doubtful, whether errors are to be attributed to want of judgment

or

or integrity. But the admeasurement being made according to geometrical rules, is subject to the review of others; and though mistakes are scarce possible to be avoided in numerous calculations, yet a surveyor risks the reputation of his abilities by those which are only accidental; and therefore must be very regardless of his own interest, before he will subject himself to the disgrace of any which are wilful.

"As there are two distinct branches of this business, consisting of the general survey of all the lands in the field, and the particular survey of each proprietor's estate, it is usual to commit the execution of it to two different persons, that their accounts may be a check upon each other; and if upon examination they tally, or nearly so in every part, it is to be presumed that they are both right. If they differ materially in any particular spot, it is necessary that they go out and review it together, and the mistake is by these means, for the most part, very easily discovered. It is reckoned that there will always be a small difference between a general and particular survey, arising from the more unequal surface which prevails over the ridges and balks of furlongs, than upon the hades or outlines thereof.

"The consequence of this is, that the particular will somewhat over-run the general survey, where both are measured exactly, because the lines of it are taken over the ridges, where there is the greater inequality; but the variation in this case is very inconsiderable, and the method of adjusting it easy*."

"The survey ought always to be laid before the Commissioners the beginning of October, that they may be able to proceed directly upon the allotments, which for

---

* Essay on the Nature and Method of Enclosures, p. 51.

many

many reasons should be no longer deferred. The rights and interests of the former occupiers, who will have then gathered their crops, are coming to a conclusion. If any fallows have been made, the season for sowing winter corn is at hand. If any parts of the fields have been laid down with grass-seeds, the future proprietors thereof will suffer daily in the loss of their herbage, and perhaps also in the destruction of it by the treading of large cattle, if the heavy rains should fall early. And besides all this, the proper season for planting commences soon after the fall of the leaf; and in strong clays, the growth of quick-sets depend very much on their being early planted. All these reasons make it highly expedient and beneficial to proprietors, to have every thing which concerns their enclosure, entirely settled by the beginning, or at the farthest, by the middle of November; which cannot be done, unless the survey is completed and laid before the Commissioners early in October; after which the situation of the allotments being fixed, they are to be measured and staked out, and each person's share of mounding to be ascertained; all which, in a field of any considerable extent, will require a month or six weeks at least, to adjust finally, from the time of the delivery of the survey*."

---

* Essay, &c. p. 58.

SECTION II.

OF THE VALUATION.

This is the branch of the business of enclosure and allotment, which demands much knowledge and great experience, as well as an unsuspected integrity. The gentlemen who have been employed in many enclosures, will always be chosen in preference to young beginners, who must be trained up by gradual exertions under the wing of experienced Commissioners. These are obvious truths, and rarely departed from in practice, through some little local jealousies, without the parties themselves suffering from want of confidence. That such a necessary measure of confidence may, in some cases, have been abused, cannot be denied; but the bad reputation attending them, has had a good effect, and, perhaps upon the whole of the business, may have been beneficial.

" In the enclosure of common fields, an estimation made of the yearly value, by the acre, of all the plots and parcels of ground contained therein, is essentially necessary. This office is sometimes undertaken by Commissioners themselves, but more frequently by some neighbouring farmers mentioned in the act, or chosen by the proprietors with the consent of the Commissioners, for that purpose. There are three properties very essential to the right discharge of it; viz. understanding, attention, and integrity. Without a general knowledge of the nature and uses of land, a man is totally unqualified for this branch of business; and this is the reason why many
Commis-

Commissioners, and among others, the Author, has always declined taking part in it; well knowing, that whatever caution and integrity they may exert in the execution of it, those qualifications cannot in this case make amends for any defects of judgment. Nor ought the most experienced to be too confident of their understanding in these matters.

" There are few concerns of more serious consequences to individuals, than that, by which their property is to be for ever ascertained: and therefore it ought not to be done without the most mature deliberation, and careful attention to every circumstance, that can in any degree affect its value. A cursory view of the surface will not suffice for this purpose.

" There should be a critical examination of its soil, as well as of the herbage which it produces; an inquiry into its latent qualities, whether it contains any thing noxious to any species of profitable cattle. Whether particular seasons are not adapted to it, and how far it is affected by the present. What management it has been under for a course of years past, and the like. To these should be added a due regard to its situation for convenience; and a consideration of the different expense of enclosing, according to its great or less intrinsic value. These are the principal objects which ought to determine the judgment of every honest man on such occasions.

" And after all, the most skilful will differ in their opinions upon these subjects; nor is there any other way to be assured of their integrity, but by their general good character, or by obliging them to confirm their sentiments with an oath, to be taken before the Commmissioners by each of the quality-men upon the delivery of their book*."

---

* Essay on the Nature and Method, &c. p. 47.

" Though

"Though an impartial estimation is one of the most essential means of procuring equal justice to all parties, and what every proprietor has reason to be anxious about; yet it may not be an improper caution to suggest, that it is very ill-judged to raise frivolous objections from selfish motives, which will probably answer no other purpose, but to take up the time of the Commissioners, and by consequence to swell the bill of costs, and create an additional expense upon the enclosure*."

---

* Essay, &c. p. 50.

SECTION III.

ALLOTMENTS.

This branch of public enclosure is necessarily produced by the preceding steps, being in fact no more than the re-division of the lands among the former proprietors, according to that proportion of value, resulting from the valuation already taken. It depends so much on local situation and convenience, as to admit scarcely of any general rule: each case of enclosure stands singly on the circumstances of the spot. Contiguity to the residence or farmeries of the proprietors is so much esteemed, that the immediate value of the lands must in some cases be made to give way to this general object of desire: able Commissioners put a just value on every circumstance, and so balance their arrangement, as usually to give as much satisfaction to all parties, as perhaps is possible in difficult cases.

SECTION IV.

AWARD.

The award is the legal establishment and register of the changes made in the property by the enclosure. If discontents arise, they are founded on the allotments; but in relation to the award itself, the most usual complaint is founded only on the time of making it. This has in some cases been delayed so long, as to occasion complaints, which apparently have been reasonable; and such cases have produced in several modern acts, a clause enforcing the award within some specified period.

SECTION V.

OF FENCES.

There is not a single step in the whole business of enclosing that does not demand particular attention; the heavy expense to which the measure has in many instances been carried, has thrown a damp upon it through various districts of the kingdom; and excited so much opposition to all proposals to enclose by act of parliament, that whatever may be the improvement in view, the very word raises alarm. Whatever therefore tends to lessen expense, must be beneficial. That of fences is extremely heavy, and therefore merits much attention.

The circumstances that particularly call for it are:

I. Arrangement of the Fields according to the Soil.
II. Size of the Fields.
III. Enclosing without Subdivisions.
IV. Position of the Fences.
V. Sort of Fence.

§ I.—*Arrangement of the Fields according to Soil.*

The practice generally followed, of tracing the lines of the fences in such directions as to form square enclosures, has

has nothing to be objected to where the soil is without material variations. But where changes of soil occur, and the open fields contain both wet and dry lands—such as are adapted to the turnip culture, and such as are too wet for that plant; tracts that may be proper for sainfoin, and others of a very different description; such a plan is attended with great inconveniences, and ought carefully to be avoided. These occur in every article of the farmer's business. He must often have two crops in one field, which is alone a great objection. He must make a difference in the time of giving many of the operations of tillage; and the whole management applied ought to vary with the soil. The expense of going to and from fields, and of making broken days' work in each, induces a neglect of necessary caution; and if unfavourable weather occurs, loss is the consequence. For these, and many other reasons, obvious to every practical man, attention should be given to tracing the lines of fences, so as to have every part of a field as similar in soil as possible.

§ II.—*Of the Size of Fields.*

Where a particular attention to shelter from bleakness of situation do not render exceptions necessary, a general rule is, to make the size of the new fields proportioned to that of the farm; and they are found to vary from five to ten acres on a small scale; to fifty or sixty on a large one. Shelter against cold winds; and a necessity of many open drains, into which to conduct covered ones, will always have a tendency to make small enclosures convenient.

In the case of grass-lands, the size may be larger than for arable. It has been a debated point among the writers on husbandry, whether large or moderately sized fields be most advantageous to live stock; and so much may be said on both sides, that probably the point will not easily be settled; and in such cases, motives remote from the immediate question will decide the conduct of those who sketch out the new enclosures. If they are to be fed by dairy cows brought home for milking twice a day, the fields should be smaller than for fatting stock, which being once distributed, should be left with few removals. Digging ponds is expensive, yet every field should have water. The expense of subdividing is considerable, and must be attended to.

Mr. BAKEWELL was a great friend to small fields; but he used one argument founded more on economy than on the well-doing of stock: he contended that where coals were of a certain price, the hedges answered as well as any other part of a farm. I have seen some very large fields that have been grazed without inconvenience. At Croswick, in Northamptonshire, one of 202 acres, supported a greater stock, in the opinion of the proprietor, than it would have done had it been in small pieces. Mr. WESTCAR, in Buckinghamshire, has a field of 300 acres: if he thought division would pay, I take it for granted it would be divided. Several parks that are fed by joist stock support and fatten it so amply, that the owners have quoted the cases in proof of the benefit of large fields.

" In enclosing waste lands in a bleak situation, and much exposed to the violence of any particular wind, it would be of the first consequence not to adhere to the custom of proportioning the fields to the size of the intended farm, but to make them very much smaller than in more sheltered parts; and many fences should be made at the same time, to begin to windward, and make the hedges in rows across it; and although the first might not thrive well, in all probability the second would do better, and the more were planted the more they would thrive. The greatest enemy to vegetables are strong winds, and their velocity is much broken by trees and hedges, as these entangle the atmosphere, and prevent its rushing on so furiously over the surface: wherever we find the wind blowing from a very extensive plain, and particularly over the sea, we find the plants on the first land that meets it all shrinking therefrom, and the branches put forth towards the land to be far more luxuriant than those towards the sea or bleak wind. This is generally attributed to what us farmers call sea air; but I conceive it is only caused by the velocity of its motion. I have observed along the sea coast of Wales, in Devonshire, and other countries towards the British Channel, particularly near the Start Point, that there is not a tree to be seen on any of the rising grounds that face the sea within a few miles of it, but in the vallies they thrive amazingly; the surface of the latter place being hilly, trees grow up quietly until their tops reach the rapid current of air that flies on at a certain distance above the hedges, when their heads have the same appearance as if they were taken off with a scythe, and never grew higher. There was in ancient times trees on the highest mountains in Wales, for on the turf grounds, which are most on mountain tops, vast number of their trunks now remain under the surface; others rooted in their native soil, and broken down close to the stump: but should trees be planted there at this time they would not grow; the velocity of the wind would starve them. When trees throve on these hills, the whole country was covered therewith, so each grew behind the shelter of the other. There is a large wood belonging to Sir Thomas Mostyn, near Barmouth, which begins near the sea, and continues far into the country: the first row of trees, or, rather oak shrubs nearest the ocean, are very short and small, little higher than the fence, and there is a progressive advance of their height and bigness towards the land, until they become large and tall wood, although the ground continues to rise. I have been informed, that if a thermometer be placed so as to oppose the current of the wind, and another just by, but sheltered from the violence of its motion, that that exposed to the wind will be much lower than the other. This accounts for the half starved appearance of the plants that are on the tops of the hills, and in bleak situations; for I make no doubt, but often in the months of May and June, a thermometer exposed in one of these places to a high wind, would be as low as it often stands in January and February. Such sudden changes from heat to cold to most plants at the time of their vegetating, must always be injurious and often fatal. For these reasons, I would recommend all those who enclose bleak lands, to make the fields small, and planted with trees in them, if possible to make them grow*."

§ III.—*Of Enclosing without Subdivisions.*

Hitherto it is taken for granted, that the new enclosure is formed into subdivisions, but it is necessary to remark, that in many cases there is no absolute necessity for this.

---

* George Matthews.

I shall

I shall touch upon this circumstance first in relation to arable, and secondly for grass-land.

Except in very bleak situations, a thickly enclosed country is unfavourable to the growth of corn: all shade is mischievous, and the free course of the wind highly advantageous in drying wet land; and in harvesting the crops on all kinds of land. Those who have been adverse to enclosing have not failed to dwell on this point; and it has generally been admitted. Hedges it is true may be kept in a dwarf state so low as not to injure crops, but they are no longer to be relied on as sufficient fences, and instead of yielding fuel, they become a regular and, so far, a barren expense.

Hence it certainly merits attention, whether the land may not be profitably cultivated in an open though in a *several* state; surrounded only by the ring fence of the farm. If this can be effected, the saving of expense would in many cases be considerable. Sheep under a good shepherd may be fed any where, even on balks between corn, on the space of a few feet, as I have many times seen abroad without the smallest damage; but their shepherds are more skilful than ours. For the consumption of clover, trefoil, &c. the difficulty, if any, could only force a management that ought to be universal—that of soiling all great cattle; in which the crops go twice as far, with a dunghill twice as large. With sheep there is no difficulty; and as to feeding the stubbles with hogs, they may be herded, though with more trouble than sheep.

It deserves notice, that in old enclosed countries where the fences are not all of white-thorn, and absolutely free from gaps, hedges are trusted to for safety which they do not afford; and when you see new enclosures in which the utmost possible attention is not given to nursing up the quick, the same spectacle is apparent. The farmer's losses are so great, yet a heavy expense annually submitted to, that fences prove a nuisance; and if he knew the full advantages of soiling (so little generally understood) he had far better be without them.

Upon the whole, it is presumed that subdivision fences in arable farms have in many cases been made at a great expense, wherein they might very well have been spared. It ought not therefore to be undertaken as a matter of course, but a due discrimination of circumstances well made and considered.

In respect to fields intended for grass; the question will depend on the decision of another, to which sufficient attention has not been given:—Is it profitable to summer-feed cows and fatting stock at home in stalls or yards, rather than suffer them to range the fields in the common manner? The system of stall or yard-feeding is better understood in some other countries than it is in England. We are not however without experiments here, which have been attended with ample success. These will without doubt be particularly detailed in the *General Report* on that subject: the benefits are numerous and great. The grass goes much farther; double the stock is kept; the quantity of manure raised is more than doubled, and of greater value per load. The animals are kept free from flies, which drive them into ponds, and ditches, and pits, where they pass the heat of the day, or drive about the fields, to the destruction of more grass than they eat. These are great objects, and deserving of much attention.

The only objection made to the practice, deserving notice here, is, that the universal method in England is different; and that rich grass-lands would be damaged by mowing. Fifty years ago this objection might have been made to soiling horses; a practice that has now crept into almost every county of the kingdom, and general in Kent and Hertfordshire. Old prejudices are done away, and
the

the new method is so much approved, that it will probably become general among all but the worst and poorest farmers. In regard to mowing, the case is very different from that of hay; for which the grass is left so long (so much longer than it ought to be) that the grazing pasture is injured by it; but for soiling it is begun much sooner, and repeated twice, thrice, and on rich land oftener: and this cutting is less injurious than trampling. The dung arising in the yards affords a much better manuring than what is dropped about the fields, to injure spots, or be carried aways by the flie. But this is not the place fully to examine a question of so great importance; it is introduced here merely as a caution against embarking in great expenses, which *may* not be necessary.

§ IV.—*Position of the Fences.*

A question has been started, whether the lines of hedges which form enclosures, should be drawn out on the higher or on the lower parts of the field where there are hill and dale, and the operator has his choice? It has been contended, that by live stock being drawn for shelter to the hedge, much dung will be left near it, and that rains will, if the fence be on the hill, distribute the effect over the surface of the field; whereas, if the fence be in the vale, the same cause will wash it at once into a ditch, brook, &c. There is a little truth in this observation, but the conclusion must be too weak to influence the position of the fence. The soil may probably be dry or wet; if wet, the fence-ditch must be marked out where it will best answer the purpose of a drain, a motive for its position far more powerful than that just recited.

recited. If the soil be dry or poor, or the situation bleak, and there is a choice of position, it will probably be placed where it will grow the best; for nursing up a quick-hedge in an unfavourable position, is so tedious and expensive an operation, that every means should be taken to accelerate it. In mountains and moors, where shelter is highly valuable, fences are of stone, and the walls may be placed as high as you please; but if there be not a plantation between double ones, the shelter will be little or none.

§ V.—*Of the Sort of Fence.*

A very elaborate Report on this subject has been presented to the Board, and printed under their auspices, to which the more curious reader may be referred; but at present it will be necessary only to notice the most usual fences that have been adopted in executing the various parliamentary enclosures that have taken place. Some notes to this purpose will be found in the Appendix to this Report (No. XVI.) As the present work is not a treatise on practical agriculture, and will still leave the desideratum of a more minute detail upon the whole economy of fences, the present reference it is conceived will answer the purpose of this general inquiry.

SECTION VI.

ROADS, BRIDGES, &c.

The expense of roads, bridges, and other public works, which attend many parliamentary enclosures, necessarily varies with the particular circumstances of each individual case. In some it forms a very heavy expense; in others it is comparatively light; and there are instances in which these objects, as well as that of fencing, are put under the management of distinct Commissioners, named from among the inhabitants of the parish enclosed; a plan which has been found to be attended with considerable advantages.

There are three things to be particularly attended to in laying out roads over new enclosures: 1st, the convenience of the public; 2d, the ease of the parishioners, as far as it can be considered without intrenching too much upon that convenience; 3d, the convenience and beauty of the several estates, where regard can be paid to such circumstances without interfering greatly with the two former. As to the first, it is certain that the straighter they are laid out the more commodious they are, so that there is no remarkable inequality in the ground, and there was a certainty that they would be put into sufficient repair; but as it seldom happens that considerations of this kind do not clash with straight lines, Commissioners are always induced to reconcile the convenience of the public with the ease of the parishioners; and this they think is better done by sometimes carrying roads a little about, for the sake of directing them over sounder ground,

or

or by reducing their number, when the public is not materially incommoded by it; supposing it more eligible to travellers to take a little circuit for the sake of a good road, than to go in a straight line over a bad one. It will happen in some cases, that a little alteration of the direction of a road will render the allotment of estates in the neighbourhood of it much more commodious. All estates should be laid contiguous to a public road, and also be as compact as possible within themselves. When both these points can be secured by a small deviation, Commissioners will perhaps be justified in doing it from such motives; though certain liberties of this kind are not to be taken wantonly, nor ought the public to be incommoded for the private convenience of any bod whatever.*"

---

* Essay on the Nature and Method of Enclosures, 1766, p. 99.

SECTION VII.

DRAINAGE AND IRRIGATION.

Drainage has been a very common article of expense in a great number of enclosures, demanding large cuts and canals for the conveyance of superfluous water; the object has been found of the first importance, and such improvements effected by it as have trebled, and even centupled the value of large tracts of land. The fens of Cambridgeshire offer a spectacle which proves clearly the general drainage of enclosed lordships; for the great increase of complaints in the fens, and which caused the application for the Eaubrink cut, have been occasioned, as I was assured by many persons on the spot, by the rapidity with which the waters from heavy rains in the parishes bordering on the fens, or from which the descent lies thither now comes, compared with the periods when it rested in the former open fields till exhaled by evaporation :— a sure proof of the immense improvement wrought in all those parishes by the drainages effected by enclosing. But with respect to irrigation, cases are rare. The following, however, sets an example, which it is to be hoped will have many imitations.

Irrigation by Enclosing.—Upon the enclosure of the parish of Ridgemont, near Woburn, His Grace the late Duke of Bedford procured a clause (and the same is in that of Maulden and Crawley) in the Act, to enable him to irrigate, by carrying a canal through the property of other persons, paying them compensation for damages;
and

and as this is one of the most important improvements in the business of enclosing that ever took place, I shall here insert the whole clause.

"And whereas certain parts of the parish of Ridgemont might be greatly improved by irrigation, or watering into valuable meadow lands, if the waters of certain springs, rivulets, and brooks, in the said parish, were at times diverted and carried along the declivity of the hills in carriages or ditches on the proper level for such purpose; and whereas such carriages will, in some instances, in their course to the land intended to be watered, pass through and over the estate and lands of other persons, and in some instances through old enclosures; and whereas certain lands within the said parish might also be greatly improved by proper and competent drains and ditches being cut and continued through the vallies and ground below such land; be it therefore enacted, that the said Commissioners shall and may direct and appoint some competent person (making him a reasonable compensation for his trouble therein) to take the levels, and examine the practicability and extent of the improvements which may be made by irrigation and drainage within the said parish of Ridgemont, and to report the same to the said Commissioners, who shall be authorized and empowered to scour out, deepen, straighten, divert, alter, change, rise, sink, or embank all, or any of the ancient brooks, rivulets, springs, ditches, and water-courses within the said parish, for the purpose aforesaid; and to set out, appoint, construct, and make all such new carriages, ditches, trenches, tunnels. bridges, water-gates, sluices, and drains, as well in, through, over, and upon the lands and grounds hereby intended to be divided and enclosed as aforesaid,

as

as in, over, through, and upon any ancient enclosures or other lands or grounds within the said parish (except gardens), or across and under any public or private road, as they shall judge necessary for the purpose of irrigating or draining any of the lands and grounds within the said parish, which from their situation may be capable of such improvement; and the said Commissioners are hereby authorized and required to make such satisfaction as they shall think proper, to the proprietor or proprietors of such ancient enclosures or other lands, not hereby intended to be divided and enclosed, for any damage done their lands, in the constructing, making, and maintaining of any carriages, ditches, water-courses, trenches, drains, tunnels, bridges, water-gates, sluices, or drains, in, through, or thereon: and the said Commissioners shall apportion and assess the expense of satisfaction for damage done to old enclosures, and of the digging, making, and constructing the necessary carriages, ditches, tunnels, drains, bridges, water-gates, sluices, or dams, for the purpose of conveying the water upon, and taking the same off the land again, as aforesaid, upon such of the said proprietors to whom the said lands shall be allotted and belong, in proportion to the benefit their estate will severally derive from such irrigation and drainage: and the money so assessed shall be levied and recoverable in the same manner as the money for the purpose of passing this Act, and carrying the same into execution, is hereinafter directed to be levied and raised; and the Commissioners are hereby directed, in and by their award hereafter mentioned, to order, direct, and appoint at whose expense, at what time, and in what manner the said carriages, ditches, tunnels, drains, bridges, water-gates, sluices, banks, dams, and other requisites

quisites for irrigation and draining, shall thereafter severally be repaired, scoured out, cleansed, maintained, and renewed; and at what times, and in what proportions, the said water shall be used by the several proprietors for the purpose of irrigating as aforesaid: and the several proprietors of lands irrigated as aforesaid, and their respective servants shall, thereafter, at such times as the said Commissioners shall in their said award direct, have free access in, to, and upon the estates of any other person, doing as little damage as may be, and keeping and passing along upon the banks of such of the carriages, ditches, rivulets, or brooks, which bring or convey the water to or upon their respective lands, and along the banks of such drains, ditches, or brooks as convey the water from or off their said lands, for the purpose of opening, shutting, or regulating the water-gates or sluices, or of removing any obstruction to the course of the waters."

"In consequence of this clause, levels were taken in the three parishes before mentioned, to ascertain what lands could be watered, and the allotments so marked, that the ditches of the limitation fences might be the main water-carriers on the highest possible level: no difficulties occurred in these instances, because in general the tracts below these levels were bogs, or boggy bottoms, which, however valuable in the prophetic eye of an enlightened mind, were in no estimation amongst the proprietors in general: and when all such shall become equally well informed, still the application of this clause will be of infinite consequence in a multitude of cases at present unthought of; and had equal wisdom guided the proprietors in the many hundreds of bills that have passed the legislature, thousands of acres would have been irrigated,

gated, to the amazing increase of the benefits which have flowed from enclosures in general.

The works made pursuant to this clause, in the parishes of Ridgemont, Crawley and Maulden, I viewed with much attention, and should fully explain, were it possible, without the assistance of maps*.

* Annals, v. xli. p. 539.

SECTION VIII.

EXPENSES.

There have been two methods of providing for the expenses of the measure of enclosing; first, by levying assessments upon the proprietors, proportioned to their property, usually according to the poor-rate. Second, by selling portions of waste lands or commons sufficient to pay part, or the whole of such expenses. Where the latter is practicable, it is a most easy and beneficial method of providing for the demands of the measure.

It is to the expense of procuring separate acts of parliament to which must be attributed the slow progress made in enclosing; and which will for ever lay a direct prohibition on the application of the measure to all small commons, wastes, or open fields. These expenses have arisen and increased so much, that multitudes set themselves in opposition to the proposal in every part of the kingdom; they dread demands which they are not able to satisfy; and must be deterred from consenting, by seeing so many persons whose means have been so exhausted by these expenses, that when the allotments came into their hands, the power of cultivating them was gone. This raises such an opposition, that, if it do not preclude the measure, it adds at least to the expenses, already so great.

In the examination by order of the Board, in 1800, the following particulars were gained:

Acres on an average enclosed, 1612, nearly what has
been

been found to be the average of all the enclosures that have been authorized by parliament.

The act, 497*l.*
The survey, 259*l.*
Commissioners, 344*l.*
Fences, &c. 550*l.* 7*s.* 6*d.* (Appendix, No. XVII.)

Hence it appears, that in the ratio of 500*l.* per act, 2591 acts would now cost at least THIRTEEN HUNDRED THOUSAND POUNDS; which sum, in case such a number of acts were in future to pass at no greater expense, would nearly be taken from the faculties of those whose undiminished capitals are, in most cases, requisite for the preparatory improvements of the land; a circumstance ruinous to small proprietors.

Notes, in reply to the Committee of the House of Commons.

" In my parish is great abundance of coal and good limestone, and about nineteen thousand six hundred acres of heath-down and waste land, lying undivided, and not stinted; several acres of which would re-imburse every expense of improvement; but the proprietors of these commons are deterred from dividing and enclosing them, solely from the intolerable expense attending the obtaining acts of parliament necessary for the purpose.

" HUGH NANNEY, Vicar,
" Haltwhistle, Northumberland."

" I cannot omit this opportunity of saying, that the expense of the enclosure has been so enormous, as cordially to disgust the majority of proprietors. The community may perhaps gain some little by it hereafter; much

much from the size of the land enclosed they cannot, but most of the individuals concerned, will ever have cause to regret that the Bill obtained the sanction of the Legislature. The expenses usually arising in the operation of an Enclosure Bill, call loudly for parliamentary interference.

"THOMAS ALSTON WARREN,
"Curate of Kensworth, Hertford."

"In the enclosure of Hartingfordbury, a plan was formed to escape the charges (so often very heavy) which are made by Commissioners; that of naming in the bill three neighbouring gentlemen for Commissioners: Mr. BYDE, of Ware-park, Mr. NICHOLSON CALVERT, and the Rev. Mr. BROWNE. By this mode, no other expense is incurred than is absolutely necessary; these gentlemen, of course, taking nothing, but acting as friends to the parties. If this plan could be more commonly pursued, which surely it might be, enclosing would not be so much complained of*."

"Although the money arising from the sale of tracts of the common was far from being adequate to the purposes intended by the Act; yet these sales have answered a very valuable end, in easing the proprietors of the bulk of that enormous load of expenses that generally attend divisions; and have consequently given vigour to the proprietors (the poor ones especially), in breaking up, and pushing the improvements on their several allotments, at a more early period than has generally been practised on the division of other commons; and even long before there is any probability of executing the award of the Commissioners†."

---

* Hertfordshire Agriculture, p. 44.
† Essay on Divided Commons, by a Farmer, p. 23.

CHAP. IV.

PRODUCE OF THE KINGDOM INSUFFICIENT FOR ITS CONSUMPTION.

A MODERN Writer of considerable talents*, has explained some important principles of population, in a manner that not only does great honour to his knowledge and penetration, but tends powerfully to convince the Legislature of this kingdom, that the increase of the people very far outruns the productiveness of our Agriculture; and has by a chain of satisfactory reasoning proved, that if measures be not speedily taken to increase our Agriculture, we may expect the early recurrence of scarcity, under circumstances probably more dangerous than those we have already experienced.

The reader will scarcely fail to combine such results with the present state of the countries bordering upon the Baltic.

Accounts will be inserted in the Appendix to these papers, which will shew that the late and actual state of importation, tend as strongly as they can tend, to confirm those opinions which represent this country in respect to its agriculture, combined with its population, to be in a most dangerous state.

The export of manufactures, the general extent of

---

* Mr. MALTHUS.

commerce,

commerce, even the universal prosperity seen through so many classes of the people, are all so many causes of increasing population; and if, with such powerful and operating principles of augmentation, the national Agriculture is not equally impelled, the consequences must be severely felt upon every trifling deficiency of crop. That Agriculture is not thus proportionably increased or improved, the regular import of corn is a clear proof.

Our situation in these respects is such as to call for great, and even immediate attention to the agricultural state of the kingdom. No person can seriously reflect on the last scarcity in this country, and on the proportion of the twenty millions sterling paid for corn which came from the Baltic, and compare such an import with what the present state of those countries permits us to expect from them, perhaps for many years to come, without seeing some reason for apprehension. Nothing can place the kingdom in any degree of security, but taking effective measures to prepare, as much as human efforts can prepare, for evils of the most dangerous tendency. The more this subject is examined, the more imperiously it will be found to call for immediate and adequate exertions. The wisdom of the Legislature will determine what those exertions should be; but it is conceived that it is peculiarly within the province, and indeed, the strict duty of a Board of Agriculture, to point out whatever appears to them to tend forcibly, under Divine Providence, to place the national subsistence upon a secure foundation.

No means can tend more powerfully, it is to be hoped, to such an end, than to ascertain the certainty of the fact, that the Agriculture of the kingdom is at present insufficient to feed it. The obvious necessity of setting this

fact

fact in a clear light, will apologize for the details which it is necessary to give. (Appendix No. XVIII.)

Sir Geo. O. Paul, Bart. in the tract which I have often quoted, has a remark on this subject which is very just.

" The prominent evil which has given birth to the present design, is the sudden conviction of a fact, which, though far from a *new* observation, has not, until now, been pointed to our feelings.

" *This flourishing kingdom, on an average of crops, does not produce a supply of the ordinary articles of food for its inhabitants**, *whilst there are* 18,000,000 *of acres of land lying in waste*†, *which are convertible to culture, and capable of being rendered productive of the various articles of human sustenance.* Dependent on foreign markets for the supply of the ordinary deficiency of our own produce—if the supply fails in those markets, an *absolute* want takes place, without any peculiar visitation of Providence on our own island. Should the crop *not* fail in the countries of our foreign markets, but should other countries be purchasers at the same market, whose wants should be greater than our own; the price we shall pay will not be regulated by *our own* wants, but by those of such other countries —In a country where the supply is less than the demand, the home price will be regulated by the price at which the article can be brought into the home market, which is to make good the deficiency; and if this price, thus aug-

---

* See, " Representation of the Lords of the Committee of Council, upon the state of the Laws for regulating the importation and exportation of Corn, 1790."

† See, " Appendix (B) to the First Report of the Select Committee of the House of Commons, appointed to take into consideration the means of promoting the improvement of the Waste Lands," &c.

mented,

mented, should be advanced beyond a due relation to the earnings of labour, a *relative* want must be the consequence. Such, it appears, is now the situation of this kingdom, and such that of the labouring agricultural poor*."

Should it be contended that the principles so ably explained by Mr. MALTHUS, demand the admission that any increase of cultivation will be attended by a corresponding increase of people, and consequently that the benefit will be but partial: the observation is admitted to be just; but the proportion of surplus produce above the consumption of the cultivators is so considerable, that the advantage is a very essential one which flows from every increase of agriculture. By the population returns it appears:

Total enumeration for England and Wales 9,343,578
Scotland 1,599,068
                                                        ──────────
                                                        10,942,646
Of which, employed in agriculture:
In England 1,713,289
Scotland 365,516
                                          ───────── 2,078,805
                                                     ──────────
                                                     8,863,841

Hence the fact appears to be, that two millions employed in agriculture, feed (besides themselves) near nine millions of other persons; and consequently that any objections tending to lessen the importance of an increase of cultivation, do not deserve attention.

This able Writer has also a remark which I have heard

---

* Observations on the General Enclosure Bill, by Sir G. O. PAUL, Bart. 1796, p. 5.

much misrepresented in argument, as if it proved something against the cultivation of British wastes: "The great obstacle to the amelioration of land, is the difficulty, the expense, and sometimes, the impossibility of procuring a sufficient quantity of dressing. As this instrument of improvement therefore is in practice limited, whatever it may be in theory, the question will always be, how it may be most profitably employed? and in any instance where a certain quantity of dressing and labour employed to bring new land into cultivation, would have yielded a permanently greater produce if employed upon old land, both the individual and the nation are losers*."

Then it has been said, why require a general power to enclose, seeing, that it will probably be attended with a deviation of dressing and labour from lands that would pay better?

The original passage is not quite correct, in bringing *dressing* into the question; but the application of the remark to the wastes of England, &c. is entirely erroneous in those who make it.

The culture of a waste tract, when added to a farm already in cultivation, is in many cases much more likely to give additional dressing to the old land than to take any from it: of this I have seen many instances; and it would not take Mr. MALTHUS, more than a morning's ride from Cambridge, to see some himself. The practice of paring and burning produces great crops, which are all taken from the new land, and consumed on the old, to the very great amelioration of the old cultivated fields. Nor is there a waste bog or fen any where to be found, capable of draining, but the same effect would

---

* Essay on the Principles of Population, p. 479.

result, provided the husbandry of paring and burning be understood in the country where such wastes are found.

In the case of drier moors and heaths, the application of the same practice, in some cases with the addition of lime or marl (dressings to which there is no other limit than that of expense), has the same effects, and produces very beneficial crops, without requiring dung; and on the poorest soil, without any other dressing than what the consumption of its own produce will yield. The fact to those who have a practical knowledge of the subject, speaks for itself; but very many instances might be given. The article *dressing* should therefore have been left out of the observation.

In regard to *labour*, the case certainly *may* be different: we can suppose exertions to be made on waste land at the expense of old cultivation, in a district where hands are scarce. The thing is *possible*: I do not conceive it probable in any part of this kingdom. If a contiguous farmer undertakes the work, we are to suppose he would do it for his profit; but this would not be the result, were he to draw his hands for it, from the necessary demand of his old cultivation: these men are too cautious and prudent, to make it necessary for the speculative politician to be under any apprehensions of the sort. If the work be executed on a larger scale, by a stranger establishing a new farm, and thus creating a new demand for labour, he must, if hands are scarce, attract them by higher prices than common; or, which is nearly the same thing, by giving piece-work to men usually at day wages. If he does this, is it not a proof that he does it with the expectation of profit? and does not this expectation prove that the waste ought to be cultivated? It is the best and the surest proof of that proposition.

What

What is here mentioned, is sufficient to remove any apprehension of an improper deviation of labour, or dressing.

But it has been said, that the capital might be better employed on old cultivated lands. I beg to ask, who is the proper judge of this? the farmer out of business with money in his pocket—or the politician in his night-gown and slippers? This is surely a case which should be left to the conviction of individuals. Let it be remembered, that the want of farms is felt in most of the districts in this kingdom; and when capital, and skill, and industry, are ready to be invested, and would immediately be invested on these wastes, if obstacles were removed by a power of enclosing, it surely cannot be urged with the smallest degree of propriety, that such exertions would be any deviation of dressing, or labour, or money, from lands already in cultivation.

Another objection to cultivation has been hinted, which may raise a smile, and that is, Mr. WILLIAMS's idea, that luxuriance of vegetation deteriorates the climate of the country: that were all the kingdom in the state of the South Downs and Salisbury Plain, the climate would be much better. Let the assertion rest on the opinion of the author; or if you please, be taken for granted; what conclusion will you draw from it? To change our cultivation for desarts, and our people for sheep? This is not the author's meaning; and I have no intention to misrepresent him: suffice it, that the idea is mentioned. It does not demand a serious discussion.

Let us then come to the great fact, that the kingdom has not for many years past fed itself; and does not effect it at present. The corn trade proves this.

" From

GENERAL REPORT ON ENCLOSURES. 107

" From 1708 to 1773, the average annual exportation of wheat* has been 222,121 quarters.

From 1773 to 1804, it has been only 5400 quarters.

From 1700 to 1756, only two years occurred when importation was wanted.

From 1773 twenty-five years have occurred when we could not subsist without an importation; the average annual amount of which has been 346,874 quarters.

From 1646 to 1686, the average annual price was 2*l.* 4*s.* 4*d.*

From 1686 to 1756, it was 1*l.* 15*s.* 2*d.*

From 1785 to 1790, the average annual importation was 107,978 quarters.

The price, 2*l.* 5*s.* 5*d.*

From 1790 to 1795, the importation was 298,583 quarters.

The price, 2*l.* 14*s.* 8½*d.*

From 1795 to 1800, the importation was 617,935 quarters.

The price, 3*l.* 12*s.* 3½*d.*

From 1800 to 1803, the importation was 827,763 quarters.

The price, 4*l.* 7*d.*

Thus have our imports increased, and the prices gradually advanced with them.

In the five years previous to 1800, the balance was above three millions sterling against this country, in imports and exports of corn.

In one unfortunate year, viz. from the 5th of January,

---

* The exportation of wheat alone is here mentioned, but it may be necessary to observe, that from 1710 to 1760, the average annual exportation of grain were near 600,000 quarters; and that the value of the corn exported was an advantage to the nation of above 600,000*l.* annually.

1800,

1800, to the 5th of January 1801, above eleven millions, sterling were paid to foreign countries, for corn and rice imported into this kingdom, besides large sums expended on bounties.

In the four last years we have paid 25,375,027*l.* besides 2,224,491*l.* granted in bounties.

Such has been the fluctuation of price, that in the year 1800 8*l.* per quarter was given for wheat; the average now is not above 2*l.* 13*s.*, a price at which the agriculturist cannot grow it*."

Average import for ten years, ending 1803:

Wheat	592,055	qrs.
Flour	221,243	cwt.
Deducting three years of scarcity, average of the remaining seven	391,325	qrs.
Flour	122,455	cwt.
Value of the import in the years 1800 and 1801, near	£.24,000,000	
Ditto in ten years	£.40,000,000	

In 34 years, from 1770 to 1803, there were eight years in which the export exceeded the import; the amount in all, 1,446,312 quarters, not equal to the import of the single year 1801, or wheat and flour 1,495,429.

Bounties on import in eight years, 1796 to 1803, 2,826,947*l.* †

A circumstance also which deserves great attention in the present state of the North of Europe, is the comparatively small quantity of corn which we have at any time been able to get from North America.

" Average of wheat and flour imported from the

---

* Annals xlii. p. 181.

† Memoir presented by the President of the Board to the Treasury, 1805.

North of Europe, for twelve years and from the States of America previous to 1796:

	qrs.	bush.
Wheat and flour from the North of Europe for twelve years, per ann.	127,819	4
Greatest quantity ditto in one year	329,281	
Average of wheat and flour from North America for twelve years	27,525	5
Greatest quantity from ditto in one year	93,724*	

" The greatest quantity of wheat ever imported into Great Britain in one year from the north of Europe, during a century preceding 1796, was 329,281 quarters, but in the last mentioned year we imported 753,356 quarters of wheat, and 15,535 cwt. of flour, equal to about 5178 quarters viz. from

	Wheat.	Flour.
	qrs.	cwt.
Denmark	17,184	
Sweden	18,174	
Russia	102,126	702
Prussia	296,180	
Poland	126,790	
Germany	192,902	14,832
Total from the North of Europe	753,356	15,534
Importations from America	2,697	143,833
Total importation	756,053	159,367†"

But perhaps a more lamentable circumstance than even in these imports, is that of their continuing to the present moment. By a late (and hitherto unpublished) ac-

---

* Question of Scarcity, 1800, p. 64.

† Lord SHEFFIELD's Remarks on the Deficiency of Grain, Part I. p. 20, 1800.

count procured by the Board, this fact appears:

In 1804, about 440,000 quarters of wheat were imported;
In 1805, about 900,000 quarters;
and in 1806, near 300,000; and as these years have been of moderate plenty, it shews clearly the alarming deficiency of our produce. (See Appendix, No. XVIII)

For various other documents tending to throw a light on the corn trade of this kingdom, see the Appendix No. XVIII.

CHAP. V.

NECESSITY OF A GENERAL ENCLOSURE.

THE necessity or the propriety of a general measure of this sort, must be proportionate to the proofs already adduced of the benefits which have resulted from the enclosures that have taken place under distinct acts of parliament; and it must also be in proportion to that increase of population which may be expected to take place in future in this kingdom. As the capital employed by the national industry is rapidly increasing; as the commerce and manufactures, and general activity of the people are at present flowing in a tide of prosperity; and as the political and civil liberty, and consequent happiness of the people, which most powerfully influence the increase of human societies, never diffused their blessings more generally, we have every reason to expect the people will increase as rapidly as heretofore; and if provision be not made for ensuring a corresponding increase of cultivation, the consequences must be dangerous, perhaps fatal. This consideration cannot be duly examined without the obvious conclusion resulting, that a General Enclosure Act is absolutely and essentially necessary to the prosperity, peace, and safety of the kingdom.

The call for a General Enclosure has been nearly universal throughout the kingdom; and not among persons only of one or two descriptions, but in almost every rank and situation of life. This common opinion has been the

result

result of conviction, that enclosures produce more food for mankind than commons and open fields; and the severity of the evils felt in two scarcities, impressed these ideas so much more forcibly on the public mind, as to influence, in a great measure, not only the conversation, but very warm hopes that the legislature would, in its wisdom, gratify the desires of so large a proportion of the proprietors of the kingdom.

In the Appendix (No. XIX.) is collected some of the observations upon this point, which the documents in the possession of the Board afford.

§ I.—*Of the Progress that has hitherto been made towards attaining a General Enclosure Act.*

On the Law and Practice of North Britain, in regard to the Division of Commons, and the Alterations which might be made therein.

" If any person entertain an idea that a General Enclosing Bill is an impracticable measure, his doubts will probably be removed, when he is informed that such an Act was passed about a century ago in Scotland, and has been found to answer the purpose which was thereby intended. As that Act is distinguished by its simplicity and conciseness, it may not be improper to give it a place in this Report.

" *Act concerning the Dividing of Commonties, passed in the Parliament of Scotland,* 17th *July,* 1695.

" Our Sovereign Lord, with advice and consent of
" the estates of parliament, for preventing the discords
" that

" that arise about commonties, and for the more easy
" and expedit deciding thereof, in time coming, statutes
" and ordains, that all commonties, except the common-
" ties belonging to the King and royal burrows in
" burgage, may be divided at the instance of any having
" interest, by summons raised against all persons con-
" cerned before the Lords of Sessions, who are hereby
" empowered to discuss the relevancy; and to determine
" upon the rights and interests of the several parties
" concerned; and to grant commissions to sheriffs, stew-
" ards, baillies of regalitie and their deputies, or justices
" of peace, or others, for perambulating and taking
" all other necessary probation, which commissions shall
" be reported to the said lords, and the said processes
" ultimately determined by them; and where mosses
" shall happen to be in the said commonties, with power
" to the said lords to divide these said mosses among the
" several parties, having interest therein in manner afore-
" said; or in case it be instructed to the said lords that
" the said mosses cannot be conveniently divided, His
" Majesty, with consent foresaid, statutes and declares,
" that the said mosses shall remain common, with free ish
" and entry thereto, whether divided or not; declaring
" also, that the interest of the heretors having right in
" the said commonties, shall be estimat according to the
" valuation of their repective lands or properties, and
" which divisions are appointed to be made of that part
" of the commontry that is next adjacent to each heretor's
" property."

" From this Act it appears how simple the regulations are, which a century ago were thought sufficient, in a part of the kingdom not distinguished for the scarcity of its wastes; and under the provision of that Act many

extensive

extensive commons have been divided, in a manner that has given satisfaction to the particsinte rested therein. By this law, it is proper to observe, that a division may be procured at the instance of any one having interest; but the expense of obtaining that division, though instituted at the suit of one, is defrayed by the whole parties concerned, in proportion to their respective shares.

" However excellent this law is justly accounted, and however useful it has proved, yet there are two alterations in it which might render it still more effectual than at present. The first is, that of taking away the exception ingrossed in the statute, by which no common can be divided, in which either the Crown, or any Royal Borough is interested. For this exception no good reason can be assigned, and it probably originated from a jealousy which might naturally occur at the formation of a new system, but which the experience of almost a century ought, before this time, to have totally removed.—The second alteration might be adopted with great advantage from the practice of England. By the Scotch Act, the Court of Session is empowered to grant commissions to sheriffs, justices of the peace, or others, for perambulating and taking all other necessary probation, or, in other words, ascertaining the extent of the commons, &c. and the result of the investigation is directed to be reported to the Court of Sessions, to be finally determined on by them. Questions, however, respecting the rights of parties, &c. are heard bfore the Court of Session alone. Where the common is of great extent, this is attended with great expense, and much delay. The number of questions which may arise, is more than a court of law, having a great deal of other business to go through, can always attend to. It would be

infinitely

infinitely better, therefore, were the Court of Session to nominate Commissioners, not less than three, nor more than five, who should be entrusted with the same extensive powers which are given to the Commissioners in England, when appointed by private acts of parliament. They ought not only to have the power of nominating surveyors, &c. but all questions arising in course of the proceedings ought, in the first instance, to be heard before, and decided by them. After they have given their award, it may then be brought under the cognizance of the Court of Session with effect, and all parties conceiving themselves injured, may then have an opportunity of complaining, and of having their case fairly considered by the court. Every one must see how much easier it is to determine any litigated point after it has been once decided upon, than if it had never received any former judgment. The parties would, in many cases, probably acquiesce in the decision of the Commissioners, and at any rate the great object would be attained, of having the business effectually done, and the common speedily divided, every delay in which must be attended with considerable loss both to the parties interested and to the public.

" It is impossible on this occasion for your Committee not to remark the benefit which may often be obtained by comparing the laws of England and Scotland, and ascertaining the advantage of which they are respectively possessed. It may often happen, that combining the principles of the two codes may be as useful to the laws, as an union of the two legislatures has proved advantageous to the strength, the security, and the happiness of both kingdoms; and where circumstances will admit of it, there cannot be a doubt, that it would be desirable to establish the same system of jurisprudence, or

at

at least of agricultural legislation and police over the whole island*."

Report from the Select Committee of the House of Commons, on Bills of Enclosure.

" The Select Committee appointed to consider of the most effectual means of facilitating, under the authority of parliament, the enclosure and improvement of waste, unenclosed, and unproductive lands, commons, common arable fields, common meadows, and common of pasture in this kingdom, and to report the same, with their opinion thereupon, to the House, have, pursuant to the order of the House, considered the matter to them referred, and agreed upon the following Report.

" Your Committee, in considering the subject referred to them, have principally had in view the impediments to enclosures under the authority of parliament, arising from the expenses incurred in such procedure; and have consequently endeavoured to trace the nature and amount of those expenses, as far as the various and complicated circumstances attending them would admit, through the several stages of the transaction; the result of which they shall, in the first place, proceed to lay before the House.

" Your Committee find that a meeting is frequently convened by public advertisement, for the purpose of considering the propriety of applying to parliament for an intended enclosure; at which it sometimes happens, that persons not interested in the business, attend; and that the expenses of such meetings, usually held at some

---

* Report on Waste Lands, p. 30.

inn,

inn, as well as that of the advertisements, are often charged in the solicitor's bill.

"A petition to parliament is then prepared, the expense attending which rarely exceeds the sum of two guineas.

"Notices of the intended application are then, in pursuance of the standing orders of this House, to be affixed to the church door of each parish in which the lands to be enclosed are situated, for three Sundays in the month of August or September, the expense of which naturally varies, according to the number of parishes, and the distance of the churches from the residence of the solicitor or agent concerned; it being usual for only one person, if possible, to be employed for this purpose, in consequence of the necessity of his attending afterwards in town, to prove the fact before the Committee on the petition. The charge in general appears to be from one to three guineas for each parish.

"The draft of the bill itself is either copied by the solicitor in the country from some former act, as far as circumstances will admit, or prepared originally by the parliamentary solicitor; in both which cases, it is obvious that a number of similar clauses, either required by the orders of the House, or authorized by general practice, are constantly inserted. The proportion of these general clauses to the provision of a local and peculiar nature, cannot be precisely ascertained; but your Committee have reason to suppose that they may, in some instances, amount to two-thirds, and in others, not to more than two-fifths of the whole. The expense of preparing and copying this draft being charged by the sheet, must depend upon the length of it, which must in all cases be increased by these general clauses.

"The practice of the legislature requiring proof of the
consent

consent of a certain number of the parties interested, by their actually signing the bill, it is necessary to employ a proper person, and sometimes more than one, to procure this, and afterwards to attend in London to prove it before the Committee of both Houses. As it is occasionally necessary to travel to a considerable distance, and into different parts of the kingdom, for this purpose, the expense attending it is in such case considerable, and in one instance it appears to have amounted to between seventy and eighty pounds, to procure the consent of one individual. It is also stated to your Committee, that the great number of consents supposed to be necessary, according to the present practice of parliament, whether three-fourths, according to the ideas of some, or four-fifths, according to the ideas of others (for there is no fixed rule), is a great bar to enclosure. Your Committee are thence led to submit it to the wisdom of the House, whether it may not be expedient in future, to allow the proof of a less number of consents, provided they amount to a decided preponderance, to be sufficient for obtaining a bill.

" The bill having been brought in, read a first and second time, and committed, it is necessary to bring witnesses to town, to prove that the orders of the House have been complied with in the foregoing particulars, and to verify he allegations in the preamble. All this is attended with different degrees of expense, according to the number of persons employed, the distance of their residence from the metropolis, and the accidental delays which may retard the progress of the bill to the House of Peers; when the same person must again attend to be sworn at the bar of the House, and afterwards examined before the Committee. In cases where the bill meets with opposition, this must necessarily be considerable; and in all it is sufficient to deserve attention.

" The

"The subsequent progress of the bill through parliament is subject to the payment of the several fees particularly specified in the Table annexed to this Report. The amount of these, it is evident, must vary according to the size of the bill, the number of interests affected by it, and the opposition it may happen to meet with.

"The length of the bill chiefly operates as an increase to the expense in this stage of proceeding, by the additional charge of engrossing and printing. The only other incidental expense, not yet noticed in this part of the transaction, is that of a town, or parliamentary solicitor, usually some person whose experience in such business, and acquaintance with the forms of parliament, render his assistance particularly desirable; and that of a country solicitor, whose local knowledge, and immediate connexion with the parties interested, in many cases makes his attendance also material. The charge of the former, for his whole service, is usually twenty guineas; but in controverted, or any complicated cases, considerably more: that of the latter is subject to necessary variations, according to the length of the attendance, and other circumstances, but must in most cases be considerable.

"When the bill has received the sanction of the Legislature, the usual mode of carrying it into effect through the intervention of Commissioners, give rise to charges and expenses of a different nature. The necessity of peculiar qualifications, as well as a reputation for experience and integrity, in persons employed for this purpose, has usually confined the choice of them within no very enlarged limits; and the expediency of dispatch, without the additional expense of multiplied litigation, has suggested the necessity of investing them with a summary,

summary, and, in most cases, uncontroulable jurisdiction; unless where any flagrant instance of misbehaviour, of which no instance has been stated to your Committee, might subject them to the animadversion of a criminal court. This latitude of confidence, however necessary for some of their functions, may in some cases lead to abuse, particularly in the charges which may be occasioned by neglect in not proceeding regularly, and with as little interruption as possible, in the dispatch of the business entrusted to them.

" Your Committee find that it is usual to appoint three Commissioners; the attendance of two of them is requisite to give effect to their acts; and that the sum allowed to each for his trouble and expense is about two guineas for each day of necessary attendance, exclusive of charges for his journey, in some cases, not only from their residence to the place of meeting, but from considerable distances to which their other avocations may have carried them.

" It appears to have been the practice of late years, for the Commissioners to appoint a clerk to draw up the minutes of their proceedings, which he may thus be prepared to authenticate in case of litigation, to which the Commissioners themselves are a party, and to assist them with his advice in legal questions. The country solicitor employed to prepare the bill is generally appointed the clerk; which seems now to be recognized by the standing orders of the House, requiring books of account in all cases to be left at his office.

" It appears to your Committee, that the clerk receives in general, emoluments equal to the Commissioners, besides his legal perquisites for business done as a solicitor, for which his charges are separately made. The expenses incurred, both on his account, and that of the Commissioners,

missioners, for att ndance at the regular meetings, necessarily depend on the number of such meetings, but it has been stated to your Committee, that these are sometimes rendered more frequent than is necessary, by the practice of the same Commissioners transacting the business of two enclosures on the same day, which must necessarily interfere with the dispatch of one or both of them; that meetings are sometimes held at which little or nothing is done, and that charges are sometimes made for the attendance of all the Commissioners, where one or more may not actually have been present, though they may afterwards have signed the minutes of the proceedings.

"Acts of Enclosure commonly require a survey to be made either by the Commissioners, or by some person employed by them, and a map to be prepared from it; both which are generally done by a surveyor specially appointed for the purpose, who also frequently makes all the calculations for the Commissioners, and stakes out the several allotments; for all which the charge made is one shilling and sixpence per acre, besides a guinea and a half per day for attending the Commissioners, and an allowance for making a reduced plan. It also appears to your Committee, that the clause above-mentioned, is usually construed so literally, that a fresh survey and map are often ordered, though there may have been one of each in existence, fully or nearly adequate to the purpose; and that in some counties a practice has prevailed of employing two surveyors, one to take a general, the other a particular survey. In some instances, another description of persons is appointed by the Act, called quality-men, whose business it is to value the land.

"Other expenses incidental to an enclosure, are the setting out, forming, and putting in repair the necessary roads,

roads, and fencing the several allotments, according to the direction of the Commissioners. The former being kept for a certain time under their particular controul, are often in consequence the occasion of delaying the execution of the award to a much later period than would be otherwise necessary. The expense of the latter, particularly the public fencing, have, in some instances, been very considerable.

" The last procedure of the Commissioners is the making and enrolling their award, which is required by the several Acts to be written on parchment, and of which one copy is sometimes required to be deposited in the parish church. This being subject to considerable stamp duties, and often of great length, is consequently attended with a proportionate expense. Your Committee find, however, that it has been the practice of late years to reduce the size of the award as much as possible, by omitting the recital of the principal clauses of the Act, and the proceedings of the Commissioners, formerly inserted, and by referring to schedules annexed. Yet even under these restrictions it has been stated to your Committee, that they have sometimes extended to the length of sixty-seven skins of parchment.

The last possible proceeding provided by the Act, is the appeal given to the quarter-sessions against such acts of the Commissioners as are not thereby declared to be final and conclusive, and particularly against the rates they are empowered to make for the payment of the expenses. The delay and expenses attending this part of the proceeding, must of course be casual and uncertain.

" Your Committee having thus laid before the House the several charges incidental to the present mode of procuring and carrying into effect Bills of Enclosure, proceed, in the next place, to state such observations as have
occurred

occurred to them in the course of the inquiry; and to suggest such alterations as may, in their opinion, by diminishing those charges, tend to facilitate the cnelosure and improvement of the wastes, common fields, and other unproductive lands of the kingdom.

" The first head of expenses which appears to them capable of retrenchment, is that which arises from the practice of proving by parole evidence the requisite notices, the consents to the bill, and the allegations of the preamble. If the wisdom of parliament should see fit, for the sake of facilitating the means of general improvement, to depart in this respect from their accustomed usages, your Committee conceived that it might be provided by an Act, to be passed for that purpose, that affidavits of the truth of these facts might be taken, under the penalties of perjury, before one or more neighbouring justices of the peace; which being properly authenticated by them, might be admitted as sufficient *prima facie* evidence before both Houses, without precluding either, if circumstances should appear to require it, from adopting the present mode of investigation, by *viva voce* testimony. Your Committee apprehend that forms of such affidavits, adapted to the several objects which they may be designed to prove, might be annexed to the Act, so as to enable not only the agents to substantiate the facts within their knowledge, but distant proprietors, at the same time that they signify their assent, to authenticate their having done so.

" The form of the bill itself necessarily comprising, as before stated, many provisions of a general nature, has next attracted the attention of your Committee, and they are of opinion, that it would tend much to reduce the expense both of drawing and copying the bill, and of printing and engrossing it, if all such clauses as should appear

appear from the general practice to be necessary and usual in all Bills of Enclosure, were to be incorporated in one General Act, and be thereby declared to be applicable *(mutatis mutandis)* to all future enclosures to be made under the authority of parliament, as well as to all such matters as should not be otherwise especially provided for by the particular bill.

" The next general object that has occurred to your Committee, is the charges of the solicitor, whether acting as such, in the necessary conduct of the bill through parliament, or, after it has passed, in the additional capacity of clerk to the Commissioners. Should the alterations before suggested, as to the mode of proof before the two Houses, be adopted, your Committee are led to hope, that these charges would necessarily be reduced; and that in many cases, where the measure met with no opposition, the attendance of the solicitor, or any other person from the country, might be dispensed with: but while the existing charges, whatever they may be, are undefined in their nature, and subject to no controul but through the medium of an expensive litigation, abuses will in many instances exist. Your Committee see no remedy for these, unless it should be found practicable to ascertain the nature of such charges with some degree of precision, and then to subject them to taxation in the same manner as costs in the courts below, either by some officer of those courts, or by officers of the two Houses of Parliament, or others specially appointed for that purpose. The particular duty and charges of the clerk to the Commissioners might, as appears to your Committee, be prescribed by the general or particular Act, and like that of the Commissioners and surveyors, controuled by the sanction of an oath of office.

" With respect to the Commissioners themselves, upon whose

whose ability and integrity so much depend, it might not perhaps be expedient to subject them to similar controul, lest men of respectability should be deterred from engaging in so laborious and useful an employment; but the abuses above noticed, might perhaps be remedied by defining in some degree the number of hours which ought actually and *bona fide* to be devoted to each meeting, and requiring that it should not be occupied by attention to any other business; and also by regulating, according to the place of residence of each Commissioner, the charges to be allowed for travelling expenses. With a view to ascertain how far the former of these regulations had been complied with, it might be desirable that the clerk should be required to keep a register of all the days and times employed in the business of the enclosure; which, as well as the books of account, should be open to the inspection of all persons concerned.

"On a full consideration of the subject of parliamentary fees, properly so called, which has occupied much of the attention of your Committee, they see no ground to recommend to the House any general regulations on that head. As a suitable recompense for the time, attention, and abilities of the several persons to whom they are payable, they find no reason to object to their usual amount; and from a comparison of it to that of the other expenses necessarily incidental to this procedure, they are not inclined to think it can in general operate as a discouragement to this mode of improvement. In particular instances, however, which are not unfrequent, of small wastes and commons, it is obvious that the whole expense of conducting an enclosure, under the authority of parliament, must always bear so large a proportion to the value of the land to be divided, as to preclude the possibility of improvement in that mode. It seems to your

your Committee worthy the consideration of the House, how far it might be advisable, in certain cases of such a description, to be ascertained either by the number of acres, or value of the land (in addition to the general regulations above suggested), to remove such part of the impediment as is more immediately under its controul, by providing that such bills should only be considered in the payment of fees, as single bills, and be entitled to any other indulgence which parliament in its wisdom should see fit.

"Your Committee ground this recommendation on the supposition, that such portions of land could by no possibility be brought into cultivation in the ordinary mode, and that therefore the reduction proposed is not so much to be considered as a diminution of probable and accustomed perquisites to the officers of the two Houses, as the means of making that productive of emolument to a certain amount, which would otherwise never be at all available to that effect.

"On the whole, your Committee have thought they should best fulfil the intention of the House, in referring to them to consider of the most effectual means of facilitating, under the authority of parliament, the enclosure and improvement of the waste and other unproductive lands of this kingdom, by confining the regulations they might suggest, to such points as appeared to them simple and easy of attainment; by which the expense attending enclosure, under the present system, would be considerably diminished, and the plan would in other respects be improved. And if the suggestions they have ventured to recommend, should have the good fortune of meeting with the approbation of Parliament, they flatter themselves that such expenses, instead of being great and undefined, would be so moderate, and in general so capable

of

of being estimated, that, in so far as regards large enclosures, the principal objection to the present system would be done away, and a great encouragement would be given to improvement.

" 1. That in order to promote the cultivation and improvement of waste, unenclosed, and unproductive lands, commons, common arable fields, meadows, and common pastures in this kingdom, it may be expedient to adopt such regulations as would diminish the expense of enclosing and improving the same, under the authority of parliament.

" 2. That in order to diminish the expense of bills of enclosure, it may be expedient that regulations should be adopted by the two Houses of Parliament for the admission of affidavits, authenticated by the certificate of one or more magistrates, as sufficient evidence of the notices, the consents, and the allegations in the preamble of such bills, instead of the parole evidence now required; unless where the latter should appear at the time to be necessary from particular circumstances.

" 3. That for the same purpose it may be expedient that a general law should be passed, comprising all such provisions as by experience have been found necessary in most bills of enclosure, to which all such bills in future might refer.

" 4. That in order to diminish other expenses incidental to bills of enclosure, it may be expedient that provision should be made in such general law, for taxing the charges of the solicitor, regulating the conduct of Commissioners, and preventing any unnecessary delay in carrying such bills into effect.

" 5. That in the case of small enclosures, not exceeding 300 acres, it may be expedient to provide, that such bills should be considered, as to the payment of fees, only as single

single bills; and that those for the enclosure of smaller tracts of land, not exceeding 100 acres, should be subject only to the payment of half the fees due on a single bill; the admeasurement in both cases to be provided in the same manner as is proposed by the second resolution regarding notices and consents."

As to difficulties, if the necessity of the measure had been once formally adopted and declared, all would, of course, be analyzed; to examine the nature and extent of difficulties is half to conquer them; but without such examination they may, for what any one knows to the contrary, be mere bugbears.

We have seen, in other difficult cases, bills of experiment altered and amended again and again. Was the income tax without difficulties, and great difficulties? And how many acts have been passed to bring it even to its present degree of efficiency? Why not proceed in the same way with an enclosure bill? Try the experiment for a year; and in those points where great difficulties arise, remove them by successive efforts.

Those who contend against the practicability of the measure, and are examining every step of the progress of a bill, in order to see each difficulty, are employed to little purpose.

Let difficulties go with the authority delegated; they are of a special nature, arising out of the circumstances of every case. It is in vain for parliament to attempt to analyze these. The men to whom power is given, and who meet in the district of the enclosure, will be much better able to examine these difficulties than a judicature 200 miles off, before which witnesses can be brought only by those whose wealth enables them to contend any where.

The

The objections which I have heard on the score of difficulties are radically weak : if the measure be effectively provided for by a due grant of authority, these difficulties are, relative to the Act, quite beside the question. It is, on the contrary, necessary to prove, that they are of a nature which respectable Commissioners could not disentangle, nor one of the Judges of England try in the form of an appeal.

The great object seems to be, to find a proper court or judicature to which Parliament should delegate its powers; to which it should transfer its tenderness in touching private property.

Are precedents wanting for such delegation of power over private property ? What think you of delegating an unlimitted power of taxation to every vestry in the kingdom, filled with as low and ignorant people as are to be found in it ?

Three or four parish-officers make a rate for 36s. in the pound, with no other controul or examination than the signature of a couple of justices, and an appeal to a quarter-sessions: and at this moment* many millions are probably raised in this summary manner. Does this show that Parliament cannot, consistently with itself, delegate a power over a parcel of beggarly wastes and commons, which are nuisances to every body ? You give a power to an ignorant, and even to an interested set, to tax with much failure in the object of the intention; and yet you will not delegate a like power into better hands, in order to attain an end in which it is impossible you should fail ! Can such a plea be real ?

There are several means of delegating this power. It might be lodged in the quarter-sessions. The assizes might be better; but the judges and juries have as much

---

* Written in the time of the scarcity.

business already as they can perform. Though it be worthy of attention, that all the roads in Ireland are made under the authority of the grand-juries assembled at the assizes, they give the power, possess the controul, and audit the accounts. If the sessions were not thought competent, Commissioners from the most respectable people for rank, fortune, and character, in every county, and meeting at the most central town, might be appointed: or such Commissioners might be chosen in every hundred, wapentake, or lathe, for this business.

For such an object, at such a moment as the present, the first men in the district would voluntarily and cheerfully undertake the business at no other expense than paying their clerk.

To such Commissioners might safely be referred the power of regulating the payment of surveyors, and Commissioners of Enclosure, and the controul of the law charges.

Appeals must go somewhere; and I see no better mode of trying them, than by appointing a thirteenth Judge; who should hold an assize for this express purpose once a year in every county.

Should the *nullum tempus* of the Clergy be objected, as I have heard it, against all general acts, one public act, passing annually, to recognize and confirm all the specific agreements of the year, would do away the objection.

But one word more:—take care of the interests of the poor; they will pay for wastes (in saving rates) treble the rent of all your other improvements put together.

It is much deserving of attention, that relative to one county, what may be called a General Enclosure Act, did once pass, is at present the law of the land, and has been acted on for the purpose intended, without any inconveniences resulting from it. The Act I allude to is the following:

12 ANNE,

12 ANNE, CAP. 4.

An Act for making Enclosures of some parts of the Common-grounds in the West Riding of the County of York, for the endowing poor Vicarages and Chapelries for the better support of their Ministers.

Whereas, in the West Riding of the county of York, there are divers parishes of great extent, and very populous, which hath occasioned the erecting of divers chapels of ease for the benefit of the inhabitants; but there being very small, or no settled provision, made for the maintenance of the ministers that perform divine offices in those chapels, or for the vicars of many of the parish-churches within the said West Riding; and there being large commons or waste-grounds within many of the said parishes, which yield little or no profit or advantage to any person, it would be a great advantage and encouragement to the vicars and ministers there, if they might, by enclosing some parts of the commons and said waste-grounds, improve the same, for the benefit of themselves and their successors: may it therefore please your most excellent Majesty, at the humble suit of the justices of the peace, gentlemen, clergy, freeholders, and other inhabitants of the said Riding, that it may be enacted: and be it enacted by the Queen's most excellent Majesty, by and with the advice and consent of the Lords Spiritual and Temporal, and Commons in Parliament assembled, and by the authority of the same, that from and after the nine-and-twentieth day of September, which shall be in the year of our Lord, one thousand seven hundred and thirteen, it shall and may be lawful for any of the inhabitants of any parish in the West Riding of the county

of

of York, wherein any such chapels of ease, as aforesaid, now are, or hereafter shall be erected or built, and wherein there are large wastes or commons, with the consent of the lord, or lords of the manor wherein such waste-ground lies (and if there be above two lords of such manor, then with the consent of the major part of them), and with the consent of three parts of four of all freeholders and others, who have any right of common therein, according to their number, and the value of their respective estates, to enclose any part of the wastes or common-grounds within such parish (or chapelry therein), not exceeding sixty acres, or a sixth part of such common-land, where the said sixth part shall not exceed sixty acres, and to settle the same in trustees and their heirs, for the benefit, and as a maintenance and support of such ministers as shall not have a settled provision of above 40*l*. per annum; and shall reside within the same parish or chapelry, and perform divine offices in the parish-church or chapelry therein, according to the use of the Church of England, and be licensed by the Archbishop of York, or the guardian of the spiritualties, any former law or usage to the contrary notwithstanding.

2. Saving always, and reserving unto all lords of manors, and other owners and proprietors of royalties within the said Riding, their heirs and assigns, all and all manner of mines, and quarries of stones, coal, and ore, and other mines; with full power and free liberty to dig, get, and sough for the same, in and through any such enclosures that shall be made pursuant to this Act; and the same so got, with carts, wains, and carriages, to take, lead, and carry away.

3. And be it further enacted by the authority aforesaid, that after any such enclosure and settlement, it shall not

be

be in the power of any trustee or minister, or any person whatsoever, to alienate and employ any of the profits of any such enclosed lands to any other use or uses, but only for the support and maintenance of the vicar or minister who shall serve the cure (if it belong to a vicarage), and to the minister that performs divine service in the chapel, according to the usage of the church of England (if it be appropriated to any chapel), and not otherwise.

4. And be it further enacted, that it shall and may be lawful for any of the trustees and their heirs, from time to time, by any writing or writings, under their hands and seals, with the consent of the vicar or minister, for whose use such enclosure is made, to be testified by his being made a party to, and signing and sealing such writing, to demise or lease any common or waste grounds, or any parcel or parcels thereof, that shall be enclosed by virtue of this Act, for any term or number of years, not exceeding one-and-twenty, so as upon every such demise or lease, there be reserved, payable half-yearly, during the said term, as much rent as can, at the making such lease, be really gotten for the same; and that such rent be made payable to, or for the only use and benefit of such vicar and minister of such vicarage or chapelry, and their successors, and so as no fine, income, or other consideration be taken for the same.

5. And it is hereby enacted, that all leases made of such enclosures in any other manner, shall not be good or available in the law, but shall be *ipso facto* void.

6. And be it further enacted by the authority aforesaid, that if any action, suit, or information, shall be commenced or prosecuted against any person or persons, for any thing that he or they shall do, or cause to be done, in pursuance or in execution of this Act, such person or persons, so sued in any court whatsoever, shall and

may

may plead the general issue of not guilty; and upon any issue joined, may give this Act, and the special matter in evidence; and if in any such suit, the plaintiff or prosecutor shall become nonsuit, or forbear prosecution, or suffer a discontinuance, or if a verdict shall pass against him upon a demurrer, then, in any of the said cases, the defendant or defendants shall recover full costs, for which he or they shall have the like remedy as is allowed in any case where costs are to be recovered by any former law.

7. And be it further enacted, that this Act shall be taken and allowed in all Courts within this kingdom, as a Public Act.

8. And whereas some manors within the said West Riding, do belong to her Majesty in right of the Crown; be it further enacted by the authority aforesaid, that by and with the consent of her Majesty, her heirs and successors, and with the consent of three parts of four of the freeholders and others, who have right of common therein, according to their number, and the value of their respective estates, it shall and may be lawful to enclose any part of the wastes or common grounds of such manors, not exceeding sixty acres, or a sixth part of such common-land where the said sixth part shall not exceed sixty acres; and to settle the same in trustees and their heirs, for the charitable purposes afore-mentioned; any law or statute to the contrary thereof in any wise notwithstanding.

The above local Act of Parliament is very little known out of the county of York; but it is an experiment that has been attended with such salutary effects, as to merit the attention of the public in general, especially in such parts

parts of the kingdom as abound with waste lands and small livings. There are curacies in Yorkshire, that at the beginning of this century were not worth more than ten or twelve pounds a year (exclusive of free gifts), that have, partly owing to this Act, been augmented to near ten times those sums.

The way the inhabitants proceeded was this: they first of all marked out so much of a common as was valued at two hundred pounds. They then applied to the trustees of Queen ANNE's bounty, who were ready to advance the like sum, whether the subscription was in land or in money, provided it was *bona fide* of that value. With this two hundred pounds they purchased land as near the allotted waste as they could, and this allotment being immediately enclosed, and cultivated, in a manufacturing part of the county, where every blade of grass towards the keeping of a cow or horse, is worth more than in most farming districts, it is not surprising that the incomes of the poor clergy have been so much improved. But what is more worthy of notice at this time is, that, simple as the Act is, and that a less proportion of consents is required than is usual for other Acts for Enclosures, tradition has not handed down to us any accounts of the least disputes or complaints amongst the neighbouring freeholders. It is the wish of many persons, that one object of the Board of Agriculture may be to introduce such laws as may facilitate the enclosure of such small wastes, as, though well worth draining and liming, will scarce admit of the expense of an Act of Parliament. The experience drawn from the effects of this local act, may perhaps afford them some hints and encouragement to attempt so useful an undertaking.

APPENDIX.

No. I.

From the Report of the Committee of the Board of Agriculture.

IT would certainly have been extremely desirable, had it been in the power of your Committee to have furnished the Board with an exact statement of the extent of Waste Lands in the kingdom: that, however, could not be effected, without an expense to which the funds of the Board were totally inadequate. It is a subject, however, which is well entitled to the consideration of Parliament, whether a survey of them ought not to be made, either at the public expense, or at the charge of those to whom the property of such wastes belong. In the interim, a general, though not an accurate idea of their magnitude and extent, will be given in the following statement, partly founded on the reports transmitted to the Board by its different surveyors; partly on calculations made from the county maps, where they have distinguished the waste from the cultivated land; and partly, where both these sources of information failed, from such other means of ascertaining their extent, as your Committee could have access to.

It may be necessary, however, to premise, that under the general name of waste lands, your Committee comprehend not only commons, where there is an intermixture of property, but also such land as lie open, uncultivated, and unenclosed, yielding nothing but coarse and common herbage, heath, furze, and other productions of little value, though no right of commons has ever been exercised thereon. It was impossible for your Committee to distinguish the one from the other: and they naturally imagined, that the Board might wish to form, as early as possible, some general idea of the total extent of the unproductive lands in the kingdom, reserving it for future inquiry to ascertain the distinctions between them.

General

General View of the Amount of Waste Lands in the Kingdom of Great Britain.

I. ENGLAND.

County.	Statement, on what founded.	Distinction of Lands.	Number of Acres.
Bedford*	County Report, p. 11	Commons and waste lands	108,500
Berks	Ditto, p. 59	Forests and commons	40,000
Bucks	Ditto, p. 32	Wastes	6000
Cambridge	Ditto, p. 193	Wastes and commons	185,300
Chester	Ditto, p. 8	Wastes, including peat, bogs, and mosses	60,000
Cornwall	Ditto, p. 56, 57	Wastes, including furze, crofts, &c.	505,655
Cumberland	Ditto, p. 34	Wastes and commons	492,000
Derby	Ditto, p. 38	Wastes, and not employed in husbandry, one-third of the county	239,492
Devon	Ditto, p. 65	Waste lands, one-fifth of the county	320,000
Dorset	Ditto, p. 5	Waste lands	86,000
Durham	Ditto, p. 43	Waste lands, about	130,000
Essex	Calculated from the county map	Waste lands and forests	27,693
Gloucester	County map	Wastes and forests	28,500
Hants	County Report, p. 32, 35, 41, 43	Waste lands and forests	188,650
Hereford	County Report, p. 27	Waste lands	20,000
Herts	Ditto	Wastes	4500
Hunts	General information	Wastes, including fens	20,700
Kent	County map	Wastes and commons	12,220†
Lancaster ‡	County Report, p. 52	Wastes, moors, & marshes	108,500
Leicester	Ditto, p. 46	Waste lands	20,000
Lincoln	Ditto, p. 112	Commons, wastes, and un-embanked salt marshes	200,000
Middlesex	Calculated from the county map	Common sand heath	13,080
		Carry forward, -	

---

* The common fields and meadows, the commons and waste lands, of the county of Bedford, are stated by the surveyor at 217,000 acres; of which, it is supposed, one-half is waste or common.

† By the County Report, since printed, 20,000.

‡ The quantity of waste land in the printed copy of the Report of Lancashire, ought to be altered to 108,500 acres.

Monmouth

APPENDIX.

County.	Statement on what founded.	Distinction of Lands.	Number of Acres.
		Brought forward,	
Monmouth	General information	One-fourth waste	67,520
Norfolk	County Report, p. 5, 18	Wastes, including warrens	143,346
Northampton	General information	Commons and fens	45,000
Northumbd.	County Report, p. 7	Wastes and mountainous districts	450,000
Notts	Calculated from the county map	Waste lands and forests	67,880
Oxford	Ditto	Wastes and commons	37,880
Rutland	County Report	Unenclosed land, one-third of the county	50,000
Salop	From the county map	Wastes and commons	131,612
Somerset	County Report, p. 22	Wastes and commons, fens included	100,000
Stafford	Ditto, p. 22	Waste lands, &c.	141,760
Suffolk	Ditto, p. 19	Waste lands	100,000
Surrey	Ditto, p. 25	Commons and wastes	96,000
Sussex	Ditto, p. 95	Wastes and commons	90,000
Warwick	Ditto, p. 37	Wastes and commons	120,000
Westmor'land	Ditto, p. 6	Three-fourths of the county uncultivated land	405,120
Wilts	General information	Wastes and downs	200,000
Worcester	County Report, p. 17	Waste lands	15,000
York—			
East Riding	General information	Wastes and commons	254,588
West ditto	County Report, p. 140	Wastes and commons	405,173
North ditto	Ditto, p. 140	Wastes and commons	442,000
	Total wastes and commons in England, -		6,259,670

II. WALES.

County.	Statement, on what founded.	Distinction of Lands.	Number of Acres.
Anglesea	County Report	Wastes and commons	5000
Brecknock	Ditto, p. 39	Ditto	256,000
Cardigan	Ditto, p. 30	Ditto	206,720
Carmarthen	Ditto, p, 21	Ditto	170,666
Caernarvon	General information	1-3d of the county waste	102,333
Denbigh	Ditto	1-4th of the county waste	102,500
Flint	Ditto	1-4th waste	40,000
Glamorgan	Ditto	1-4th waste	107,200
Merionethshire	Ditto	1-3d waste	166,666
Montgomery	County Report, p. 12	Wastes and commons	250,000
Pembroke	Ditto, p. 21	Ditto	22,222
Radnor	Ditto, p. 16	Ditto	200,000
	Total in Wales, -		1,629,307

III. SCOT-

APPENDIX.

III. SCOTLAND.

County.	Statement, on what founded.	Distinction of Lands.	Number of Acres.
Aberdeen	County Report, p. 127	Unimproved lands	374,400
Argyle	General information	Wastes and mountainous districts	787,733
Ayr	Ditto	Moorish waste	218,454
Banff	Ditto	Wastes and hills	290,000
Berwick	County Report, p. 10	Moor, moss, &c.	126,000
Bute, and the rest of the Hebrides	Hebrides Rep. p. 60	Moors, wastes, &c.	2,880,000
Caithness	County Report	Wastes and commons	368,000
Clydesdale	Ditto, p. 71	Moors, &c.	250,000
Clackmanan	General information	Wastes and moors	25,000
Dumbarton	Ditto	Wastes	164,266
Dumfries	Ditto	Wastes and commons	200,000
Elgin	Ditto	Ditto	350,000
Fife	County Report, p. 1	Hill, moss, &c.	64,000
Forfar	Ditto, p. 1	Wastes, in English acres	71,875
Inverness	General information	5-6ths waste	1,694,933
Kinross	Ditto	Wastes	25,000
Kirkcudbright	Galloway Report, p. 1	2-3ds waste, in English acres	366,734
East Lothian	General information	Wastes	55,000
West Lothian	County Report, p. 5	Ditto, in English acres	14,336
Mid Lothian	Ditto, p. 7	1-3d waste	76,800
Mearns	General information	Wastes and commons	164,266
Nairn	Ditto	Ditto	10,000
Orkney	Ditto	Ditto	700,000
Perth	Ditto	5-6ths waste†	1,321,600
Renfrew	Ditto	1-6th ditto	24,533
Ross and Cromarty	Ditto	5-6ths ditto	1,480,000
Roxburgh	County Report, p. 58	Heath and hill pasture	250,000
Selkirk	Ditto, p. 15	Ditto, in English acres	145,000
Stirling	General information	Wastes and commons	120,000
Sutherland	Ditto	5-6ths waste	1,232,000
Tweedale	County Report, p. 1	Wastes, in English acres	169,360
Wigton	Galloway Report, p. 1	Moorlands, ditto	198,934
		Total in Scotland, -	14,218,224

The following will be the total amount of waste lands in the united kingdom:

		Acres.
In England,	7,888,777	6,259,470
Wales,		1,629,307
Scotland,		14,218,224
		22,107,001

—*Report on Waste Lands*, p. 10.

---

* Exclusive of 1000 square miles, or 640,000 acres, of rock and sand.
† There must be an error here. Total of the county, 4,068,640; 5-6ths of this would be 3,390,530.

NO. II.

No. II.

Acres in the Counties of England, as detailed in the Returns to Parliament of the Poor-Rates; drawn up under the Inspection of the Right Hon. GEORGE ROSE.

	Reports to the Board of Agriculture.	Mr. Rose.
Bedford,	307,200	275,200
Berks,	438,977	476,160
Bucks,	518,400	478,720
Cambridge,	443,300	439,040
Chester,	676,000	650,880
Cornwall,	758,484	900,480
Cumberland,	970,240	958,080
Derby,	720,640	689,280
Devon,	1,600,000	1,592,320
Dorset,	775,000	722,560
Durham,	610,000	665,600
Essex,	1,240,000	976,000
Gloucester,	800,000	718,080
Hereford,	781,440	621,440
Hertford,	451,000	385,250
Hunts,	210,000	220,800
Kent,	832,000	935,680
Lancaster,	1,129,600	1,155,840
Leicester,	560,000	522,240
Lincoln,	1,893,120	1,783,680
Middlesex,	217,600	190,080
Monmouth,	352,000	330,240
Norfolk,	1,094,400	1,288,320
Northampton,	550,000	617,600
Northumberland,	1,267,200	1,157,760
Notts,	480,000	495,360
Oxford,	450,000	474,880
Rutland,	105,000	128,000

Salop,

APPENDIX. 143

	Reports to the Board of Agriculture.	Mr. Rose.
Salop,	890,000	897,920
Somerset,	1,000,000	991,360
Southampton,	1,212,000	981,120
Stafford,	780,800	765,440
Suffolk,	800,000	1,002,240
Surrey,	481,947	519,040
Sussex,	933,360	935,040
Warwick,	618,000	629,760
Westmoreland,	540,160	462,080
Wilts,	878,000	821,120
Worcester,	540,000	431,360
York, East Riding,	819,000	811,520
—— North Riding,	1,311,187	1,351,680
—— West Riding,	1,568,000	1,685,120
Wales,	4,705,400	5,200.000
Total,	37,909,455	37,334,400

NO. III.

No. III.

WASTES.

"Needwood Forest is a most interesting spot. Here near 10,000 acres of one of the finest soils of the kingdom lie in a state of nature.

"This forest is stocked with deer, horned cattle and horses; but no sheep are suffered to feed on it. The supposed stock may be about 3000 deer, and 3000 of all the other kinds in the summer; but much fewer in winter. The keeping of the 3000 horses and horned cattle, charged at 12*s.* per head for the summering, amounts to 1800*l.* or about 4*s.* per acre, upon the whole extent of the forest; and this sum of 4*s.* per acre is all the advantage that a neighbouring very intelligent farmer supposes the public derive from this tract; the deer not being managed in any system for the public advantage, or for the supply of subsistence and employment of the bulk of mankind. I shall add for them to the above account 1*s.* per acre, and 5*s.* per acre as the total value of the forest to the public in its present state. I estimate the capital employed in stocking the forest at 5*l.* per head upon 3000 in number, or 15,000*l.* Although these, not being constantly kept there, cannot wholly be called forest stock, yet I will suppose that which ought to be taken off on this account to be made good by advantages arising from the deer. The capital then employed in stocking the forest will amount to 15,000*l.* or about 1*l.* 12*s.* 6*d.*

per

per acre, and its value to the public, in its present state, as land, about 2300*l*. per annum.

" The extent of the forest, by an ancient survey alluded to by the Commissioners of Crown Lands in their last examination of it, is 9220 acres: of this, in case of enclosure, I will suppose 1000 acres ought to be reserved for wood-land. This may be done about the glens and impracticable spots, and in other places where thriving oaks are the most promising: there they ought to be fenced off, and reserved in clumps and coppices, which would be both an ornament to the country, and a nursery for stout oak timber. Two hundred and twenty acres I will suppose occupied by the lodges, and other small enclosures. This is already in an improved state; 8000 acres will then remain for improvement. The moment that these shall have been enclosed, and buildings for occupation erected on them, they will be worth for a term, as many guineas per annum, and would be improved to a higher value. The amount of capital employed in such improvement in buildings, enclosure, crop, stock, &c. might on this rich land be 20*l*. per acre. Deduct the present capital, 1*l*. 12*s*. 6*d*. per acre, remains increase, 18*l*. 7*s*. 6*d*. per acre, which upon 8000 acres, adds 147,000*l*. to the national capital. By improving this tract, the increased annual product would probably be 5*l*. per acre, or 40,000*l*. per annum*."

" Cannock-Heath is the most extensive waste in the county of Warwick, but its extent cannot be determined with accuracy; I estimate it at about 40 square miles, or upwards of 25,000 acres. Large tracts of land on the north and west parts of this waste consist of a good light soil, adapted to the turnip and barley culture; the east and south parts are a colder gravelly soil, in many places

---

* Stafford Report, p. 102, 103.

covered

covered with heath to a large extent; yet I have no doubt but the whole may be brought into cultivation ; and that some of our enclosed land now under cultivation is not at all of a superior quality to this waste.

" Sutton Coldfield is also a very extensive waste, of no other use but as a sheep-walk, or rabbit-warren : that part of it in Staffordshire contains, according to an estimate by a very intelligent resident near the spot, about 6500 acres; and he supposes the additional waste land between Litchfield and Birmingham, including Bromwich-heath, Aldridge-common, Walsall-wood, Whittington-heath, and Weeford-hills, will raise the amount of Sutton Coldfield to 10,000 acres : their value in their present state amounts by his information, to 3s. 6d. per acre; and if enclosed would rise to 10s. 6d. per acre for the first twenty-one years, and afterwards be greater. The other principal wastes in the county, are those of Swindon, Wombourn, and near Stewponey, in the south; Morredge, Wotley-moor, Stanton-moor, Hollington-heath, Caverswall-common, in the north. In other parts of the county we find Calf-heath, Essington-wood, Snead-common, Wyrley and Pelsal commons, Tirley, Ashley, and Maer heaths; Swinnerton, Tittenor, and Shelton heaths; Houlton, Milwich, Hardwick, and Fradswell commons, and many others ; and upon a retrospect of the whole, I cannot put our practicable waste lands, or such as are capable of being brought into cultivation, at less than 100,000 acres. Their present value as sheep-walks amounts to 3s. per acre per annum: the value enclosed, and after one round of cultivation (tithe free) will amount to 15s. per acre, and improve by enclosure and cultivation, 12s. per acre, or 60,000l. per annum. The present capital or value of stock belonging to such land, may be estimated at 10s. per acre, or 50,000l.; the capital of the land, when enclosed

enclosed and cultivated, including buildings, fences, crops, live stock, implements, and furniture, would amount to 15*l*. per acre, or 1,500,000*l*.

" The addition to the national capital, by such general enclosure and improvement in this county, would amount to 1,450,000*l*. This land also, would make many farms, which, with a due proportion of labourers' tenements, would employ a population of 20,000 persons, children and families included, in cultivation and other occupations connected and dependent thereupon; would furnish food for double that number, and would maintain also at least double the present number of sheep; if sheep stock should become the chief object, independent of other stock, which at present draw no nourishment or subsistence from this tract. Those farms would produce a proportion of corn: the wool also of the sheep might be increased in weight and improved in quality, by a due attention to rams and breeding stock. A general enclosure and improvement by cultivation, of all the wastes of the kingdom, would, by greatly increasing the national capital, have a proportionable effect upon the revenue; and it is astonishing that the colonization of distant countries should have been so much encouraged, while the cultivation of our own country remains so far from being finished or perfected*."

" In this county (Lancashire) there are large tracts of waste lands, not less than 108,500 acres, according to Mr. YATES's statement, who took the pains to calculate the number for this particular purpose. He makes the lands under the denomination of moss, or fen lands, to be 26,500 acres. Moors, marshes, and commons to amount to

---

* Stafford Report, p. 108.

82,000

82,000 acres. Why seek out distant countries to cultivate, while so much remains to be done at home?

"At Lancaster there is an excellent salt marsh, adjoining the banks of the river Lune; and of which about 500 statute acres belong to 80 of the oldest freemen of the corporation of Lancaster, or their widows, and the trustees of this charity, the corporation. This marsh is pastured, and divided into what are termed orl grasses, that is, a privilege of turning one horse, or two cows of any size, to summer upon this common; so that a poney is reckoned equal to two oxen, however small the horse, or large the ox. The number of grasses, or gates, is equal to that of privileged burgesses, namely 80, and two more to the trustees of the charity, or 82 gates; and which, if lett, are worth at present from 1*l.* 10*s.* to 1*l.* 11*s.* 6*d.* per summer. Seven years ago they would not lett at 20*s.* a gate.

"Now this marsh, if divided into fields of a proper size, is so fertile, that it would immediately be worth 3*l.* per acre; and if improved, worth 5*l.* per acre, per annum.

	£.	*s.*	*d.*
The present value is 82 summer grasses at 1*l.* 11*s.* 6*d.*	129	3	0
And suppose the winter herbage worth	50	0	0
Total	179	3	0
But if enclosed, its annual value would at 3*l.* per acre per annum, be	1,500	0	0
Excess	1,320	17	0
If improved at 5*l.* per acre would be	2,500,000	0	0
Excess	2,320	17	0

"Such

"Such statements cannot require any comment to recommend them to public attention, and that too in a neighbourhood distressed for enclosed land; being bound up on one side by this marsh, and on the other side by a moor, which extends to the very borders of the town; a moor too, which manifests itself capable of being made into fertile land, as is evident from small enclosures under cultivation, which the industry of some cottager has improved from the waste.

"In the neighbourhood of Preston, lies Preston-moor, about 500 acres of good land, and abounding with excellent marl, but which at present lies under water, which might be easily removed. Fulwood-moor, too, in the same neighbourhood, about 1000 acres, and Caddeley-moor, which belongs to the Crown, and many more which might be enumerated, and which remain in a state that disgraces the county[*]."

"There is a large tract of land in this neighbourhood, I should think, consisting of from eight to ten thousand acres, in an useless state; but of much better quality than any upon the Cotswold-hills: I mean the Forest of Whichwood, at present the best nursery for idleness and thieves in this kingdom. What a pity, that so valuable a piece of land, and so easily converted into tillage, should be suffered to remain in its present state, when it is acknowledged that the land under cultivation at present, in this kingdom, is insufficient to produce a proper quantity of food for its inhabitants!

"The Minister of Westwell, Oxfordshire."

---

[*] Lancashire Report, p 86.

No. IV.

No. IV.

Effect on the Poor, of the Enclosures which took place during the first Forty Years of His present MAJESTY.

County.	Parish.	Effect.
Bedford	Potton	I presume the poor are sufferers.
	Tutvy	To my knowledge, before the enclosure, the poor inhabitants found no difficulty in procuring milk for their children; since, it is with the utmost difficulty they can procure any milk at all. Cows lessened from 110 to 40.
	Maulden	Previous to the enclosure, a general system of trespass existed.
	Souldrop	The condition of the labouring poor much worse now than before the enclosure, owing to the impossibility of procuring any milk for their young families.
Berks	Letcomb	The poor seem the greatest sufferers; they can no longer keep a cow, which before many of them did, and they are therefore now maintained by the parish.
Bucks	Waddesdon	Poverty has very sensibly increased: the husbandmen come to the parish, for want of employment: the land laid to grass.
	Tingewick	Milk to be had at 1*d*. per quart before; not to be had now at any rate.

County.

County.	Parish.	Effect.
Bucks	Bradwell	Fewer hands employed; rates increased.
	Castlethorp	Less work for the people.
Cambridge	March	The poor much benefited: rent of a common right, 8*l.*; raised to 20*l.*
Chester	Cranage	Poor men's cows and sheep have no place, or any being.
Dorset	Tolpudle	Poverty increased.
Durham	Lanchester	Many cottagers have been deprived of the convenience of keeping a cow, without any recompense in any other respect. The proprietors do not consult the welfare of the labourer so much as they might, without any injury to themselves, and with very little more trouble to their agents.
Gloucester	Todenham	Nothing increased but the poor; eight farm-houses filled with them.
Hants	Upton Gray	The poor injured.
Herts	Offley	The poor have not the same means of keeping cows as before.
	Norton	Cottagers deprived of cows, without compensation.
Hereford	Willington	Live-stock of the poor gone.
Leicester	Rutcliffe	A great defalcation in cheese and pigs, occasioned principally by taking away the land from the cottager.
Lincoln	Donington	Cottagers' cows (140) lost by the enclosure.
	Uffington	Town herd of cows reduced one-third, to the great injury of the poor.
Norfolk	Totterhill	The poor injured.
	Shottesham	Cottagers' cows much increased.
	Ludham	Obliged to sell their cows.
Northampton	Passenham	Deprived of their cows, and great sufferers by loss of their hogs.

County.

County.	Parish.	Effect.
Stafford	Ashford	All their cows gone, and much wretchedness.
Wilts	Ramsbury	Their cows reduced.
York	Ackworth	The parish belonged to near 100 owners; nearly the whole of whom have *come to the parish* since the enclosure, or changed the quantity of their lands.
	Kirkburn	The enclosure has proved of singular advantage to great landowners and their tenants; but the labourer who, previous to the enclosure, had his cow-gate, and from thence derived considerable nourishment to his small family, was deprived of this aid by his inability to enclose, therefore was under the necessity of selling his tenement to his richer neighbour, and deprived his family of a comfortable refuge.
	Ebberston	Have lost their cows.
	Tibthorpe	Lost their cows, and sold their tenements.

"Milk has diminished, owing to the farmers finding the profits of grazing larger, and the unwillingness of too many agents and proprietors to accommodate industrious cottagers with small parcels of land to keep a cow.

"J. WALKER,
"Minister of Lanchester, Durham.

"It has been a general observation, applicable to every division of common in this parish, that the resources of the small proprietors (and they are principally here of that description) have been for the most part so entirely exhausted

exhausted by the expenses of obtaining the Act, of solicitors, surveyors, commissioners, making new roads, &c. that they have been incapacitated for cultivating their allotments in a proper manner. The mischief has gone farther; for it has rendered them less adequate to cultivate the ancient lands, for which such shares of common were allotted. It is believed, that had the proprietors come to the cultivation of their allotments in their full strength, unimpaired by the above causes, that the quantity of produce, both in the new and ancient lands, might have been increased to an inconceivable degree in this parish.

"W. WILSON,
"Rector of Wolsingham, Durham."

In addition to these authorities, may be added the result of other inquiries, made in a journey already noted.

County	Place	Date of Enclosure	Effect on the Poor.
Bedford	Sandy	1797	The poor injured.
	Eaton	1795	Their cows much lessened.
Hunts	Warboys	1795	Many kept cows; now few. They were certainly injured.
	Ramsey	1796	Cottagers' cows lessened.
	Holywell	1800	Cottagers' cows much lessened.
	Alconbury	1791	Many kept cows that have not since: they could not enclose, and sold their allotments. Left without cows or land*.
Cambridge	March	1793	Those who had property in their cottages were benefited: those who were tenants were ruined.
	Wimblington	1792	The same.
	Long Stow	1796	Several kept cows, who have them no longer.

* The enclosure has, without question, been injurious to the poor. This was the account they gave me themselves; Mr. NICHOLSON, the curate, confirmed it, and Mr. HOLMES very candidly admitted it. Their own account to me, at Mr. NICHOLSON's, was, that several who kept cows before, were, upon the enclosure, forced to part with them, and have kept none since. The cottage allotments going to the landlords, were thrown together, and the inhabitants left without cows or land. Those who had allotments given in lieu of their rights, not being able to enclose them, were forced to sell, and became as the rest in this respect. Before the enclosure, milk could readily be bought; poor people could lay out a halfpenny, or a penny, every day; but nothing of the sort to be got since: some not a halfpenny in a month, and others not in three.—*Annal*, xliv. p. 199.

Cambridge

APPENDIX. 155

County			
Cambridge	Abington	1770	All the allotments thrown to one person. The cows of the poor people disappeared, and they suffered so much, as to stop enclosing for many years.
	Morden Guilden	1799	Greatly alarmed at the Act passing. Their cows will all go.
	Streatham	....	Abhor the idea of enclosing, because they must lose all their cows.
	Weston Colville	1776	The cottagers who had *rights*, are placed in a better situation; the rest lost their cows.
Norfolk	Hilborough	1769	They suffered.
	Fincham	1772	Their cows gone.
	Shouldham	1794	Injured in fuel and live-stock.
	Garboisethorp	1794	The poor kept twenty cows before; now none.
	Lexham	1795	Their cows lessened.
	Sedgford	1795	Injured.
	Fellthorp	1779	Much injured.
	Bintry	1795	Much injured.
Suffolk	Barton Mills	1794	Their cows annihilated.
Essex	Parndon	1795	Their little allotments all sold; could not enclose.
Hants	Basingstoke	1786	Injured.

That the injury, which, in these cases, seems really to have been received, flowed from inattention to the property or customs of the poor, and by no means of necessity from enclosure, appears from the following cases.

APPENDIX.

County.	Place.	Date of Enclosure.	Effect on the Poor.
Cambridge	L. Wilbraham	1797	An allotment never to be occupied but by cottagers.
Norfolk	Carleton	1777	Their interests much improved.
	Marham	1793	They did not suffer.
	Heacham	1780	Little allotments assigned of two to ten acres: they keep cows, and are very comfortable.
	Brancaster	1755	Well treated.
	Salt House	1780	Ditto.
	Sayham	1798	Very well treated.
	Langley	1800	Well treated.
	Shropham	1798	Ditto.
	Shottesham	1781	Ditto. Their cows increased.
	Old Buckenham	1790	Well treated.
	Northwold	1796	Many bettered: their allotments can neither be let nor sold from the cottages.
Suffolk	Barnady	....	Ditto.
Essex	Naseing	....	Their live-stock greatly increased, and a worthless crew changed to industrious labourers.

" The

"The rise of poor-rates in many of these parishes that have been enclosed having kept pace with the increase in other parishes, is another proof that there has been something deficient in the principles which have conducted them. Above 60,000 acres of commons have been enclosed in the places here registered; in the following the rise is noted particularly:

	Acres of Common.	s.	s.	d.
Lidlington	497	1 to	4	6
March	3440	Doubled to 1300*l.*		
Chattris	4320	2 to	4	6
Abington	80	0 —	2	6
Wilbraham	569	More than doubled.		
Hillborough	420	Doubled.		
Fincham	647	Trebled.		
Hethersett	430	5 to	10	0
Barton Mills	300	4 —	13	0
	10,603	20 to	53	0

"These are selected merely because the old rates, the new, and the commons are all minuted. The rise has been equal in the rest. It should therefore seem, that notwithstanding the increase of employment, yet there has been some contrary current which has been bearing heavily against the face of such employment. On the contrary, if a right use had been made of a very small portion of these commons, poor-rates might have been done away altogether.

"Commissioners of enclosure are little apt to confess any thing against them, but I met with three in one county who furnished me with observations that merit notice.

"Mr.

"Mr. FORSTER, of Norwich, after giving an account of twenty enclosures in which he had acted as a Commissioner, stated his opinion on their general effect on the poor, and lamented that he had been accessary to injuring 2000 poor people, at the rate of twenty families per parish. Numbers in the practice of feeding the commons cannot prove their right, and many, indeed most who have allotments, have not more than one acre, which being insufficient for the man's cow, both cow and land are usually sold to the opulent farmers. That the right sold before the enclosure would produce much less than the allotment after it, but the money is dissipated, doing them no good when they cannot vest it in stock.

"Mr. EWEN, a Commissioner in the same place, observed, that in most of the enclosures he has known, the poor man's allotment and cow are sold, five times in six before the award is signed.

"Mr. BURTON, of Langley, a very able Commissioner, wished for a clause in all acts, on the principle of that of Northwold, which makes the allotment inalienable from the cottage, as he admits there is a considerable benefit in the poor people having land enough for a cow, from two to four acres, according to the soil*."

FUEL.

"In Dorsetshire, in Hampshire, and in many other counties where coals and wood are wholly out of the reach of the cottager, and where the furze of large growth is scarce, the indigent inhabitants obtain their fuel from extensive wastes, so little productive of a substance suited to the application, that the setting out a

---

* Annals, xxxvi.

small

small part (as proposed) if not protected in a state of cultivation adapted to the purpose, will not secure to them a requisite compensation. Poor inhabitants who live on the borders of the forests and other wastes, and who may not possess any one of the real and defined rights; yet frequently exercise an undenied privilege of pasturing a cow, horse, or ass which assists them in their means of obtaining a livelihood. Waste lands have been occupied in some sort, as the common estate of those who have no other; they are spaces of the earth on which every man walks in freedom, and imagines he is committing no trespass. In the view of this law, let us suppose all wastes to be cultivated and enclosed—every man not possessing a share of landed property, will be a trespasser when he steps off the highway. In suggesting these observations, I am for an instant, adopting the language of those who see a great private injury attendant on this general good, and who oppose themselves to enclosures on these plausible grounds;—but if the national produce can be so much increased as to feed a people who are now not fed, and at a price proportioned to the earnings of that people, the smaller interests must give way. I certainly shall not argue, because I do not think, that in order to preserve an airing ground for those who possess no portion of the landed property, or grouse shooting for those who are land-owners, the Legislature should suffer any lands to remain unproductive*."

" The privilege or usage of cutting fuel being admitted as a right, and the justice and equity of ratifying it being declared by the preamble of this clause, the enactment, with benevolent intention, proceeds to require the Commissioners to provide for this right by a determinate

---

* Observations on the General Enclosure Bill, by Sir G. O. PAUL, Bart. 1796, p. 22.

mode, to the amount of a proper and reasonable satisfaction, so far ' as the judgment of the Commissioners may enable them to determine what shall be proper and reasonable ;' but this specific instruction is relieved, by giving to the Commissioners the very general alternative power, ' to establish and declare any other mode, in case they shall think expedient so to do.'

" As I fear it will be found more easy to design a reasonable satisfaction for this privation, than to establish it with permanent propriety, I shall offer the remarks which have occurred to me in contemplating the difficulty. Considering the perpetual variation in number of inhabitants to which parishes must be liable in the course of time, and by change of circumstances, it is impossible, with a view to posterity, to ascertain what shall be, in effect, a proper and reasonable part, as a satisfaction to all future parishioners, for a right over the whole. So different are the properties of waste lands, that it would be equally impracticable on this account, by any positive enactment, to fix a specific proportionate quantity, as ' proper and reasonable to fulfil the purposes of the preamble', on very poor moors where there is no wood. Peat or furze, the substance cut for fuel, is no more than a kind of turf, half formed from the successive growth and decay of the ling or heath plant ; large portions of the whole, now over-run by the cottagers, would scarcely afford ' a proper and reasonable supply of fuel for a class of inhabitants continually increasing in numbers (as we must presume) in consequence of the enclosure*.' "

" Whether it would not be a more eligible plan to set a-part smaller portions, to be cultivated to the particular

---

* Observations on the General Enclosure Bill, by Sir G. O. Paul, Bart. 1796, p. 31.

purpose?

APPENDIX.

purpose? Would it not answer better to the community, that allotments should be assigned in trust, to be sold or lett on a lease, as a fund to purchase coals or other ordinary fuel? It is certain, that the produce of much labour is lost, by time employed in cutting and collecting a substance so unfit for the purpose to which it is applied. If (as we are to presume, as a consequence of a general spirit of enclosure) the work of the labourer, who now seeks his fuel over desolate wastes, should be required in the productive pursuits of husbandry, at adequate and reasonable wages, it may be proved, that so far from obtaining this fuel gratuitously, he buys it more dearly than they who purchase coals at a moderate price. Or suppose (reasoning farther on the same principle), that no portion of land should be withdrawn from the general into specific allotments for this purpose, but that a similar fund was obtained, by an assessment to the like annual amount over the whole waste, or over an agreed part of it, by way of fire-rate. The setting out large portions of land for a produce to which it may not be suited, is to make an improvident use of it. That future bodies of men, in perpetual succession, will so perform their duty in a trust, as to create and preserve an annual cultivated produce, is to presume upon more active virtue than should be depended upon for the efficacy of any plan. Or finally, on this untried ground, where it is evident we have no result of extensive experience to fix our judgment, would it not rather be advisable, after admitting the right, and enjoining the Commissioners to consider the compensation, wholly to generalize their powers, and enable them to adopt such means as may appear most suited to local circumstances? The difficulty to find a substitute in kind, for what must (at least) be considered as a sensible

priva-

privation of a habit, has, I know, occurred to gentlemen who reside on the borders of the vast wastes of Dorset and Hants: to these and to similar situations, the above observations are more particularly applicable. Although the last mentioned clause has admitted the justice and the equity of a claim for ' a general usage to which the poorer class of the inhabitants may be entitled, or may have exercised and enjoyed," as separate and distinct from a claim as owners of tenements or other real property which may entitle them to specific allotments, yet I observe, that the principle of allowing compensation for the loss of such usages, is admitted so far only as regards fuel: no retribution or substitute is proposed for any usage or privilege which may have been exercised and enjoyed by persons of this description, in depasturing cows or other cattle, on the wastes to be enclosed. Some special Enclosure Acts have provided for setting out allotments of land for this purpose, to be fed and depastured in common*."

Northwold, in Norfolk: Fuel.

Clause.—" And be it further enacted, that the said Commissioners shall in the next place assign, set out, and allot unto the owner or proprietor of every commonable messuage within the said parish of Northwold, such part of the fen grounds within the said parish, as shall, in the judgment of the said Commissioners, be sufficient to supply, or admit to be cut and taken thereout, yearly for

---

* Observations on General Enclosure Bill, by Sir G. O. PAUL, Bart. 1796, p. 40.

ever, a quantity of turf or flag for firing, equal to, but not exceeding, 12,000 flags, or 12,000 turves, in a year, as a compensation or recompense for the right of such owner or proprietor to cut turf or flag for firing upon the fen grounds within the said parish; and every allotment which shall be made from the said fen grounds for firing to the owner or proprietor of any commonable messuage, shall, from and after the execution of the award, be annexed to, and be inseparable from the commonable messuage in respect of which such allotment is made; and the owner or proprietor of such commonable messuage, his heirs or assigns, shall not alien, assign, or convey such allotment to any person or persons whatever, save and except such person or persons to whom the commonable messuage in respect of which such allotment is made, shall be aliened, assigned, or conveyed."

NO. V.

No. V.

COTTAGERS' LAND.

"A gentleman having been employed by the Board of Agriculture to examine a district of country in the counties of Lincoln and Rutland, where it is common management for the poor to have land and cows, and reports having been made from 48 parishes containing 753 cottagers, it is proper to state, that those 753 cottagers have amongst them 1195 cows, or, on an average, one and a half, and one-thirteenth cow each. Not one of them receive any thing from the parish! nor did, even in the late scarcities. The system is as much approved of by the farmers as it is by the poor people themselves. They are declared to be the most hard-working, diligent, sober, and industrious labourers who have land and cows, and a numerous meeting of farmers signed their entire approbation of the system. In the above-mentioned parishes, rates are, on an average, $17\frac{1}{2}d.$ in the pound; and, but for exceptions of some families who have not land, of certain cases and expenses foreign to the inquiry, they would not be $1d.$ in the pound.

"In nine parishes, where the proportion of the poor having cottages amount to rather more than half the whole, poor-rates are $3\frac{1}{4}d.$ in the pound.

"In twelve parishes, where the proportion is less than half, but not one-third, poor-rates are $9\frac{1}{2}d.$ in the pound.

"In

APPENDIX.

"In ten parishes, where the proportion is something under a fourth, poor-rates are 1*s.* 6*d.* in the pound.

"In seven parishes, where the proportion is but merely one-sixth, poor-rates are 4*s.* 1½*d.* in the pound.

"And in thirteen parishes where few or none have cows, poor-rates are 5*s.* 11*d.* in the pound.

"The poor in this considerable district being able to maintain themselves without parish assistance by means of land and live stock, and to do it at the same time so much by their industry and sobriety, and consistently with an honest conduct clearly marked by the entire approbation of this system by the farmers, &c. their neighbours, is a circumstance which, well considered, does away a multitude of those objections and prejudices which we so often hear in conversation; and it proves, that the instances which sometimes are said to occur, of men who have land and stock being thieves, to be either exaggerated, their possessions perhaps mistaken, from confounding them with their poor neighbours, or that the number of such offences are not at all greater than are found amongst any other class of people. Such ideas are absolutely contradicted in this part of Lincolnshire, where the cow system is general. Cases may, however, occur of such offences in certain parishes, and yet not amount to any fair foundation for an argument against the system[*]."

"*Mayfield, Sussex.*—Here is a case which proves the assertion in the preceding article: a family chargeable when there was no scarcity, ceased to be chargeable in scarcity, from a cow being given by the parish[†]."

---

[*] Annals, xxxvi.
[†] Annals, xxxvi. p. 502.

"*Chattris,*

"*Chattris, Cambridgeshire.*—About a hundred small cottages have been raised of late years on the common, so close to each other as to admit only a path around them: very few have gardens: many were built by the owners, who inhabit them, and did not cost more than 10*l.* or 12*l.* The proprietors have no relief from the parish*."

"I cannot close these answers without remarking the very laudable conduct of a principal land-owner in this parish, Col. SIBTHORPE, M. P. for Lincoln, who has rendered many of his inferior tenants comfortable, by permitting them to rent small parcels of ground: they are now enabled to keep a milch cow—bring up a few young sheep, and kill one or two large pigs. Were this plan universally adopted, the labourers in villages would never be heard to murmur; our poor-rates would be considerably diminished, and our markets would be better supplied with articles of food—cheese, butter, &c. &c.

"CHAS. WRAY HADDELSEY,
Curate of Tetney, Lincoln."

"A variety of cases, in many districts, detailed in the work quoted, prove clearly, that wherever there is a hope of occupying land, it operates beyond all the powers of calculation. How these men were able to effect their object, surpasses inquiry: that they saved money with this view is palpable, because in most of the cases the erections have been the work of regular carpenters and masons, who could not have been employed without a

---

* Annals, xxxvi. p. 498.

considerable part of the expense being provided for; and this accordingly I found the case, for where mortgages had taken place, it was only for a part of the expense, in many instances for only a small part, and in some, not a few, without any assistance at all.

" And here it is deserving of great attention, that during the very period in which the poor have become wholly dependent, and burthened their parishes to an enormous amount, these cases of saving frugality and industry have occurred in a few places with no other motive or instigation but the prospect of becoming the proprietors of their own cottages. What a powerful motive has this proved to render them such striking exceptions to a whole kingdom*!"

" It will be a very beneficial consequence of Enclosure, if small portions of ground can be allotted to attend the inheritance of cottages. The convenience will certainly be greater, if such portions can be set out ' near or adjoining to the cottages to which they are allotted;'—but as to any thing in the nature of gratuity or benefaction, which the style of the preamble seems to affect, I am greatly mistaken if the clause (taken together) admits of any such construction. Proprietors of cottages seem to be confounded in idea with the poor tenants who inhabit them; whereas they are objects perfectly distinct. The cottages in agricultural villages generally belong to the principal land-owners, if not part of the manorial estate. The carpenter, the smith, or the mason, may probably possess a cottage or tenement, to which may be annexed a right of common; but as to the poor husbandman, who is alone an object of charitable purpose, it is

---

* Annals, xxxvi. p. 506.

rare

rare indeed that he has an house of his own. Setting aside therefore the bounty of the clause, I have only to consider its justice and its use, as appropriating an occcupancy of the land, to that of the cottages of the parish.

" The accommodation of vicinity proposed, will in most instances be impracticable. Wastes and commons are generally situate at a distance from the villages to which they belong : by the power of exchange given at the end of the clause, something may be done to accommodate this difficulty, but even this wise provision cannot be applied to a very general effect.

" It is provided, that ' the owner of the cottage shall pay for the fences of his specific allotments; and if he has not the money, he shall mortgage his property for the cost. This may wear the face of justice, but I deny that it is equity, if by that term is meant equal proportionate advantage. I am not as yet convinced, that if all the waste land of the kingdom could at once be enclosed, it would pay five cent. on the capital employed. For this doubt I may be called to account by my fellow advocates for the measure; fortunately it is a proposition regarding which it would be useless to contend, for if he who calculates the advantages on the lower scale, sees the measure as indisputably politic, still more so must it be esteemed by the adherents to the more sanguine expectation. Being so far a sceptic as to the mass of pecuniary advantage, my opinion is of a little doubtful tendency as to the fractional part which is the object of this clause. By reference to pages 59 and 60, it will appear that this claimant is in common with others to pay his ' quota towards all costs, charges, and expenses of dividing, alloting, laying in severalty, and all other costs and charges incident to or attending the same.'

" As

"As I must presume the framer of this clause did not mean to fix an extreme pressure on this class of proprietors, I shall consider this circumstance as an oversight, and merely reason on the inequality of putting the small claimants to enclose separately for themselves. Suppose a claim to be on the smallest scale, or that, without any claim, it should be determined to set out allotments of garden-ground to cottagers of the vicinage; and suppose (as directed by the clause) the Commissioners to order each parcel to be substantially fenced and maintained, ' the cost of which to be paid by the person to whom the allotment is given:' I then contend, that, taking an average value of waste land, it would, in the case of the claimant, be no retribution for his claim, nor in the other case, would it be a gratuitous grant. Both of them would pay the value of the land enclosed, and the one would lose the value of his claim, or perhaps, be taxed for having asserted it. Suppose a third of an acre of land, worth 15$l.$ per acre, to be allotted for each garden: to enclose a third of an acre substantially on all sides, and to support and maintain the fence to maturity, will cost 10$l.$; but suppose you reckon but the half enclosure to each share, it will be 5$l.$, which is the value of the fee, besides the expense of clearing the land. Suppose each owner of a cottage to have a claim of one pasture for a cow or other animal, and the proprietor of a large farm to have a claim for ten such pastures: and suppose two acres of land to be allotted to the one, and twenty acres to the other: the person who surrenders his one pasture, gives up what is of more relative value or convenience to him, than a tenth of what the larger claimant has surrendered; whilst what the cottager receives will be at an expense to him of a third of

the

the whole sum of the allotment to the greater proprietor; it will be three times the expense per acre. Twenty acres of ground to be fenced on all sides, will cost 80*l.* which is 4*l.* per acre. Two acres, to be fenced in a similar manner, will cost 26*l.* ar 13*l.* per acre*."

---

* Observations on the General Enclosure Bill, by Sir G. O. PAUL, Bart. 1796, p. 44.

No. VI.

COMMONS ENCLOSED.

March, in Cambridgeshire.

First year,	2800 acres of cole, fed, at 42*s*.	£.5880
	100 oats, 8 qrs. at 21*s*.	8400
	540 pasture, at 70*s*. ,.....................	1890
	3440	£.8610
Second year,	700 cole seeded, 5 qrs. at 40*s*. a last	£.14,000
	2100 oats, 10 qrs. at 20*s*.	21,000
	200 wheat, 4 qrs. at 50*s*.	2000
	440 pasture, at 70*s*.	1540
	3440	£.38,540
Third year,	100 cole, fed, at 42*s*.	£.210
	2700 oats, 10 qrs. at 20*s*.	27,000
	200 wheat, 4 qrs. at 50*s*	2000
	440 pasture, at 70*s*. .,..................	1540
	3440	£.30,750
Fourth year,	2700 oats, 10 qrs. at 16*s*.	£.21,600
	300 wheat, 4 qrs. at 50*s*.	3000
	440 pasture, at 70*s*.	1540
	3440	£.26,140

Fifth

APPENDIX.

Fifth year,	200 of cole, fed, at 42s.	£.210
	1840 oats, 10 qrs. at 16s.	14,720
	400 wheat, 4 qrs. at 50s.	4000
	1000 pasture, at 50s.	2500
	3440	£.21,430
Sixth year,	200 cole, fed, at 42s.	£.210
	1540 oats, 10 qrs. at 20s.	15,400
	200 wheat, 4 qrs. at 60s.	2400
	1500 pasture, at 50s.	3750
	3440	£.21,760
Seventh year,	200 cole, fed, at 42s.	210
	800 oats, 9 qrs. at 24s.	8560
	140 wheat, 3 qrs. at 70s.	1470
	2300 pasture, at 50s.	5750
	3440	15,990

First year,	£.8610
Second ditto,	38,540
Third ditto,	30,750
Fourth ditto,	26,140
Fifth ditto,	21,430
Sixth ditto,	21,760
Seventh ditto,	15,990
	£.163,220

Thus in seven years this single enclosure has produced 163,220l.*

---

* Annals, xlii. p. 321.

" The

"The aforesaid commons had not been ploughed for time immemorial, previous to the Enclosure: and they were much over-run with rushes, thistles, broom-weed, rough grass of little value, and other rubbish, which (as I frequently for 21 years before the Enclosure, told the commoners) were a just cause of reflection upon their good sense, for suffering such valuable land to lie neglected.

"Immediately after the Enclosure, probably 3000 acres of the said commons were ploughed and burnt (the wise custom of the fen country), and sown with cole, fed off with sheep, and then with oats chiefly, and perhaps on the average there might be 400 acres of wheat on the high land formerly commons. The value of the cropping grown for the first three years on the enclosed commons, was at least 20,000*l.* per annum. The parish has been greatly enriched by the Enclosure, so that even those commoners who were most averse to the Enclosure, now thankfully admit its great utility; and have some cause to thank me for the active part I took to promote the Enclosure. The poor have been much benefited by the measure, by having much more labour in cultivating the land. The quantity of both oats and wheat are now considerable from the Enclosure, and ever will be considerable.

"The Minister of March,
Cambridge."

"The vast benefit* of enclosing can, upon inferior soils, be rarely seen in a more advantageous light, than upon

---

* Although it may be a received opinion with many, respecting enclosing depopulating the parishes, yet, from carefully searching the registers of many parishes, in the Kesteven division of this county, and comparing

upon Lincoln-heath. I found a large range which was formerly covered with heath, gorse, &c. and yielding in fact, little or no produce, converted, by enclosure, to profitable, arable farms; lett on an average at 10*s.* an acre; and a very extensive country, all studded with new farm-houses, barns, offices, and every appearance of thriving industry; nor is the extent small, for these heaths extend near 70 miles, and the progress is so great in 20 years, that very little remains to do.

" The effect of these enclosures have been very great, for while rents have risen on the heath from nothing, in most instances, and next to nothing in the rest, to 8*s.* or 10*s.* an acre, the farmers are in much better circumstances, a great produce is created, cattle and sheep increased, and the poor employed. The rectory of Navenby, one of the cliff towns, has become greater than the total rent of the lordship was before.

" From Lincoln to Barton was all, or nearly all, heath, but now enclosed by Acts of Parliament. And for five,

---

ing the result with a similar one, made by a gentleman in Boothy-Graffoe hundred, published in the Gentleman's Magazine for 1782, p. 74, I find Enclosures to have produced a very little variation in the number of births and burials; and it may be necessary to observe, that the places wherein I made my inquiry, have likewise had no manufacture, or other partial circumstance, to influence any increase or decrease of the people. And that there are other causes capable of increasing the number of inhabitants in a parish, besides a manufacture, I will produce Domington as a proof.

A Mr. Cowley, and others, gave to that place, for charitable uses, an estate, which, by an enclosure, &c. has so much improved, as to become of the yearly value of six hundred pounds. Notwithstanding this circumstance, the poor-rates are above double what they were before the improvement of the estate; arising from the lower class of persons gaining settlements in the parish by every means in their power, merely through the expectation of benefiting by the said charity.—*Mr. Cragg, MS. of the Board.*

six, or seven miles every way around Hackthorne, the same within twelve or sixteen years; and of that tract, the heath part was not more than 1*s.* 6*d.* to 2*s.* an acre; large sheep-walks, with pieces tilled alternately, now lett at about 10*s.* tithe free; and the result otherwise has been, that the tenants live much better, and shew, in every circumstance, signs of greater prosperity. The land is universally kept in tillage.

" Around Norton-place, or rather longitudinally from it to Kirton, &c. open heath did lett for 2*s.* an acre; now for 8*s.* tithe free; some however rising to 15*s.*; and this general, except near Lincoln, where it is much higher. In Kirton, of which Mr. HARRISON has the tithes, lambs and wool paid him about 30*l.* a year on five acres; from which may be collected how favourable open fields and heaths were to rearing sheep; for in this parish, now under the plough, except the vale-lands, proper for grass, the quantity of sheep is considerable, and a great culture of turnips to winter-feed them.

" There are few instances of the benefit of enclosing commons, greater than that of Long Sutton: the Act passed in 1788, by which near 4000 acres of common became several property; the rent of it, before enclosing, was 1000*l.* a year, or 500 rights, which lett the messuages at 40*s.* each more for the right; the whole now letts from 30*s.* to 50*s.* an acre, and about half of it is ploughed. Before this Act, the old enclosures were subservient to the common, but now the common is subservient to those; and, if all are included in the account, there is now more live-stock kept than before, and of a much better kind; though above 2000 acres have been ploughed up, to yield an enormous produce*."

---

* Lincoln Report, p. 77.

" By

"By the Acts for enclosing Barton, Barrow, and Goxhill, no less than 17,000 acres are rendered productive, to the infinite advantage of the community*."

"The value of these lands before the enclosure were, open arable lett at from 4*s*. to 9*s*. per acre, of something less than three roods; little parcels for 10*s*. or 12*s*.; average about 6*s*. 6*d*."†

"The advantages that arise from enclosing, in respect to increase of produce or value, must entirely depend upon the modes of management pursued after the enclosing takes place. From the abundant crops produced by land which has never grown grain before, the occupier vainly thinks that it will always continue to do so; and the deception is still increased by the stimulating effects of lime; but alas! after having got nine or ten crops, the golden prospect vanishes; the farther they proceed, the more they are convinced of their error; and growing corn having become a losing trade, the land is left to grass. But what can it produce? Already exhausted by repeated corn crops, and over doses of lime, it remains a spectacle of the bad effects of such culture, and a warning to others to avoid the same course. Even under this treatment, the increased value is in the ratio of three or four to one: had these lands been continued in tillage only three years at one time—the first year oats; second, fallow, turnips, or rape; the third, wheat or oats, or (if the soil suited) barley, sown up with clover and ray-grass, and depastured with sheep for three, four, or five years, according to circumstances and situations, we will venture to say the land would have gone on improving from rotation to rotation; would have been more profitable, and put on a

---

* Lincoln Report, p. 83.
† Lincoln Report, p. 82.

very different aspect to what it does at present, and have been worth double the rent it now letts for*."

Ramsey, in Hunts.

"*Improvement.*—Very great indeed: I viewed it with pleasure. Mr. POOLEY shewed me a considerable part of it; all seems to be under cole, and oats, and wheat, or now burning for the present crops of cole. I saw many of cole, that will in all probability yield half a last an acre. Oats very abundant, and wheat that promises four quarters. Paring and burning effects the whole; and the ditches, instead of posts and rails, and quicks, are all cut out in peats, which go off by water for the various towns that are around Whittlesea Mere, &c. These pay the making—expense 6*d.* a perch for finishing. There are 250 acres of cole now on this common.

Course:

"1. Pare and burn for cole, which is fed, and then seeded.

"2. Oats.

"3. Wheat.

"4, 5, 6, and perhaps 7, Grass seeds, and then pare and burn again.

"*Produce.*—Suppose the whole 500 acres thus cropped, which it nearly will be, there will be 71 acres of cole, 71 of oats, 71 of wheat, and 284 of grass. One division of this grass, or 71 acres, will probably give more profit to the public than the whole common, fed as it was by mares and foals, &c. did before the enclosure.

---
* Cumberland Report, p. 186.

The average produce may be laid at 5*l.* an acre, at the least, probably much more.

"*Culture.*—One or two circumstances merit notice. The paring is done by the fen plough, and it is burnt for 4*s.* 5*s.* and to 6*s.* an acre. A man and a pair of horses will pare above an acre a day. Mr. POOLEY does it at twice; the second in the contrary direction, to take the spots missed at the first. I saw his operations, as well as ploughing, sowing half a peck of seed an acre, and bush-harrowing; all performed in a most husbandlike manner. Some of his finest crops now on the ground were sown so late as September; but at that season he sows three quarters, and even a peck an acre*."

Warboys, Hunts.

" The high fen and commons of this parish offer as extraordinary an instance of improvement, in consequence of enclosure, as can any where be met with. Mr. LONGLAND has 400 acres of the fen, which he has cultivated by paring and burning, and sowing coleseed: this is first fed, and then seeded; oats succeeded; then wheat, with which seeds for three or four years. There are now 500 acres of coleseed in this fen, much of which promises fair for producing half a last of seed per acre. What a spectacle is this! Take the present price of seed, and here is 25*l.* an acre; then ten quarters of oats, then four or five (and sometimes more) quarters of wheat: the fee simple of the land presently becomes a small consideration, when compared with the value of the produce. Where will the visionary theorists that declaim and write against paring and burning, hide their heads? Hide them they must in this country†."

---

* Annals, xliv. p. 57.   † Annals, xvxvi.

Raveley,

Raveley, Hunts.—Enclosed 1786.

" *Improvement.*—Mr. Pooley had an allotment of the common, of which there were 300 acres, which he pared and burned, and sowed coleseed; the crop, half a last an acre: he then sowed wheat, and got five quarters and a half an acre; wheat a second time, five quarters*."

" In fifteen enclosures in which Mr. Burton of Norfolk has been Commissioner, there are 10,800 acres of common land; about half converted to arable, and proper for the five-shift husbandry. One thousand acres for wheat, producing 5000 coombs, at 24s. 6000l.: 1000 barley, 8000 coombs, at 12s. 4800l.; 1000, oats second crop after wheat, 8000 coombs, at 10s. 4000l.; 1000 acres of turnips will feed 500 bullocks or cows, which will pay for the turnips only, 5l. a head, or 2500l.; and 1000 acres of grass, with the offal turnips, will feed 4000 sheep in winter, and fattened by a part of the new lay grass to be off by June. The sheep, for the turnips and grass, will pay 3000l.: there remains 5000 acres of pasture, which will support 500 bullocks, bringing them forward for turnips to 3l. per head, or 1500l.: and there may also be summer-kept 4000 sheep, which, with wool and profit on carcass will pay 2000l. And besides all this, 200 cows at 6l. or 1200l.

Wheat,	6000
Barley,	4800
Oats,	4000
Bullocks,	2500
Sheep,	3000
Bullocks,	1500
Sheep,	2000
Cows,	1200
	£.25,000

* Annals, xliv. p. 187.

" There are 800 acres more unaccounted for; 5000 acres of arable will take 200 horses to till it, wanting each 400 acres arable and pasture; 400 of this for corn will give 10 coombs a horse, for 30 weeks, or 2000 coombs: 150 acres remain for hay, which producing 200 tons, will, with the barns, maintain them the winter; and the 400 acres of pasture will support the 200 horses, with mares and colts in summer. The improved rent on the 10,000 acres, is for a lease of 14 years, 7725*l*. The tithe, for 14 years, about 1500*l*. a year. Capital to stock, and improvement, about 10,000*l*. being additions to farms adjoining. The interest 500*l*. Labour for said lands, including harvest, 5000*l*. Seed corn, 2200*l*. Wear and tear—the blacksmith's will be about 500*l*.; wheelwright's about 100*l*.; carpenter's 100*l*.; small seeds, 300*l*.; poor-rates on an average at 5*s*. 1031*l*. 5*s*.; capital for 500 acres of pasture, 6000*l*.; interest 300*l*. Contingencies, &c. may be estimated at 1000*l*.

Tithe,	£.1500
Interest of capital, on the arable,	500
Labour,	5000
Seed corn,	2200
Wear and tear,	700
Small seed, 1000 acres at 6*s*.	300
Rates,	1031
Interest of capital, for pasture,	300
Contingencies,	1000
	12,531
Rent,	7725
	20,256
Produce,	25,000
Expenses,	20,256
Profit,	£.4744

" This

" This calculation, which does Mr. BURTON credit, sets in a very clear light, the immense advantages which have resulted from the enclosures in which he has been employed*."

Sayham and Ovington.—Enclosed 1800.

" One thousand six hundred acres of common.

" The husbandry of breaking up the common, is to plough once for pease, oats, or cole; the two former all dibbled. Then clay 60 load an acre, of 24 bushels; and fallowed for turnips; and then the common husbandry. It may be calculated that the first year there were 600 acres of oats and 600 of pease.

For the first Year.

600 acres of oats, are 15 coombs, some broke up this year, 25.

	£.	s.	d.
This is 9000 coombs at 10s.	4500	0	0
600 acres of pease at 5 coombs, are 3000 at 14s.	2100	0	0
	£.6600	0	0

" No cole would be sown, but they cannot get all ready in time for oats and pease.

Second Year.

	£.	s.	d.
400 acres of cole, at 6 coombs, 2400 coombs at 30s.	3600	0	0
600 acres of wheat, after pease, at 8 coombs, 4800 at 24s.	5760	0	0
600 acres of turnips at 3l.	1800	0	0
	£.11,160	0	0

* Norfolk Report, p. 182.

Third Year.

	£.	s.	d.
400 acres of wheat, 6 coombs, 2400 coombs, at 24s.	2880	0	0
600 acres of turnips at 3l.	1800	0	0
6 0 acres of barley, at 10 coombs, at 12s. after turnips fed, ...	3600	0	0
	£.8280	0	0

" And this prodigious product will arise in three years, from the culture of a common which most certainly never produced 500l. in any one year, reckoning at the highest which such indefinite returns as that of an unlimited common can be estimated at*."

" Very large wastes and commons still remain in Salop. Among these, Clun forest deserves to be particularly noticed. It contains about 12,000 acres. The uncultivated state of many farms surrounding this magnificent waste, has been urged as an argument against its enclosure. It is supposed the farmers have more land than they can cultivate, and that adding to their enclosed grounds, would increase the evil. However specious this reasoning may appear, it is not true. The existence of the unenclosed land, is the cause of the surrounding farms being uncultivated, and therefore their bad state is an additional motive for the enclosure. Whilst the common continues, the adjoining farmers will, in general, consider their enclosed lands, principally, as affording winter meat for their sheep, and that without care or culture; and their time will continue to be taken up in looking after their flocks. They now pay their rents from the sale of wool; but if the common

---

* Norfolk Report, p. 156.

was holden in severalty, the profit of the wool may be continued or increased, with every other advantage of good husbandry, both to landlord and tenant. Whilst the common remains open, the landlords must be content with a very inadequate rent for their enclosed land, and without any consideration for their right of common*."

* Salop Report, p. 144.

No. VII.

Wastes Enclosed in the first Forty Years of His present MAJESTY.

Waste Land enclosed by Acts which passed in the first forty years of GEORGE III.

BEDFORD.

Podington,	842
Lidlington,	250
Odel,	400
Tempsford,	500
Northill,	266
Crawley,	248
Marston,	40
Houghton,	223
Maulden,	500
Shefford,	90
Chalgrove,	80
Caddington,	832
Sandy,	1100
Farndish,	160
Souldrop,	150
	5681

BERKS.

BERKS.

Farringdon,	842
Uffington,	1001
Langford,	207
Shilton,	289
Remenham,	85
Sparsholt,	800
	3224

BUCKS.

Westbury,	1507
Shalstone,	252
Woughton,	400
Stoke Goldington,	30
Soulbury,	300
Stoke Hammon,	429
Hitcham,	324
Wandow,	511
Little Woolston,	40
Wendover,	300
Little Brickhill,	160
Sherrington,	300
Wingrave,	1032
Emberton,	146
Wraisbury,	174
	5905

CAMBRIDGESHIRE.

Knapwell,	100
Weston Colvill,	388
March,	3400
Little Wilbraham,	800

Long

Long Stow,	200
Elsworth,	1000
Connington,	450
Milton,	441
	6779

CHESHIRE.

Weverham,	360
Kingsley,	903
Rudheath,	700
Cristleton,	277
Tarwin,	471
Frodsham,	1100
Tuskenham,	200
Macclesfield,	760
	4771

CUMBERLAND.

Morresby,	1060
Stapleton,	552
Castle Sowerby,	4500
Sebraham,	2896
Skelton,	5000
Bassenthwayte,	1810
Greystock,	654
Culgarth,	1600
Carlisle,	1800
Bolton,	5178
Farlam,	2300
Brampton,	2000
Irthington,	3679
Millfield,	3600
Upper and Nether Denton,	2886
	39,515

DERBY.

APPENDIX.

DERBY.

Harteshorn,	850
Repton,	636
Darley,	2419
Belper,	696
Stapenhill,	100
Buxton,	900
Bonsal,	1200
Crick,	200
Killamarsh,	242
North Wingfield and Stretton,	558
Shirland,	232
Tibshelf,	330
Bolsover,	1592
Ashover,	3634
Staveley,	400
Matlock,	1719
Stoney Middleton,	368
Bolstone,	98
Morley,	500
Marston,	89
Southwingfield,	251
Spondon,	471
Parwick,	927
Dale and Stanton,	103
Heanor,	500
Chaddesden,	211
Stanley,	82
Beighton,	600
Eckington,	980
Barlbrough,	608

Etwall,

Etwall, ... 834
South Normanton, ... 250
                                    ―――――
                                    22,580

DORSETSHIRE.

Portesham, ... 400
Winfrith, ... 610
West Knighton, ... 343
Hinton Marlet, ... 447
Bradford Peverell, ... 300
Maypowder, ... 331
Leigh, ... 640
                                    ―――――
                                    3071

DURHAM.

Chester, ... 2800
Norham, ... 870
Evenwood, ... 2007
Wolsingham, ... 5020
Heworth, ... 368
St. Oswald, ... 200
Thornley, ... 720
Brancepeth, ... 1701
Elvet, ... 400
Lanchester, ... 20,000
Horncliff, ... 53
Egleston, ... 800
Holy Island, ... 950
Tweedmouth, ... 650
                                    ―――――
                                    36,539

ESSEX.

APPENDIX.

ESSEX.

Navestock,	530
Great Parndon,	150
Dedham,	413
	1093

GLOUCESTERSHIRE.

Childswickham,	10
Willersey,	200
Beddington,	160
Holyrood Ampney,	374
Aston Subedge,	141
Kemerton,	600
Beckford,	302
Oxenton,	300
Woodrush,	350
Naunton,	300
Buckland,	1900
Clifford Chambers,	127
Iron Acton,	270
Winstone,	168
Mangotsfield,	262
Lower Swell,	1000
Rodmaston,	140
Maisemore,	150
Old Sodbury,	106
Aure,	97
Horton,	463
Little Compton,	603
Welford,	120
Abbots Ann,	245
	8388

HAMPSHIRE.

Kinsomborn,	215
Basingstoke,	620
Over Wallop,	650
Dibden,	200
Shipton,	419
Mitchel-marsh,	663
Nether Wallop,	641
Whitchurch,	588
	3996

HERTFORD.

Elstrée,	750
Ickleford,	40
North Mims	700
Norton,	400
Tring,	750
Hensworth,	440
Cheshunt,	1168
Pembridge,	176
	4424

HEREFORD,

Wigmore,	450
Willington,	400
	850

HUNTINGDONSHIRE.

Kimbolton,	167
St. Neots,	130
Harlford,	489

Kings

APPENDIX.

Kings Ripton,	160
Little Stukely,	134
Easton,	105
Spaldswick,	330
Little Calworth,	244
Wornditch,	205
Warboys,	2500
Somersham,	468
Pidley,	340
Ramsey,	473
Diadington,	110
Mooleswrth,	404
Bythorn,	368
	6627

LINCOLNSHIRE.

Horbling,	1400
Hecklington,	2294
Ankborough,	1000
Bourne,	4440
Kettlethorpe,	864
Bicker,	2000
Corby,	631
Bartnetby,	800
Holland,	20,225
Donnington,	3007
Billingborough,	1100
Marton,	2820
North Hickham,	350
Beckingham,	781
Benniworth,	600
Boothby,	1202
Algerkirk,	3260

Shirbeck,

APPENDIX.

Shirbeck,	277
Thorpe,	822
Helpringham,	2149
Whitten,	343
Heapham,	550
Quadring,	2262
Brampton,	470
Kirmington	800
Surfleet,	1176
Leadenham,	800
Edlington,	295
Huttoft,	265
Frampton,	1460
Canwick,	415
Martin,	1400
Ranceby,	3000
Denton,	1535
Pointon,	646
Ludford,	300
Anwick,	1400
Gedney,	1318
Tydd,	567
Barton,	1420
Covenham,	400
Dunston,	600
Moulten,	1800
Fleet,	500
Spittlegate,	1511
Hepworth,	2500
Harlaxton,	253
Tattershall,	520
Caiston,	190
Barrow,	1730

Messing-

APPENDIX.

Messingham, ... 3800
South Hykeham, ... 201
                                 ─────
                                 84,649

LANCASHIRE.

Lowton, ... 380
Chorley, ... 590
Kirkby, ... 158
Childwall, ... 350
Barnaker, ... 327
Walley, ... 2400
Blackburn, ... 980
Ditto, ... 858
Forton, ... 80
Clitheroe, ... 300
Wiswell, ... 350
Bolton, ... 250
Claife, ... 1350
Bolton Moors, ... 1000
Cartmell, ... 12,516
Prescot, ... 150
                                 ─────
                                 22,039

LEICESTERSHIRE.

Roarsby, ... 100
Quorndon, ... 141
Thurmarston, ... 680
Whetstone, ... 600
Stoney Stanton, ... 778
Charnford, ... 750
North Kilworth, ... 610
Blaby, ... 220
Ailstone, ... 140

Ashby

APPENDIX.

Ashby de la Zouch,	210
Eaton,	358
Bottesford,	1654
Appleby,	400
Kirkby,	194
Ibstock,	250
Ditto,	500
Thornton,	300
Rothly,	50
Osgaythorp,	36
South Kilworth,	300
Walton,	398
Bagworth,	200
Knipton,	785
Welburn,	1400
	11,044

NORTHAMPTONSHIRE.

Moreton Pinkney,	250
Long Buckby,	300
Harleston,	1180
Great Oxendon,	200
Cosgrove,	500
Astop,	800
Charlton,	312
East Haddon,	200
Warmington,	762
Crick,	100
Duston,	160
Desborough,	231
Clipson,	800
Harpole,	930
Isham,	140

Bulwick,

APPENDIX.

Bulwick,	100
Piddington,	140
Broughton,	180
Great Catworth,	756
Ravensthorp,	920
Coton,	420
Stamford,	234
Whittlebury,	277
Wilbarston,	200
Greens Norton,	595
	10,687

NOTTINGHAMSHIRE.

Loudham,	170
Carleton,	220
Balderton,	507
Farndon,	102
Epperstone,	70
Blidworth,	1800
Scaftworth,	400
Normanton,	260
Stapleford,	300
Southwell,	360
West Retford,	249
Hickling,	800
Sutton,	2294
Scrooby,	372
Clarebrough,	421
Farnsfield,	2064
Hallam,	470
Winthorp,	66
Ollerton,	500
Elksley,	1358

Calverton,

Calverton,	1554
Ratcliffe,	1500
Cropwell,	340
Arnold,	2000
Colgrave,	927
Eastwood,	130
Syerstone,	129
Lambley,	438
Basford,	1200
Gedling,	1209
Willoughby,	900
Woodborough,	616
Ashfield,	2000
Caunton,	200
Gringley,	2000
Gateford,	411
Linton,	300
Snenton,	343
Great Leke,	800
Keyworth,	700
Harworth,	850
Tuxford,	400
Grassthorpe, ...n............	83
Moorgate,	90
Normanton,	155
Ordsall,	80
	32,138

NORFOLK.

Snettisham,	1723
North Tuddenham,	650
Scarning,	189
Little Ellingham,	500

Sherborn,

APPENDIX.

Sherborn,	210
Rondham,	1100
Fincham,	600
Beetley,	250
Crownthorp,	71
Wreningham,	260
Telthorp,	3000
Talconeston,	416
Woodbastwick,	400
Tottenhill,	600
Winfarthing,	683
Shottesham,	320
Walpole,	2180
Tewington,	862
Old Buckenham,	795
Thornham,	260
Bentry,	200
Tilney,	431
Narford,	300
Saxlingham,	300
Acle,	350
Saham,	1150
Hetherset,	436
Bressingham,	490
Upton,	757
Ranworth,	370
Rackheath,	540
Plumstead,	606
Ovington,	730
Causton,	1200
Brook,	150
Ludham,	1050
Langley,	500

Snetti-

Snettisham,	576
Horseford,	2000
Ringstead,	1260
	28,465

NORTHUMBERLAND.

Simonburn,	5218
Elsdon,	2500
Wooller,	140
Corbridge,	4506
Langley,	566
Ovingham,	800
Fourstones,	427
Haitwistle,	10,000
Tynemouth,	1150
Long Bentone,	1800
Hexhamshire,	4060
Thorngrafton,	1700
Langley Warden,	2814
Grindon,	4250
Wark,	1350
	41,281

OXFORD.

Tringford,	230
Steeple Aston,	188
Skipton,	150
Blackbourton,	1636
Westwick,	750
Burford,	90
Cropredy,	800
Broadwell,	800

Claydoyn,

APPENDIX.

Claydoyn,	540
Tudmarton,	500
Stratton,	800
Ensham,	500
Coggs,	298
Adington,	237
Melcomb,	300
Stoke Lyne,	1186
Burford,	80
Westcot,	200
Wigginton,	1190
Hampton,	204
Alvescot,	600
Mollington,	180
Ensham,	1000
	12,559

RUTLANDSHIRE.

Wissardine,	1569
Greetham,	500
Wing,	150
Normanton,	124
Bridge Casterton,	300
Birbrook,	40
Little Casterton,	80
Empingham,	759
	3522

SALOP.

Newport,	117
Donnington,	200
Drayton,	1400
Crofton,	377

West

APPENDIX.

West Felton,	278
Shiffnal,	1093
Aston Abbots,	177
Prees Darleston,	1150
Cheswardine,	580
Worthen,	400
Seifton,	220
	5992

SOMERSETSHIRE.

East Cranmore,	380
Ubly,	901
Doulton,	1101
Crowcombe,	1000
Shapwick,	900
Compton Bishop,	300
Huntshill,	1100
Westhay,	2800
Glastonbury,	1505
Brislington,	380
Wookey,	1100
Marke,	1914
West Pennard,	119
West Harptree,	900
Bleadown,	1139
Compton Martin,	700
Edington,	968
Rodney Stoke,	753
St. Cuthbert Wells,	789
Milton,	120
St. Cuthbert,	4200
Chapel Allerton,	169
East Harptree,	1000
Pilton,	1123
Mark,	136
East Brent,	118

East

APPENDIX.

East Came,	222
Banwell,	500
North Pelkerton,	1280
Higham,	1594
Shipham,	1070
Exton,	570
Weston,	647
Huish Episcopi,	250
Moorlinch,	175
Othery,	629
Street,	500
Aller,	600
North Curry,	1752
Chewton,	2300
Ashcott,	600
Chedsoy,	300
Glaston,	74
Chilton,	227
Ditto Trinity,	270
Portbury,	950
Middlezoy,	602
Clevedon,	488
Huntspill,	50
Locking,	160
	40,625

STAFFORDSHIRE.

Elford,	660
Leek,	6800
Wigginton,	1232
Horninglow,	1200
Kinver,	1157
Ditto,	500
Trisul,	650
Rushton,	319
Culton,	670

Dilhorn,

APPENDIX.

Dilhorn,	700
Kingswinford,	1430
Uttoxeter,	250
Milwick,	500
Hirton,	250
Handsworth,	250
Colton,	90
Normancott,	191
Womborne,	980
Abbots Bromley,	900
Aldridge,	2150
Stone,	410
Pattingham,	210
Rowley,	169
King's Bromley,	920
Rocesher,	160
	22,748

SUFFOLK.

Kessingland,	400
Ellough,	116
Sotterly,	642
Uggeshal,	102
Barnby,	720
Gisleham,	230
Pakefield,	110
	2320

SURREY.

Cobham,	1314
Croydon,	1200
Walton,	3000
	5514

SUSSEX

APPENDIX.

SUSSEX.

Ringmer,	2000
Aldingborne,	400
Elsted,	290
	2690

WARWICK.

Pailton,	225
Bourton,	350
Redford,	40
Aulchester,	308
Rugby,	540
Newbold,	442
Coughton,	569
Long Itchington,	200
Coleshill,	1000
Burton,	60
Paine's Salford,	250
Lower Brailes,	300
Meredon,	286
Great Kineton,	200
Ratley,	100
Balsale,	1200
Birmingham,	320
	6390

WILTSHIRE.

Tidcombe,	395
Bremhill,	500
Pewsey,	871
Ramsbury,	30
Ayston Keyms,	727
Patney,	100
Chicklade,	439
Colerne,	238

Nether-

APPENDIX.

Netheravon,	1740
Marden,	480
Winterborne,	1506
Lavington,	633
Shrewton,	1150
Sutton,	1739
Purton,	240
Wilcott,	200
Stratford,	164
	11,152

WESTMORELAND.

Orton	5500
Long Maston,	800
Ormside,	885
Warcop,	980
Ditto,	820
Appleby,	226
Kirkby Thore,	362
Moreland,	410
Ditto Township,	400
	10,383

WORCESTERSHIRE.

Pinton,	299
Stone,	379
Emload,	353
Broadway,	360
Stoke Priory,	400
Hadsor,	147
Severn Stoke,	690
Cleve Priory,	300
Wolverley,	1277
Charlton,	500
Grefton,	100
Bellbroughton,	500

Himbleton,

APPENDIX.

Himbleton,	140
Hanbury,	340
Church Linch,	170
Dudley,	975
Harvington,	284
Fladbury,	700
Hanley,	1400
Chaddesley,	368
Lyndridge,	30
Broomsgrove,	1000
	10,712

WALES.

Hanmer,	400
Salmer,	1900
Narberth,	1800
Street Marshall,	1504
Castle Martin,	274
Hope,	3308
Mold,	4000
Lanferris,	4200
Penley,	79
Kerry,	9500
Broughton,	700
Ysceiliog	1800
	29,465

YORKSHIRE.

Burton Pidsea,	468
Hessington,	785
Clifton,	360
Sutton,	3180
Sheffling,	300
Bentham,	5000
Cropton,	2060
Braithwell,	160

Everingham,

Everingham,	283
Wadworth,	1970
Aston,	830
Naburn,	311
Cottingham,	1486
Arlingfleet,	500
Barnbydun,	600
North Ansten,	266
Hotham,	1850
Heck, &c.	2150
Bridlington,	500
Millington,	800
Sancton,	410
Sheriff Hutton,	837
Osbaldwick,	112
Elvington,	300
Ebberston,	8000
Haxby,	1300
Wiggington,	400
Nafferton,	2200
Langston,	390
Rotherham,	394
Tickhill,	1630
Skipton,	966
Upper Dunsford,	81
Bellerby,	1400
Dunnington,	1100
West Hessington,	880
Earswicke,	600
Mapleton,	300
Oxenthorpe,	2031
Brampton,	350
Welton,	220
Ditto,	170
Singleton,	200
Royston,	170

Aikworth.

Aikworth, ... 350
Market Weighton, ... 2500
Agnes Burton, ... 300
Spalding Moor, ... 6513
Rossington, ... 1063
Snaith, ... 342
Kirkby Ravensworth, ... 1820
Acombe, ... 559
Rawmarsh, ... 800
Righton, ... 1855
Goodmanham, ... 100
Kildare, ... 2944
Mulgrave, ... 424
Cawood, ... 2000
Stainbourne, ... 1100
Bilton, ... 204
Stonegrave, ... 153
Armtherly, ... 93
Cantley, ... 2063
North Newbald, ... 200
Fremington, ... 1047
Aysgarth, ... 617
Halton Moor, ... 100
Ravensworth, ... 3200
Milborne, ... 1000
Barnsley, ... 486
Tunstale, ... 300
Northoram, ... 460
Otley, ... 1246
Kildwick, ... 4000
Ecclesfield, ... 400
Sheffield, ... 729
Weston, ... 1342
Gaewelthorpe, ... 1100
Pontefract, ... 897
Kighley, ... 5000

Almondbury,	1300
Thormanby,	247
Roos,	497
Eccleshield,	600
Loxley,	2480
Leyburn,	1100
Rothwell,	500
Wykeham,	1100
St. John Beverley,	1000
Womersley,	650
Methley,	278
Huddersfield,	323
Sinnington,	1066
Moor Monkton,	600
Kidwicke,	966
Kirkby Malzeard,	2600
Kirkley Moorside,	1903
Featherstone,	450
Rightsides,	111
Yafforth,	172
Bingley,	2206
Burnsale,	1603
Birkin,	582
Giggleswick,	1400
Bramley,	670
Tickton,	234
Hutton Bushel,	1430
Sheffield,	4253
Kippax,	300
Bilton,	400
Anlaby,	1725
West Ayton,	654
Monk Triston,	280
Kirkburn,	1500
Knottingley,	246
Thornborough,	400

Armley,

APPENDIX.

Armley,	165
Marsham,	5000
Whitby,	700
Thirsk,	1235
Wakefield,	1900
Hoyland,	234
Feliskirk,	550
Elloughton,	894
Rufford,	370
Guiseley,	350
Old Malton,	1020
Kirk Ella,	104
Kimberwaithe,	230
Morfield,	424
Berwick,	2159
Selby,	734
Womersley,	176
Sowerby,	400
Kirkby Overblow,	80
Sandal Magna,	570
North Crossland,	1100
Kirkheaton,	521
Leek,	726
Birkin,	92
Dalton,	194
Skelmanthorp,	170
Kearby,	242
Thurstonland,	485
Marton,	160
Tholthorp,	904
Total,	151,124 559.942

NO. VIII.

No. VIII.

Extent of the remaining Open Arable Fields.

Warwick—50,000 acres remained open in 1796.
Oxford—There remain above 100 parishes unenclosed.
Bucks—Contains 91,906 acres of common arable fields.

By an estimate made (which however is mentioned on very insufficient authority), it is conjectured that they amount in England to 4,600,000 acres.

No. IX.

Advantage to Landlords by Enclosing.

"The following enclosures have taken place about Spilsby, &c.; among many others, Dalby, twenty-eight years ago; Driby twenty; Langton forty; Tetford twenty-five; Swayby ten; Belleau ten; Hay three; Greetham three; Ashby Puerorum five; High Toynton fifteen; also Ashby, East and West Keal, and Fulletsby; in all which, upon an average, rents have trebled by enclosure*."

"Claypool, Beckington, and Doddington, have been enclosed since 1771; were 8s. an acre when open; now 18s. 20s. and some more.

"The country west of the great north road, to Woolsthorpe, Belvoir Castle, &c. all enclosed: a Lordship, which, 32 years ago, was 300*l.* a year, is now 1500*l.* a year. All these have been greatly improved in management, entirely by enclosing; and especially in turnips and seeds, and the breeding of sheep, articles which have taken place only in enclosures†."

---

* Lincoln Report, p. 84.   † Lincoln Report, p. 88.

212 APPENDIX.

A State of certain Improvements by Enclosing and Draining.

	A.	R.	P.	Improved Value. £. s. d.	Old Value. £. s. d.	Improvement. £. s. d.	Expenditure. £. s. d.
Donnington,	1728	0	0	681 5 0	380 0 0	301 5 0	1100 0 0
Swaby,	1555	1	24	738 5 6	310 14 0	427 11 6	1967 13 0
Belleau,	649	1	14	323 8 0	274 0 0	49 8 0	
North Bauceby,	3168	0	25	1129 16 0	352 0 0	777 16 0	3399 0 0
South ditto,	2161	0	20	1010 18 7	347 0 0	663 18 7	
Normanby,	1718	3	20	1021 18 3	480 0 0	541 18 3	1320 0 0
Huttoft,	3352	0	16	2356 2 6	1800 0 0	556 2 6	2300 0 0
Hemswell,	2531	2	20	1472 2 6	630 3 0	841 19 6	1874 0 0
Legburn,	2335	2	0	973 14 7	655 0 0	318 14 7	1663 0 0
Canwick,	2059	3	38	1437 5 0	672 12 0	764 13 0	1722 0 0
Skindleby,	1028	1	25	571 3 1	285 0 0	286 3 1	800 0 0
West Enderby,	793	0	0	526 4 8	340 0 0	186 4 8	848 10 7
Anwick fields, &c.	954	0	0	708 19 0	385 3 0	323 16 0	1510 0 0
Greetham,	1275	0	29	763 2 6	400 0 0	363 2 6	1348 0 0
Hagg,	2383	2	12	1806 17 0	1560 0 0	246 17 0	2100 0 0
Kirton,	4533	0	0	3364 3 7	1168 0 0	2696 3 7	5269 16 9
Nettleton,	3549	2	32	1523 17 9	460 0 0	1063 17 9	2425 0 0
Osbornby,	1475	2	0	1323 7 0	662 0 0	661 7 0	2023 12 1
Scarthe,	1186	2	0	876 15 0	452 0 0	424 15 0	1147 1 6
Quarrington,	1500	0	0	1268 8 0	627 0 0	641 8 0	
Sleaford and Holdingham,	2221	1	20	2191 2 0	918 0 0	1273 2 0	3669 0 0
Dunsten heath and fields,	1957	0	20	1037 1 3	641 0 0	396 1 3	
Tattershall enclosure,	4003	2	18	2168 1 11	1706 11 8	461 10 3	1200 0 0
Fens. Ditto embankment,	892	0	26	838 13 9	387 19 9	450 14 0	626 0 0
Anwick fen,	1097	0	0	703 16 0	54 17 0	648 19 0	3630 0 0
							4070 0 0
The nine embanked fens from Tattershall to Lincoln,	19,418	1	34	15,534 8 0	1941 16 0	13,592 12 0	77,672 0 0
Holland fen, eleven towns,	22,000	0	0	25,300 0 0	3600 0 0	21,700 0 0	50,600 0 0*
					21,400 16 5	50,659 19 6	175,197 13 11†

APPENDIX.

" There are other parishes, that I have been commissioner for, which I have not an account of, owing to my books being from home.

" Add to the improved annual value of 72,150*l*. 15*s*. 11*d*. upon a moderate estimation, the annual produce of three times the rent; making, for the fens drained by the Witham, 127,130*l*.; for the high-land old enclosures 89,321*l*. 14*s*. 6*d*. together; for the whole, 216,451*l*. 14*s*. 6*d*. being the annual produce by cultivation.

" Upon this animating detail, I have only to remark, that the valuation of the improved rents was that of the Commsssioners; but the real rents, at this time, exceed it in many instances; thus Holland fen is here reckoned at about 1*l*. 1*s*. per acre, whereas the average is now, as appears by the minutes, about 27*s*.: but even if we suppose that no farther rise has taken place than here stated, it is a noble spectacle to see such a prodigious improvement effected. The old rent is 4*s*. 8*d*. per acre. The new rent is 15*s*. 8*d**."

RECAPITULATION.

	Old Rent.			New Rent.		
	£.	s.	d.	£.	s.	d.
Long Sutton,	0	5	0	2	0	0
Lincoln-heath,	0	1	0	0	10	0
Ditto Lincoln, to beyond Kirton,	0	1	9	0	10	0
Near Norton,	0	2	0	0	10	0
Gainsborough,	0	8	0	1	0	0
Newton,	0	3	6	1	2	6
Carry forward,	£.1	1	3	£.5	12	6

---

* Lincoln Report, p. 87.

Brought

	£	s	d	£	s	d
Brought forward,	1	1	3	5	12	6
Haxey, &c. commons,	0	1	0	0	10	0
Barton,	0	6	6	1	1	0
Wintringham,	0	7	6	1	13	0
Horton,	0	10	0	1	0	0
Winterton,	0	10	0	1	0	0
Killington,	0	4	6	0	12	6
Dalby, Driby, Langton, Tetford, Swayby, Belleau, Hay, Greetham, Ashby, Toynton, Keals, Fulletsby,	0	5	0	0	15	0
Mr. PARKINSON's table,	0	4	8	0	15	8
Claypool, Beckington, Doddington,	0	8	0	0	19	0
Woolsthorpe, &c.	0	6	0	0	18	0
Several near Grimsthorpe,	0	6	0	0	12	0
	£.4	10	5	£.15	15	8

" The rise is therefore on an average, three and a half, as appears on this table; but there can be no doubt of the rise being, in fact, more considerable, for reasons already stated, quadruple at least.

" The admirable spirit with which enclosures have gone on in this county, is a memorable proof of the enlightened energy which has pervaded it for thirty years past*."

" About Folkingham, many new as well as old parliamentary enclosures, of arable, open, and common fields; the improvement by which have been very great; lands adapted to grass have been laid down; and some better

* Lincoln Report, p. 89.

for the plough have been broken up. At Osbornby, the rents at 10*s*. were raised to 17*s*. 6*d*.; and several others in an equal proportion. The produce vastly more considerable. 1. Fallow; 2. Wheat; and 3. Beans; are now changed to, 1. Turnips; 2. Barley; 3. Clover; 4. Wheat. In some of these parishes, the old flocks of sheep, which were folded, and sold lean, are greatly increased in number, without folding, and sold fat*."

" The arable fields of Barton now lett, on an average, at 20*s*. About the town, much more; at a distance, less. The marsh land would now sell at 79*l*. an acre, near the town; at a distance 40*l*. Some ploughed land, one mile from town, 40*l*. to 50*l*. an acre. Old enclosures near the town 100*l*. an acre, for convenience. The common on the Wold, 12*s*. an acre. The parish, including every thing, may now be rented at, or worth 6000*l*. a year; it was 2000*l*.; and all the tenants better satisfied than before; 150 acres were given to the vicar for his small tithes; and 900 were assigned for great tithe, most conveniently for the impropriator. Many new farms, barns, &c. built, and more building.

" The wheat before enclosing, two quarters on the customary measure of three-fifths statute; the beans not more than two quarters: these crops are now changed to, 1. Turnips, worth 30*s*.; 2. Barley, four quarters and a half; 3. Clover, mown once, two loads per acre, worth 50*s*. and a very fine after-grass of 10*s*. an acre; 4. Wheat, four quarters. There is wheat now in the field that will be five. They formerly carted their corn and manure two miles and a half.

" Horton was enclosed 20 years ago, and advanced from 10*s*. to 20*s*. Winterton also from 10*s*. to 20*s*.

---

* Lincoln Report, p. 77.

Coalby

Coalby was enclosed forty years ago; 800 acres, now lett at 700*l.* a year, about 17*s.* 6*d.* an acre. Killingholm, enclosed about 20 years ago, was open clay arable, lett at 4*s.* or 5*s.* an acre; now 12*s.* or 13*s.* an acre*."

" Without looking minutely where the principal benefit of enclosure rests, there is certainly a sufficient balance of advantage upon the whole, to warrant the strenuous endeavours of every friend to mankind in forwarding them. It must be owned, a great deal of beauty is often spoiled by enclosures; and it seems a pity to lose scenes of pure nature, in a country so artificial as that of South Britain. This applies chiefly to very large wastes; for instance, Clun forest, is a fine specimen of smooth and extended turf, with every variation of swelling banks and retired dingles; but when it is considered how little profit is produced to those who have a legal right in these wastes, or to the public at large; what a scope is given to industry by their enclosure; and that the population of this country seems to require an extended cultivation, the latter motives must preponderate. The expense of enclosing, indeed, is often such, as to postpone the individual return for some time, but the public are immediate gainers; and where that is denied to the private persons concerned, their distant interest will still prove an ample reward to their families†."

RISE OF RENTS.

REPORTS.

Surrey.—Upon the average of many common fields, rents 12*s.* 10¼*d.*; the tenants would, if enclosed, readily pay 1*l.* 4*s.*

---

* Lincoln Report, p. 82. † Salop Report, p. 145.

Suffolk.

REPORTS.

Suffolk.—The parish of Coney Weston enclosed in 1777. Rents doubled, and the farmers much richer.

Middlesex.—Stanwell, 500 acres of waste raised from nothing to 20*s.* an acre, and the common fields from 14*s.* to 20*s.*

Hants.—A considerable quantity of land enclosed, that was raised from 6*s.* to 12*s.* an acre.

Warwick.—Open field rent 10*s.*; the same enclosed 18*s.* The expense has been on an average, when frugally managed, about 45*s.* an acre; and the improvement one-third of the rent, after allowing interest for the expenses.

Cambridge.—The general average of the rent of the enclosed arable, compared with that of the open common field arable, in the whole county, exceeds the latter in the proportion of 8*s.* per acre. In the two parishes, Childersley, which is enclosed, and Hardwicke, which remains in common field (and which parishes consist of a perfectly similar soil, and are divided only by a hedge-row), the excess of produce appears to be great.

Childersley, enclosed.	*Hardwicke, open.*	*Excess of produce.*
24 bushels of wheat,	16	8
86 ditto barley,	18	18
36 ditto oats,	18	18
20 ditto pease and beans,	8	12

To which add the exemption from the rot, which has desolated sheep-walks in most of the neighbouring parishes; whilst in Childersley and Knapwell

(both

of which are enclosed) not the least shadow of the disease has made its appearance.

Leicester.—Advance of rent from 8*s.* to 20*s.*
York, W. R.—Lord HAWKE had open land at 5*s.* 9*d.* which could lett enclosed at 20*s.*
Cardigan.—Rents doubled by enclosing.
Carmarthen.—Ditto.
Pembroke.—Ditto.
Derby.—Nearly doubled.
Somerset.—More than two-thirds.
Northampton.—Open arable from 11*s.* 6*d.* to 20*s.*
Hertford.—Nearly doubled.

Common field arable usually lies, respecting the lots of individuals, in so scattered and divided a state, that every operation of tillage, harvest, &c. is carried on at an expense considerably greater than in enclosures; the plough, the harrow, and the cart, travel a useless distance; less land is ploughed, and less manure and corn carted; hence arises the necessity noticed in the minutes, of keeping more horses upon a given quantity of land, from which results great national loss. In moving from one piece to another, the horses and implements unavoidably trample much more land than in enclosed fields, which upon wet soils is a mischievous circumstance. But all these are trifling points, when compared with the fatal shackles under which every occupier, however anxious for improvement, is bound to the courses of crops entailed by custom on a common field. A regularly returning fallow, with one, two, or three crops of corn; the beans, if any, finishing, instead of beginning the rotation, exemplifies the whole system upon soils formed by nature for turnips, clover, and various other grasses. Dry chalk thinly covered with miserable oats, where luxuriant

crops

crops of sainfoin might be at command: turnip sands under barren fallows: fertile clays, that under grass would feed the largest oxen, poisoned with water, and the crops choaked with weeds: the landlord losing rent, the tenant profit, the poor without employment, and national prosperity at a stop. What system of barbarism can be greater, than that of obliging every farmer of a parish possessing soils perhaps totally different, all to cultivate in the same rotation! What a gross absurdity, to bind down in the fetters of custom ten intelligent men willing to adopt the improvements adapted to enclosures, because one stupid fellow is obstinate for the practice of his grandfather! To give ignorance the power to limit knowledge, to render stupidity the measure of talents, to chain down industry to the non-exertions of indolence, and fix an insuperable bar, a perpetual exclusion, to all that energy of improvement which has carried husbandry to perfection by means of enclosure! Yet is all this done by the common-field system.

To flocks that are kept in the open fields, feeding on stubbles, baulks, swampy confines and fallows, in situations void of all draining, the consequence is notorious; the profit is reduced to the mere fold, and that often insufficient to pay the almost periodical losses by rot and otherwise. The reports are almost uniform on this subject.

As to common pastures, the minutes speak but one language, and that so decisive, as to convince all but the most prejudiced and interested readers. The best soils, by overstocking, are almost reduced to a par with the worst. The value of the food thus gained is so contemptible, that the best farmers despise it too much even to accept it. An utter degradation and ruin of the breed of all the animals thus supported—distempers for ever making a dreadful havock

havock—the poor without industry—the rates enormous—health depraved—and morals destroyed. Such is the uniform picture; and a more wretched or melancholy one is hardly within the compass of imagination. What a spectacle, viewing it politically, to see the produce of such immense tracts, amounting to millions of acres, minus in the national account!

To state the benefits that result from enclosing open arable fields and common pastures, is to reverse the medal; to see all their evils remedied, and all their advantages increased. By giving an exclusive property to the soil, the proprietor has his industry unfettered; he is allowed to expend his capital; he is permitted to apply his lands to whatever use will pay him best; he neither burdens his neighbour, nor is shackled by him: no barbarous customs prohibit his exertions; his talents, his energy, and his capital, are free to be employed for his own benefit; he thrives, and national prosperity follows in his train.

It is fair to estimate, in general, from the preceding notes, that the enclosing open arable fields advances the rent to double the old proportion, and this must be esteemed a fact of great importance, for it implies double, treble, quadruple, and in some cases a much larger proportion, in the increase of produce, lessening in the expenses of cultivation, and, in consequence of both, a larger mass of commodities carried free to market: advantages that are gained by a most useful employment of hands, now perhaps next to idle, and an equally beneficial employment of capitals in the most important of all investments. The landlord doubles his income; the farmer trebles his profit; the labouring poor are more regularly employed, and better paid; and all those classes of the community that reside in towns, and support the manufacture

facture and commerce of the kingdom, receive supplies in their markets adequate to the advance they make in the prosperity and population of the nation.

If such benefits flow from the enclosure of open arable fields, how much greater are those which result from converting common pasture into private property! Arable lands must be of some value at present: they bear a rent, and some times a high rent: but pastures liable to the infinite inconvenience of overstocking, flooding, want of draining, and a deficiency of every sort of improvement, have in innumerable instances proved to be of no use whatever, but on the contrary a real nuisance and mischief; yet capable, by enclosure, of carrying a rent of from 10*s* to 30*s*. an acre. This is so prodigious a benefit, that it almost mocks the powers of calculation; and when it is considered that the quantity of land thus worse than lost to the community is very great, and found spread through every county and even hundred of the kingdom, the magnitude of the object must be strongly impressed on every mind; and the clearest conviction follow, that this is a business that ought not any longer to be delayed.

No. X.

Tithe.

THE state of tithes, in certain parishes examined.

Bedfordshire.

Milton Bryant, a corn rent of 185*l*.
Eaton, one-fifth of arable, and one-ninth pasture.
Lidlington, one-sixth arable, one-ninth grass and common.
Marston, remains subject.
Shelton, corn-rent, every man distinct.
Dunton, one-fifth arable, one-ninth grass.
Risely, one-fifth arable, one-ninth grass, one-twelfth wood.

Hunts.

Diddington, one-fifth arable, one-ninth grass.
Raunds, one-fifth arable, one-ninth grass.
Warboys, one-fifth arable, one-ninth grass.
Ramsey, one-ninth grass.
Spaldwick, one-fifth arable, one-ninth grass.
Barham, one-sixth arable, one-ninth grass.
Stonely, one-seventh of all.
Holywell, one-sixth arable, one-ninth grass.
Alconbury, one-fifth arable, one-ninth grass.

Cambridgeshire.

March, 2*s*. 3*d*. an acre oats; 3*s*. 3*d*. barley; 3*s*. 9*d*. wheat; 5*s*. coleseed; pasture 4*d*. Had a composition

APPENDIX.

position by decree before for 7*s.* 6*d.* for each common-right.
Wimblington, oats 4*s.*; wheat and cole 5*s.*; pasture 4*d.*
Barrington, remains subject.
Long Stow, one-fifth arable, one-eighth grass, one-tenth wood.
Abington, 90 guineas.
Morden Guildon, remains subject.
Conington, one-fifth arable, one-eighth grass.
Elsworth, one-fifth arable, one-ninth grass.
Little Wilbraham, one-fifth arable, two-seventeenths grass.
Carleton, corn-rent.
Weston Colville, land.

Suffolk.

Coney Weston, remains subject.
Barningham, ditto.
Pakefield, ditto.
Gislam, ditto.
Barton-mills, land.

Norfolk.

Carleton, remains subject.
Banham, ditto.
Winfarthing, ditto.
Northwold, ditto.
Hilborough, land.
Fincham, remains subject.
Barton, one-seventh of all.
Shouldham, remains subject.
Ellingham, for five years, the common if not broken up 1*s.* and 2*s.* if ploughed : then subject.
Lexham, remains subject.

Ashill,

Ashill, remains subject.
Little Dunham, ditto.
Stifkey, ditto.
Heacham, ditto.
Ringstead, ditto.
Sedgeford, ditto.
Dersingham, ditto.
Brancaster, ditto.
Titchwell, ditto.
Thornham, ditto.
Salthouse, ditto.
Kelling, ditto.
Hewingham, ditto.
Felthorpe, ditto.
Marsham, ditto.
Sayham, ditto.
Ovington, ditto.
Poringland, corn-rent equal to one-tenth of improved value.
Shropham, land.
Bintry, remains subject.
Twyford, ditto.
Wallington, ditto.
Cove, ditto.
Elbow, ditto.
Hetherset, ditto.
Cranworth, common to pay 1*s.* 6*d.* first year; 2*s.* the second; 2*s.* 6*d.* the third; 3*s.* 6*d.* the fourth: then remain subject.
Wreningham, land.
Shottesham, remains subject.
Old Buckenh, free before.
Hockham, land.

Hants.

Hants.

Basingstoke, remains subject.
Odiham, ditto.

    In 24, land is given.
        3, a corn-rent.
        2, money per acre.
        2, Fixed money payment.
      42, remain subject.
        1, free before.

Total, 74

" The cultivation of grass is increased, and is more attended to since the enclosure than corn; *i. e.* oats and a species of barley, here called bigg; because corn crops tithe, grass does not—and it is the opinion of the most intelligent persons here, that nothing is so great a check to the improvement of land, or contributes so much to advance the price of corn, as the present mode of paying tithes. In our parish, which contains ten townships, and is about 50 miles in circumference, within the last 20 years the corn tithes are diminished more than two-thirds, every year producing less than the former. A vast quantity of the land is continued in grass, which would certainly be ploughed, and to great advantage, if the grand objection (tithe in kind) could be removed, and a certain and permanent commutation for tithes be established.

                        " JOHN WILSON,
                          " Minister of Burnshall, York.

" *February* 28*th,* 1801."

                                      A Copy

A Copy of the Schedule to which Corse Award refers, containing the several yearly or Corn-Rents, or Sums of Money, payable to the Vicar for the Estates of the respective Proprietors hereunder written.

Communicated by Sir GEORGE O. PAUL, *Bart.*

	Bushels.	Pecks.	Gallons.	Quarts.	Pints.	£.	s.	d.
1. William Allen,	9	2	1	1		2	17	2
2. Charles Atwood, for his freehold,	..	2	..	.	1	..	3	1
3. Ditto, for his leasehold,	2	1	..	2	1	..	13	10
4. William Barton,	5	..	..	2	.	1	10	..
5. Charles Broadstock,	4	1	1	1	1	1	6	2
6. George Bundy,	2	1	1	..	1	..	14	2
7. Elizabeth Cowley,	7	3	.	2	1	2	6	3
8. John Clark,	16	2	1	2	1	4	18	10
9. The representatives of Sarah Clark,	1	2	..	..	..	..	8	11
10. Elizabeth Dowdswell,	1	2	1	2	..	..	10	0¼
11. Sarah Edwards,	1	2	1	..	1	..	9	8
12. Henry Fowler and William Williams,	4	..	1	..	1	1	4	6
13. James Ferris,	8	2	..	..	..	1	..	9
14. William Hawkins,	52	1	..	1	1	15	9	6
15. Henry Healing,	12	3	..	1	..	3	15	8
16. Thomas Hulls,	112	1	..	2	..	33	4	7
17. Joseph Hill,	13	3	..	2	..	4	2	0½
18. William Jeffs,	4	2	..	..	..	1	6	8
19. John Jones,	2	2	.	1	..	..	15	..
20. Martha Kemble,	10	..	1	1	1	3	..	2
21. Edmund Lechmere,	32	1	..	3	1	9	11	5¼
22. Richard Loveridge,	3	..	..	3	..	..	18	3½
23. Samuel Lane,	2	1	..	..	1	..	13	0¾
24. John Lambert, home estate,	1	3	..	1	..	..	10	6¾
25. Ditto, for Chicken Croft,	..	2	1	1	1	..	4	..
26. Thomas Pensam,	6	3	..	..	.	1	19	11½
27. The church-wardens, for the poors' land,	4	2	..	1	1	1	6	11
28. Richard Ravenhill,	7	2	..	1	1	2	4	8½
29. Samuel Stone,	17	1	..	..	..	5	2	1
30. Anthony Seymour,	15	1	.	3	1	4	10	11
31. Elizabeth Wood,	93	3	1	3	..	27	16	0¼
32. Walter Wood, freehold,	6	3	1	2	..	2	1	0½
33. Ditto, leasehold,	1	1	..	2	..	..	7	8¾
34. John White,	4	2	..	2	..	1	7	0½
35. Henry G. D. Yate,	8	1	..	1	..	2	8	6¾
Total,	476	1	1	3	.	140	19	4¼

Glouces-

APPENDIX.

" *Gloucester, March* 14, 1796.

" The Corse enclosure being now, I hope, completed, the enclosed is a copy of the schedule annexed to the award which is to regulate hereafter the payment of the corn-rents to the vicar. I transmit it for your perusal, with but few comments of my own. It may however, afford some useful hints, and occasion salutary observations from your comprehensive mind, while you are devoting so much of your time and labour towards perfecting the General Enclosure Bill.

" To the test of experience I cannot have recourse, for an opinion on the utility of a general commutation of tithes for corn-rents; but I have every reason to express my perfect satisfaction with the present valuation of my corn-rent, which makes a considerable improvement (between 30*l.* and 40*l.*) beyond what I have hitherto received. The greatest harmony has as yet subsisted betwixt me and my farmers, possibly because I made no alteration in their tithes. But I believe that harmony will never be disturbed; for though they may complain of the present rise, they cannot reasonably appeal from the judgment of competent and impartial Commissioners. This is a matter of no small consolation both to the pastor and his flock. You will observe great accuracy in the valuation of the Commissioners, for they descend so minutely as to mention *quarts* and *pints*, and afterwards reduce it to *halfpence* and *farthings*. It is now fixed for ever, that every estate shall only pay according to its *quota* of corn expressed in the schedule. For instance, Mr. Thos. Hulls, who is the greatest proprietor, is charged with 112 bushels one peck two quarts, which at the average price of about 5*s.* 10*d.* per bushel, will be 33*l.* 4*s.* 7*d.* for

the

the next period of 14 years; although his estate should be brought hereafter to the highest pitch of cultivation, he will never be charged to the vicar with more than the above number of bushels. With those who are well-wishers to the Church Establishment, and consequently to the increase of the incomes of the Clergy with the advance of other people's property, it may be a question whether the plan of Corse corn-rent will be productive of that effect. But should the average price hereafter exceed the last, of 5*s.* 10*d.* per bushel, my corn-rent will rise in value at the rate of 23*l.* 16*s.* &c. for every shilling of advance in the price of corn. Time alone however must decide the point.

" I am happy that the Legislature has adopted your idea, in the clauses to enable, *but not to compel*, the Clergy and lay impropriators to commute the tithes. All compulsory measures, at this time particularly, tend to alarm, while the same end will be answered, if it be left to the slow operations of individuals.

" I have the Honour to be,

" SIR GEORGE,

" Your most obliged and most devoted

" humble servant,

" E. JONES."

No. XI.

Culture of *Wheat*.

Counties.	Enclosures.	Total Acres Enclosed.	Acres Enclosed Wheat not returned.
Bedford,	37	61,422	5783
Berks,	12	19,682	773
Bucks,	47	66,222	5805
Cambridge,	16	30,114	6250
Chester,	11	5114	....
Cumberland,	13	37,363	....
Derby,	44	37,154	4856
Dorset,	13	10,986	1146
Durham,	19	34,863	3388
Essex,	3	1343	943
Gloucester,	52	64,169	5550
Hants,	16	23,976	7975
Hertford,	10	12,977	6188
Hereford,	3	2250	1450
Hunts,	27	44,694	1470
Lancashire,	18	22,926	2300
Leicester,	86	125,776	4399
Lincoln,,	144	287,416	13,017
Middlesex,	2	987	....
Norfolk,	47	51,791	6694
Northampton,	93	155,454	5700
Northumberland,	16	39,965	1700
Nottingham,	68	90,236	5872

Oxford,

APPENDIX.

Counties.	Enclosures.	Total Acres.	Acres Enclosed. Wheat not returned.
Oxford,	41	68,480	28,690
Rutland,	13	16,480	8764
Salop,	12	6662	1800
Somerset,	50	45,841	500
Stafford,	26	27,018	2536
Suffolk,	8	6118	400
Surrey,	3	3528	....
Sussex,	3	2690	....
Warwick,	52	62,900	7364
Westmoreland,	9	10,343	410
Wilts,	37	56,885	2101
Worcester,	31	31,717	6970
York,	218	363,110	28,461
Wales,	13	31,537	13,283
	1213	1,960,189	192,538

Counties.	Acres of Wheat before Enclosing.	Acres of Wheat since Enclosing.	Acres Increased.	Acres Decreased.
Bedford,	8666	7509	....	1157
Berks,	2900	2778	....	122
Bucks,	9868	6571	....	3297
Cambridge,	3077	2780	....	297
Chester,	....	262	262	....
Cumberland,	4	866	862	....
Derby,	2301	2312	911	....
Dorset,	1321	1340	19	....
Durham,	297	1647	1350	....
Essex,	80	120	40	....
Gloucester,	8541	8641	100	....
Hants,	2270	2506	236	....
Hertford,	652	1086	434	....

Hereford,

APPENDIX.

Counties.	Acres of Wheat before Enclosing.	Acres of Wheat since Enclosing.	Acres Increased.	Acres Decreased.
Hereford, ...	....	....	....	....
Hunts, ...	5883	6361	478	....
Lancashire, ...	4	192	188	....
Leicester, ...	10,173	6380	....	3793
Lincoln, ...	18,242	22,034	3792	....
Middlesex, ...	254	92	....	162
Norfolk, ...	2602	4601	1999	....
Northampton,	19,922	14,135	....	7587
Northumberland,	143	389	246	....
Nottingham, ...	9219	8235	....	984
Oxford, ...	4882	4770	....	112
Rutland, ...	908	410	....	498
Salop, ...	140	896	756	....
Somerset, ...	817	2129	1312	....
Stafford, ...	919	1382	463	....
Suffolk, ...	160	370	210	....
Surrey, ...	240	530	290	....
Sussex, ...	....	260	260	....
Warwick, ...	8615	6435	....	2180
Westmoreland, ...	....	272	272	....
Wilts, ...	7765	8362	597	....
Worcester, ...	3075	3610	535	....
York, ...	21,632	34,159	12,527	....
Wales, ...	....	515	515	....
	155,572	165,837	28,654	18,389

Acres

Acres of Wheat increased or diminished by the Enclosure of Open Arable Fields.

BEDFORD.

Parishes.	Date.	Increase.	Decrease.
Podington,	1765	....	130
Felmersham,	1765	....	10
Tisworth,	1768	....	32
Sundon,	1769	25	....
Potton,	1774	55	....
Lidlington,	1775	....	60
Bolnhurst,	1778	....	26
Odell,	1776	....	166
Tempsford,	1777	....	50
Turvey,	1783	....	60
Risely,	1793	....	100
Milton Bryant,	1793	....	40
Pertenhall,	1764	....	60
Bedford,	1795	450	....
Eaton,	1795	....	150
Crawley,	1795	50	....
Marston,	1796	....	270
Maulden,	1796	....	20
Ridgemont,	1796	....	145
Shelton,	1796	....	38
Elston,	1797	....	20
Dunton,	1797	....	73
Campton,	1797	....	20
Bedford, St. Mary,	1797	....	34
Chalgrove,	1797	5	....
Little Beckford,	1798	....	30
Caddington,	1798	66	....
Sandy,	1798	17	....

Overdean,

APPENDIX.

Parishes.	Date.	Increase.	Decrease.
Overdean,	1800	....	150
Souldrop,	1800	....	17

BERKS.

Ashbury,	1770	32	....
Letcomb,	1772	60	....
N. Kinksey,	1776	170	....
Stanford,	1783	....	84
Shrivenham,	1789	....	125
Blewbury,	1793	10	....
Shelton,	1794	40	....
Shrivenham,	1796	....	40

BUCKS.

Swanbourne,	1762	....	375
Waddesdon,	1774	....	133
Winslow,	1766	....	264
Little Harwood,	1766	....	55
Shalstone,	1767	....	12
Olney,	1767	20	....
Loughton,	1768	....	57
Cublington,	1769	....	35
Gundon,	1769	....	170
Goldington,	1770	55	....
Aylesbury,	1771	....	135
Whitechurch,	1771	....	150
Tingewick,	1773	....	80
Stokeham,	1774	....	80
Hartwell,	1776	20	....
Hardwicke,	1778	....	60
Hanslope,	1778	....	50
N. Marston,	1778	....	99
Brerton,	1779	....	143
Preston,	1781	....	65

Bowbrick-

234   APPENDIX.

Parishes.	Date.	Increase.	Decrease.
Bowbrickhill,	1790	....	55
Bradwell,	1788	....	60
Wondock,	1788	....	96
L. Woolston,	1791	....	56
Castlethorp,	1793	....	30
Wendover,	1794	....	100
Akeley,	1794	....	10
S. Claydon,	1795	....	180
Padbury,	1795	....	200
Aston Abbots,	1795	8	....
L. Brickhill,	1796	50	....
Grandborough,	1796	....	107
Wingrave,	1797	....	150
Stoke Mandeville,	1797	....	10
Wing,	1797	....	54
Thornborough,	1797	....	26
Weston,	1798	8	8

CAMBRIDGE.

Abington,	1770	40	....
Knapwell,	1775	20	....
Weston Colville,	1777	210	....
Chippenham,	1791	75	....
March,	1792	400	....
Little Wilbraham,	1797	130	....
Great Wilbraham,	1797	20	....
Swaffham,	1798	....	100
Long Stow,	1798	....	84

DERBY.

Wiln,	1763	....	35
Repton,	1766	20	....
Normanton,	1768	....	42
Ockbrook,	1772	....	40

Shirland,

APPENDIX. 235

Parishes.	Date.	Increase.	Decrease.
Shirland,	1777	25	....
Weston,	1786	....	30
Melbourne,	1787	....	10
Sawley,	1787	....	40
Spondon,	1788	....	28
Cunaston,	1789	....	15
Doveridge,	1791	....	20
Ilkeston,	1794	15	....
Etwall,	1797	....	85

DORSET.

Langton,	1761	....	40
Portesham,	1762	....	50
Winfrith,	1768	8	....
W. Knighton,	1779	....	27
Tolpudle,	1794	....	40
Handley,	1796	30	
Hinton,	1797	....	20
Gossage,	1797	17	....
Wyke,	1797	50	....

DURHAM.

Wolsingham,	1769	....	15
Bolam,	1782	....	157
Ryton,	1794	20	....

ESSEX.

Parndon,	1795	40	....

GLOUCESTER.

Child Wickham,	1763	....	25
Stow,	1765	....	25
Hatherop,	1766	....	80
Haselton,	1766	....	20
Stow,	1766	....	20

Willersey,

Parishes.	Date.	Increase.	Decrease.
Willersey,	1767	....	100
Bibury,	1767	40	....
Coln,	1769	80	....
Bledington,	1769	....	124
Notgrove,	1770	....	30
Aston suburbs,	1771	....	30
Quinton,	1772	....	100
Kemerton,	1772	50	....
Beckford,	1773	....	48
Stratton,	1771	10	....
Oxenton,	1774	....	60
Adlestrop,	1775	....	30
Condecote,	1777	30	....
Sherborne,	1777	213	....
Siddington,	1778	15	....
Buckland,	1779	....	72
Ablington,	1779	100	....
Salperton,	1780	70	....
Winstone,	1782	....	7
Oddington,	1786	....	32
Mangotsfield,	1788	20	....
Lower Swell,	1789	64	....
Rodmaston,	1792	....	100
Broadwell,	1792	36	....
Aldsworth,	1793	....	50
Naisemore,	1793	50	....
Old Sodbury,	1794	....	20
Coln, St. D.	1797	20	....
Little Compton,	1794	40	....
Longborough,	1794	40	....
Cold Aston,	1795	....	15
Guiting, P.	1798	70	....

HANTS.

APPENDIX.

HANTS.

Parishes.	Date.	Increase.	Decrease.
Abbots, Anne,	1774	46	....
Highclere,	1781	40	....
Upper Clatford,	1785	....	60
Upper Wallop,	1786	35	....
Broughton,	1789	80	....
Shipton,	1792	20	....
Mitchel-marsh,	1796	35	....
Nether Wallop,	1796	....	30

HERTS.

Lilly,	1768	80	....
Offley,	1768	10	....
Ickleford,	1776	...	7
Norton,	1796	84	....

HEREFORD.

Willington,	1794	40	....

HUNTS.

Leighton,	1766	77	....
Yaxley,	1767	....	100
Kimbolton,	1769	....	50
St. Neots,	1770	10	....
Brampton,	1772	....	51
King's Ripton,	1772	40	....
Woolley,	1772	50	....
Little Stukeley,	1773	....	47
Easton,	1774	27	....
Ellington,	1774	....	120
Elton,	1779	....	83
Little Catworth,	1780	....	60
Barham,	1780	....	9

Wornditch,

238   APPENDIX.

Parishes.	Date.	Increase.	Decrease.
Wornditch,	1795	....	10
Warboys,	1795	175	....
Somersham,	1796	90	....

LINCOLN.

Parishes.	Date.	Increase.	Decrease.
Wintringham,	1762	40	....
Horbling,	1764	....	146
Fotherby,	1764	10	....
Stainton,	1764	50	....
Heckington,	1764	80	....
Rothwell,	1766	40	....
Cockerington,	1765	80	....
Aukborough,	1765	....	35
Bourn,	1766	....	350
Grimoldby,	1766	58	....
Corby,	1766	....	50
Kiddington,	1766	40	....
Barnetby,	1766	102	....
Newton,	1767	....	35
Scamblesby,	1767	10	....
Woodhall,	1767	20	....
Billingborough,	1768	....	100
Threckingham,	1768	....	30
Morton,	1768	....	100
North Hickham,	1769	10	....
Ingham,	1769	....	100
Great Willingham,	1769	35	....
Barnoldby,	1769	80	....
Ancaster,	1769	60	....
Westborough,	1770	82	....
Scawby,	1770	52	....
Welton,	1770	....	13
Boothby,	1770	57	....

Winter-

APPENDIX. 239

Parishes.	Date.	Increase.	Decrease.
Winterton,	1770	....	200
Waddington,	1770	30	....
Boothby,	1771	165	....
South Reston,	1771	....	40
West Ashby,	1771	30	....
Welton,	1772	10	....
Little Toynton,	1772	14	....
Market Raisin,	1772	20	....
West Halton,	1772	....	40
Hameringham,	1772	22	....
Hemingby,	1773	10	....
Hackonby,	1773	....	150
Brinkhill,	1773	5	....
Ancaster,	1773	8	....
Horsington,	1773	....	25
Whitton,	1773	....	10
East Keal,	1773	....	20
Spridlington,	1774	10	....
Oumby,	1774	60	....
Heapham,	1774	50	....
Tetney,	1774	70	....
West Keal,	1774	....	20
Timberland,	1774	....	120
Fulletby,	1795	44	....
Gundby,	1776	....	10
Upton,	1776	79	....
Welby,	1776	35	....
Raithby,	1776	....	25
Killingholm,	1776	170	....
Kirnington,	1777	....	13
Swinstead,	1777	....	9
Ruskington,	1778	....	50
Hackthorn,	1778	200	....

Thimbleby,

APPENDIX.

Parishes.	Date.	Increase.	Decrease.
Thimbleby,	1778	70	....
Huttoft,	1779	....	26
Brattleby,	1779	20	....
Donnington,	1785	....	35
Canwick,	1786	....	78
Derrington,	1787		10
Rauceby,	1788	....	246
Denton,	1789	....	84
Ludford,	1791	....	276
Nettleton,	1791	....	100
Anwick,	1791	....	35
Hemswell,	1792	....	40
Tealby,	1792	....	120
Uffington,	1792	....	42
Dunston,	1793	40	....
Allington,	1793	35	....
Sleaford,	1794	....	60
South Witham,	1794	20	....
Shillington,	1794	....	50
Faldingworth,	1794	7	....
Bennington,	1794	45	....
Hagworthington,	1795	10	....
Scartho,	1795	88	....
Ropsley,	1795	109	....
Luddington,	1796	....	100
Stoke,	1796	....	10
Swayfield,	1797	....	40
Messingham,	1798	40	....
LEICESTER.			
Roarsby,	1761	....	15
Hungerton,	1762	....	30
Quorndon,	1762	11	....
N. Broughton,	1764	....	10

Wetstone,

APPENDIX.

Parishes.	Date.	Increase.	Decrease.
Wetstone,	1764	4	....
South Stanton,	1764	....	50
Sharnford,	1764	....	55
Wartnaby,	1764	18	....
Scalford,	1765	70	....
North Kelworth,	1765	....	50
Grimston,	1765	6	....
Houghton,	1765	....	10
Burton, Old,	1765	....	110
Lubenham,	1766	....	120
Waltham,	1766	....	20
Blaby,	1766	12	....
Courtesthorpe,	1766	....	20
Cosby,	1767	....	40
Ailestone,	1767	....	50
Little Sheppy,	1768	....	50
Eaton,	1769	43	....
Thurlaston,	1769	....	36
Saddington,	1770	....	110
Foxton,	1770	....	135
Bottesford,	1770	170	....
Appleby,	1771	....	200
Saltby,	1771	....	15
Sproxton,	1771	....	27
Heyham,	1771	....	90
Skeffington,	1772	....	32
Stapleford,	1772	....	8
Rutcliff,	1774	....	40
Ibstock,	1774	....	53
Bowden,	1776	....	275
Syston,	1777	....	34
Gilkerton,	1777	....	120
Hathern,	1777	....	84

Castle

APPENDIX.

Parishes.	Date.	Increase.	Decrease.
Castle Donnington,	1778	..	60
Little Whatton,	1778	..	63
Barkby,	1779	..	31
Thornton,	1779	..	90
Leire,	1779	..	48
Long Clauson,	1779	..	20
Kibworth,	1779	..	300
Croft,	1779	14	..
Stonesly,	1780	..	30
Swinford,	1780	15	..
Montsorrel,	1781	..	20
Rothley,	1782	..	175
Orton,	1782	..	10
Tugby,	1784	..	50
Osgathorp,	1785	..	20
Mowsley,	1788	..	193
Humberston,	1788	..	115
Thrussington,	1789	..	120
Groovy,	1789	..	10
Ratley,	1789	..	40
Lutterworth,	1790	..	150
Harby,	1790	..	70
Barston,	1791	..	22
Church Langton,	1791	..	200
Slathern,	1792	..	20
Walton,	1792	..	28
Redmill,	1792	90	..
Queenborough,	1793	..	26
Barresby,	1794	..	115
Bagworth,	1794	..	50
Sutton Cheney,	1794	..	26
Diseworth,	1794	..	80
Misterton,	1796	..	30
Twyford,	1796	..	70
Dunton Basset,	1796	..	125

Knipton,

APPENDIX.

Parishes.	Date.	Increase.	Decrease.
Knipton,	1797	..	34
Swithland,	1798	..	20

NORTHAMPTON.

Parishes.	Date.	Increase.	Decrease.
Morton Pinkney,	1761	..	153
Eydon,	1761	29	..
Woodford,	1763	..	70
Warkworth,	1764	..	38
Everdon,	1764	..	20
Stoke Albany,	1764	..	8
Newnham,	1764	..	100
West Haddon,	1764	..	150
Syresham,	1765	..	20
Wellingborough,	1765	..	300
Denford,	1765	..	30
Long Buckley,	1765	..	110
Harding Stone,	1765	..	350
Spratton,	1765	50	..
Great Dodington,	1766	..	140
Kingsthorp,	1766	60	..
Shenford,	1766	..	15
Great Oxendon,	1767	..	178
Would,	1767	..	50
Cosgrove,	1767	..	145
Upper Middleton,	1769	..	75
Pattishill,	1770	..	52
Earls Burton,	1771	..	80
Weldon Weston,	1771	..	100
Aldwinckle,	1772	..	50
King's Sutton,	1772	..	25
Passenham,	1772	..	44
Moulton,	1772	60	..
Newbottle,	1772	..	18
Ackchurch,	1772	..	73
East Haddon,	1773	..	68

Helledon,

244   APPENDIX.

Parishes.	Date.	Increase.	Decrease.
Helledon, ...	1774	..	60
Staverton, ...	1774	..	204
Gretton, ...	1774	15	..
Warmington, ...	1774	..	90
Potterspury, ...	1775	..	250
Braunston, ...	1775	60	..
Cranford, ...	1775	10	..
Scaldwell, ...	1775	..	60
Crick, ...	1775	..	300
Weedon, ...	1776	..	180
Walgrave, ...	1776	..	150
Yelvertofft, ...	1776	..	64
Yardley, ...	1776	18	..
Desborough, ...	1776	..	100
Clipston, ...	1776	..	120
Grafton, ...	1777	..	70
Killesley, ...	1777	..	121
Whilton, ...	1777	..	64
Mears Ashby, ...	1777	50	..
Welford, ...	1777	..	41
Tansor, ...	1777	..	60
Rushden, ...	1778	..	300
Harpole, ...	1778	..	100
Titchmarsh, ...	1778	..	150
Great Billing, ...	1778	..	10
Bulwick, ...	1778	..	68
Northampton, ...	1778	..	20
Barby, ...	1778	..	150
Byfield, ...	1778	..	160
Maidford, ...	1778	..	44
Braybrook, ...	1778	..	70
Wootton, ...	1778	..	135
Bowdon, ...	1778	..	120
Bugbrook, ...	1779	..	20
Badby, ...	1779	..	30

Milton,

APPENDIX. 245

Parishes.	Date.	Increase.	Decrease.
Milton, M.	1779	..	40
Kislingbury,	1779	..	130
Grendon,	1780	..	90
Brixworth,	1780	..	48
East Farndon,	1780	..	100
Little Harrowden,	1781	..	44
Piddington,	1782	..	47
Broughton,	1786	..	10
Woolaston,	1788	..	50
Polebrook,	1790	..	24
Great Catworth,	1795	58	..
Brigstock,	1795	..	36
Stanion,	1795	..	30
Ravensthorp,	1795	..	50
Stamford,	1795	..	55
Ufford,	1796	..	62
Raunds,	1797	..	380
Whittlebury,	1797	..	15
Bozeat,	1798	40	..
Welbarston,	1798	..	60

NOTTS.

Lowdham,	1765	30	..
Carleton,	1765	20	..
Balderton,	1766	74	..
Linton,	1767	..	20
Farndon,	1767	..	35
Baddington,	1767	..	158
Burton,	1768	..	35
Epperston,	1768	..	70
Rempstone,	1768	..	80
Hucknall,	1769	..	50
Normanton,	1770	..	17
Mattersey,	1770	105	..
Misterton,	1771	200	..
Cromwell,	1773	20	..

Hickling,

APPENDIX.

Parishes.	Date.	Increase.	Decrease.
Hickling,	1775	..	20
Southwell,	1775	..	30
Sutton,	1776	..	130
Clareborough,	1776	92	..
Famfield,	1777	60	..
Halam,	1777	..	80
Bleasley,	1777	..	30
Winthorpe,	1777	..	10
Kersal,	1778	..	25
Orston,	1780	..	30
Radcliff,	1787	..	40
Arnold,	1789	20	..
Whatton,	1789	..	48
North Gollingham,	1790	..	25
Colgrave,	1790	125	..
Syerton,	1792	..	22
Basford,	1792	..	50
Gedding,	1792	20	..
Orston,	1793	..	156
Granby,	1793	..	30
Willoughby,	1793	..	100
Woodborough,	1795	100	..
Elston,	1795	..	143
Upton,	1795	..	247
South Leverton,	1795	..	30
Caunton,	1795	50	..
Weston,	1796	7	..
Snenton,	1796	..	112

NORFOLK.

Snettisham,	1762	150	..
Sherborn,	1767	35	..
Beetly,	1774	..	10
Heacham,	1780	200	..
Foulden,	1780	39	..

Thornham,

APPENDIX. 247

Parishes.	Date.	Increase.	Decrease.
Thornham,	1794	60	..
Shouldham,	1794	82	..
Dunham,	1795	49	..
Bintry,	1795	12	..

NORTHUMBERLAND.

Corbridge,	1776	..	93
Haltwhistle,	1783	70	..
Elrington,	1784	10	..

OXFORD.

Fringford,	1761	..	48
Merton,	1763	..	100
Somerton,	1765	50	..
Steeple Aston,	1766	..	30
Westwell,	1770	60	..
Cropedy,	1774	..	100
Broadwell,	1775	11	..
Cleydon,	1775	..	10
Ambrosden,	1776	..	60
Alkerton,	1776	40	..
Bointon,	1777	..	50
Bucknel,	1779	40	..
Stratton,	1780	..	60
Little Tewer,	1793	10	..
Melcombe,	1793	..	20
Westcot,	1795	24	..
Hampton,	1796	..	15
Mollington,	1797	..	25
Kelmscott,	1798	50	..

RUTLAND.

Whissardine,	1762	..	20
Manton,	1772	..	102
Oakham,	1772	..	70
Wing,	1772	..	60

Preston,

Parishes.	Date.	Increase.	Decrease.
Preston,	1773	....	30
Normanton,	1793	....	23
Beltone,	1794	....	75
Bisbrook,	1795	....	80
Little Casterton,	1796	....	46
Empingham,	1794	....	90

SALOP.

Donington,	1771	27	....
Baschurch,	1777	88	....

SOMERSET.

E. and Q. Camel,	1794	....	33
Huish Episcopi,	1797	50	....

STAFFORD.

Tamworth,	1770	....	300

SUFFOLK.

Cavenham,	1772	20	....
Fuddenham,	1794	50	....
Little Barton,	1796	80	....

SUSSEX.

Ringmer,	1767	180	....

WARWICK.

Monk's Kirby,	1761	....	556
Exhall,	1761	....	142
Grandborough,	1765	....	120
Snithfield,	1765	....	18
Redford,	1766	....	50
Cubbington,	1767	....	100
Welley,	1769	....	66

Bulking-

APPENDIX. 249

Parishes.	Date.	Increase.	Decrease
Bulkington,	1770	....	70
Polesworth,	1771	....	150
Skelton,	1772	....	44
Newbold,	1773	23	....
Halford,	1774	....	74
Old Stratford,	1774	....	100
Little Itchington,	1775	....	28
Woolton,	1775	....	22
Warmington,	1776	....	38
Duston,	1778	....	30
Avendisset,	1779	....	115
Harbury,	1779	....	90
Ilmington,	1781	....	57
Burton, H.	1783	....	15
Little Brailes,	1784	....	240
Stratford,	1785	....	100
Great Kineton,	1791	....	140
Stockton,	1791	....	70
Shoteswell,	1793	....	25
Little Pellerton,	1794	....	50
Wolvey,	1794	....	150
Eatington,	1795	....	20
Ratley,	1795	70	....
Tysoe,	1796	....	97
Sherborne,	1799	....	94

WILTS.

Haddington,	1766	....	30
Enford,	1770	....	60
Tidcombe,	1771	....	10
Pewsey,	1775	....	100
Liddington,	1776	....	40
M. Lavington,	1777	17	....

Putney,

250 APPENDIX.

Parishes.	Date.	Increase.	Decrease.
Patney,	1778	50	....
Highworth,	1778	....	119
Wanborough,	1779	40	....
Chisledon,	1779	103	....
Heytesbury,	1783	29	....
Colerne,	1785	235	....
Netheravon,	1788	40	....
Berwick,	1789	....	63
Durnford,	1793	....	10
Marden,	1794	25	....
Poulton,	1795	27	....
Cheverels,	1797	30	....
Alcaning,	1797	138	....
East Knoile,	1798	....	30
Shrewton,	1798	....	40
Sutton,	1798	....	26
Purton,	1799	50	....

WORCESTER.

Pirton,	1763	45	....
Bretferton,	1765	50	....
Emload,	1765	41	....
Naunton,	1771	20	....
Broadway,	1771	....	60
Blockley,	1772	....	55
Upton Snodbury,	1774	21	....
Bredon,	1775	48	....
Cleve,	1775	10	....
Himbleton,	1779	100	....
Fladbury,	1788	....	40
Dormstone,	1790	10	....

YORK.

Burton Pidsea,	1761	74	....

Sproatley,

APPENDIX. 251

Parishes.	Date.	Increase.	Decrease.
Sproatley,	1762	....	64
Skipsea,	1762	....	126
Marfleet,	1763	50	....
Sketling,	1764	200	....
Skipsea,	1764	60	....
Thorngumbald,	1764	80	....
Brantingham,	1765	230	....
Braithwell,	1765	50	....
Everingham,	1765	40	....
Foston,	1766	65	....
Naburn,	1766	....	10
Bessingby,	1766	....	60
Beeford,	1766	100	....
Adlingfleet,	1767	180	....
Anston,	1767	22	....
Hotham,	1768	....	76
North Burton,	1768	73	....
Bridlington,	1768	....	50
Seamer,	1768	70	....
Sanéton,	1769	67	....
Elvington,	1769	....	80
Bishop Wilton,	1769	....	280
Ebberston,	1769	....	215
Haxby,	1769	....	48
Acklome,	1769	....	76
Thwing,	1769	52	....
Laughton,	1769	38	....
G. Ouseburn,	1770	200	....
W. Hessington,	1770	50	....
Butterwick,	1771	60	....
Beeford,	1771	50	....
Welton,	1771	20	....
Singleton,	1772	....	30

Terrington,

APPENDIX.

Parishes.	Date.	Increase.	Decrease.
Terrington,	1772	30	....
Ackworth,	1772	20	....
Preston,	1773	270	....
Agnes Burton,	1773	....	20
Snaith,	1773	200	....
Rudstone,	1774	....	60
Swinton,	1774	30	....
Garton,	1774	100	....
Goodmanham,	1775	50	....
Mulgrave,	1776	....	100
Foston,	1776	52	....
Bilton,	1776	....	69
Stonegrave,	1776	61	....
Arnitherby,	1776	60	....
North Newbald,	1777	106	....
Bulmer,	1777	64	....
North Dalton,	1778	40	....
Womersley,	1786	298	....
Methley,	1786	48	....
Filey,	1788	....	50
Swine,	1789	20	....
Cottingham,	1791	....	253
Bridlington,	1793	....	10
Hollyn,	1793	125	....
Walkington,	1794	....	220
Old Malton,	1796	....	30
Kirk Ella,	1796	....	64
Pontefract,	1797	6	....
		14,507	30,894

Decreased in 407 enclosures, ... 30,894 acres.
Increased in 239 ditto, ... 14,507 acres.

Decrease, ... 16,387 acres.

No. XII.

No. XII.
Barley, Oats, Pulse, &c.

Counties.	Barley.				Oats.				Pulse.			
	Enclosures.	Increased.	Decreased.	As before.	Enclosures.	Increased.	Decreased.	As before.	Enclosures.	Increased.	Decreased.	As before.
Bedford,	23	8	7	8	21	10	5	6	23	5	11	7
Berks,	8	4	2	2	8	6	2	..	8	4	3	1
Bucks,	28	18	6	4	28	13	12	3	28	19	5	4
Cambridge,	10	8	..	2	10	6	2	2	7	3	2	2
Chester,	7	2	4	1	10	9	..	1	..	..	..	..
Cumberland,	10	9	..	1	11	10	1	..	8	6	..	2
Derby,	24	12	6	6	29	25	2	2	19	4	8	7
Devonshire,	..	..	..	..	..	..	..	..	..	..	..	..
Dorset,	10	3	6	1	10	5	4	1	3	1	2	..
Durham,	8	5	2	1	13	10	2	1	2	1	1	..
Essex,	2	2	..	..	2	2	..	..	1	1	..	..
Gloucester,	41	25	10	6	38	22	9	7	40	15	20	5
Hants,	13	9	2	2	12	8	2	2	8	6	1	1
Hereford,	1	..	1	..	1	..	1	..	1	..	1	..
Herts,	5	3	..	2	6	4	..	2	4	2	..	2
Hunts,	16	4	3	9	15	6	6	3	16	2	10	4
Lancashire,	11	2	5	4	14	10	2	2	8	1	4	3
Leicester,	72	28	37	7	69	59	8	2	71	13	58	..
Lincoln,	115	75	26	14	109	78	22	9	83	14	56	13
Middlesex,	1	..	1	..	1	..	1	..	..	..	..	..
Norfolk,	28	23	..	5	27	22	..	5	16	8	3	5
Northampton,	78	36	29	13	74	50	14	10	70	3	65	2
Northumberland,	13	8	1	4	14	10	1	3	7	1	3	3
Nottingham,	50	33	9	8	46	34	5	7	44	12	24	8
Oxford,	29	14	13	2	31	29	2	..	25	11	12	2
Rutland,	9	3	6	..	6	4	2	..	9	1	8	..
Salop,	10	7	..	3	11	9	..	2	8	4	..	4
Somerset,	31	11	2	18	35	14	3	18	32	9	3	20
Stafford,	19	10	5	4	17	8	5	4	10	1	5	4
Suffolk,	7	3	..	4	9	5	..	4	7	2	..	5
Surrey,	2	2	..	..	2	2	..	..	2	2	..	..
Sussex,	1	1	..	..	1	1	..	..	1	1	..	..
Warwick,	35	14	18	3	35	19	11	5	33	4	23	6
Westmoreland,	5	4	1	..	7	7	..	..	5	2	1	2
Wilts,	30	12	12	6	30	13	11	6	27	14	9	4
Worcester,	19	10	7	2	14	6	6	2	15	8	5	2
York,	161	94	35	32	186	159	8	19	131	46	59	26
Wales,	9	4	..	5	11	8	..	3	7	3	..	4
Total,	941	506	256	179	963	683	149	131	779	229	402	143

Counties.

APPENDIX.

Counties.	Cattle.				Dairy.				Sheep.			
	Enclosures.	Increased.	Decreased.	As before.	Enclosures.	Increased.	Decreased.	As before.	Enclosures.	Increased.	Decreased.	As before.
Bedford,	18	6	7	5	22	6	9	7	25	13	6	6
Berks,	3	3	..	..	4	3	..	1	7	5	1	1
Bucks,	23	17	3	3	30	23	3	4	34	20	13	1
Cambridge,	5	1	2	2	7	1	5	1	9	4	3	2
Chester,	1	1	..	..	2	1	1	..	1	..	1	..
Cumberland,	8	6	2	.	4	4	..	..	17	1	6	..
Derby,	19	15	2	2	17	16	..	1	19	12	5	2
Devonshire,	..	..	..	..	..	..	..	..	..	..	..	..
Dorset,	4	4	..	..	6	2	3	1	7	7	..	..
Durham,	4	4	..	..	2	1	1	..	4	3	1	..
Essex,	..	..	..	..	..	..	..	..	1	..	1	..
Gloucester,	26	17	5	4	25	13	7	5	33	21	9	3
Hants,	2	..	1	1	5	1	4	..	9	5	4	..
Hereford,	2	2	..	..	..	..	..	..	2	1	1	..
Herts,	2	1	..	1	4	..	1	3	6	2	2	2
Hunts,	13	10	3	..	12	2	9	1	17	14	3	..
Lancashire,	6	3	..	3	8	7	..	1	5	3	1	1
Leicester,	57	51	4	2	47	39	7	1	65	59	5	1
Lincoln,	73	37	26	10	38	7	26	5	91	72	11	8
Middlesex,	..	..	..	..	..	..	..	..	..	..	..	..
Norfolk,	13	4	3	6	17	3	9	5	17	5	5	7
Northampton,	33	28	4	1	33	16	13	4	43	39	3	1
Northumberland,	10	5	1	4	3	..	..	3	5	1	..	4
Nottingham,	34	19	5	10	26	16	3	7	41	29	8	4
Oxford,	13	9	1	3	18	13	1	4	26	20	2	4
Rutland,	6	5	..	1	2	1	1	..	8	8	..	..
Salop,	6	4	..	2	4	1	..	3	7	3	1	3
Somerset,	26	10	..	16	26	9	..	17	28	7	7	14
Stafford,	10	5	1	4	11	7	..	4	15	7	4	4
Suffolk,	6	1	..	5	6	1	..	5	6	1	..	5
Surrey,	1	..	1	..	1	..	1	..	1	..	1	..
Sussex,	1	..	1	..	1	..	1	..	2	1	1	..
Warwick,	23	17	4	2	29	19	7	3	34	30	3	1
Westmoreland,	5	3	2	..	3	2	1	..	6	3	3	..
Wilts,	9	1	4	4	17	3	10	4	17	6	7	4
Worcester,	18	13	3	2	17	8	7	2	20	14	5	1
York,	83	48	21	14	56	26	13	17	95	47	33	15
Wales,	8	4	..	4	8	4	..	4	8	4	1	3
Total,	571	354	106	111	511	255	143	113	721	467	157	97

Counties.

APPENDIX.

Counties.	Hogs. Decrease.	Turnips. Increase.	Potatoes. Increase.	
Bedford,	1	1	2	
Berks,	....	2	....	
Bucks,	....	1	1	
Cambridge,	....	....	....	
Chester,	....	1	8	
Cumberland,	....	1	6	
Derby,	....	5	12	
Dorset,	....	....	1	
Durham,	....	7	7	
Essex,	....	....	1	
Gloucester,	2	3	3	
Hants,	1	2	....	
Hereford,	....	1	....	
Herts,	1	....	....	
Hunts,	....	....	1	
Lancashire,	....	1	2	
Leicester,	15	2	19	
Lincoln,	1	9	inc. 8	dec. 1
Middlesex,	....	1	1	
Norfolk,	....	3	1	
Northampton,	5	6	5	
Northumberland,	....	4	9	
Nottingham,	....	4	13	
Oxford,	....	4	3	
Rutland,	....	1	1	
Salop,	....	....	3	
Somerset,	....	1	inc. 12	dec. 1
Stafford,	....	3	5	
Surrey,	....	2	1	
Warwick,	....	4	1	
Westmoreland,	....	....	2	
Carry forward, ..	26	39	inc. 128	dec. 2 Counties.

APPENDIX.

Counties.	Hogs. Decrease.	Turnips. Increase.	Potatoes. Increase.	
Brought forward,	26	39	inc. 128	dec. 2
Wilts,	....	3	6	
Worcester,	....	2	4	
York,	....	36	59	
Wales,	....	....	1	
	26	80	inc. 198	dec. 2

Counties.	Artificial Grass. Increase.	Counties.	Artificial Grass. Increase.
Bedford,	3	Middlesex,	....
Berks,	1	Norfolk,	1
Bucks,	2	Northampton,	3
Cambridge,	1	Northumberland,	....
Chester,	....	Nottingham,	4
Cumberland,	....	Oxford,	1
Derby,	....	Rutland,	....
Dorset,	1	Salop,	....
Durham,	1	Somerset,	1
Essex,	....	Stafford,	....
Gloucester,	1	Surrey,	1
Hants,	2	Warwick,	2
Hereford,	1	Westmoreland,	....
Herts,	1	Wilts,	4
Hunts,	6	Worcester,	....
Lancashire,	....	York,	12
Leicester,	1	Wales,	....
Lincoln,	9		59

APPENDIX. 257

In most of the following cases (in all where the returns admitted), it is an exact proportion to the actual result; but in some, the expressions used by the Clergy, are estimated; such, for instance, as where *rather* increased or diminished, *much, considerable, greatly;* but whether in diminution or increase, the estimate made is moderate, never exceeding half the standard sum of 20, and rarely so much.

Dairy.

		20 the Standard Quantity before Enclosure.
Bedford, ...	return of 10 enclosures,	20
Berks, ...	2 ditto,	23
Bucks, ...	21 ditto,	60
Cambridge, ...	5 ditto,	12
Chester, ...	1 ditto,	23
Cumberland, ...	3 ditto,	29
Derby, ...	13 ditto,	28
Dorset, ...	2 ditto,	23
Gloucester, ...	14 ditto,	20
Hants, ...	5 ditto,	19
Herts, ...	1 ditto,	10
Hereford, ...	1 ditto,	5
Hunts, ...	10 ditto,	12
Lincoln, ...	27 ditto,	14
Lancaster, ...	3 ditto,	18
Leicester, ...	39 ditto,	42
Northampton, ...	24 ditto,	21
Notts, ...	13 ditto,	60
Norfolk, ...	12 ditto,	15
Oxford, ...	17 ditto,	33
Rutland, ...	1 ditto,	18
Salop, ...	3 ditto,	41

Carry forward, ... 546

Brought

APPENDIX.

		20 the Standard Quantity before Enclosure.
Brought forward,		546
Somerset,	return of 15 enclosures,	25
Stafford,	8 ditto,	48
Suffolk,	6 ditto,	20
Surrey,	1 ditto,	18
Sussex,	1 ditto,	17
Warwick,	27 ditto,	30
Wilts,	10 ditto,	16
Westmoreland,	1 ditto,	26
Worcester,	8 ditto,	22
York,	21 ditto,	17
		785
Average,		$24\frac{1}{2}$

" The number of milch cows kept in the village before enclosure, was not more than about 230 : they are now increased to 308.

" The Minister of Parwick, Derby."

" One thing, which had nearly escaped my inquiries, is well to be noted. I am assured, by persons who were in business before the enclosure, and are so still, that *one cow* at present produces as many pounds of butter as *two* did before; and that two sheep produce as much wool as three did before (six or seven to a tod then, and now about four). I am also informed, that when the field was open, not one cow, not one lamb, or sheep, or hog, was fatted for sale; now, several cows are fatted every

every year; many scores of lambs and of sheep (the largest part for the London market), and many hogs and porkers. But it is said there are fewer hogs kept now (where, indeed, very few are kept) by the labourers than formerly.

" This parish being within 70 miles of London, and a turnpike road through it, by which butter, &c. is sent weekly to the London market, there is a greater inducement to pasturage than would generally (it is presumed) be found at the distance of 80 or 100 miles from the metropolis.

" Perhaps I have, in some respects, exceeded the direct purport of the printed questions; but it was thought, that the advantage or disadvantage of enclosing, which it may probably come within the wishes of the Committee to ascertain, could not be estimated satisfactorily without an account of the stock as well as of grain.

"RALPH CHURTON,
" Rector of Upper Middleton Cheney, Nottingham.
" *Feb.* 24, 1801."

" Cows are decreased from 270 to 130; but this is more owing to the pernicious custom (too prevalent in this county) of the farmers giving up their dairies, than to the enclosure of the common. The decrease of young neat stock, and of swine, are both to be attributed to the above cause. And, indeed, it is highly probable, that on true investigation, this practice of giving up dairies, will prove the foundation of all the evils under which this nation is suffering, as it occasions the present extravagant price of butter and cheese, and also of all kinds of butchers' meat; and by thus increasing the price of neces-

necessaries, obliges the tradesman to raise all other articles, to answer the additional expense of maintaining his family.

" Jos. WHITE,
" Vicar of Foulden, Norfolk."

" The number of cows kept, is decreased above one half, or nearly two-thirds. This circumstance, I think, is not wholly to be ascribed to the effect of the enclosure, as the spirit of reducing the dairies pervades the whole county; and where no enclosures have of late taken place, there is as great a decrease in the number of cows, in the last seven years, as in the parishes of Shouldham and Shouldham Thorpe: therefore, the probability is, that the same diminution of cows would have ensued, had the enclosures not taken place.

" EDW. CHAPLIN,
" Minister of Shouldham, Norfolk."

" The abolition of dairies is of late become the prevailing practice; and I am credibly informed, that above 800 cows have been sold off, by different farmers, in the course of a few years, within a small compass round this town.

" The Minister of Tottenhill, with West Briggs,
" Norfolk."

" Before the enclosure, butter was to be bought at 6*d.* per pound; and milk at 1*d.* per quart, and less: now milk is not to be had at any rate, and butter not under 14*d.* per pound.

" JOHN RISLEY, sen.
" Rector of Tingewick, Bucks.

" *Feb.* 21, 1801."

" The

"The tota. number of cows in these parishes is diminished, but in what proportion I cannot say; and consequently, such articles as depend on cows, must be diminished also. The farmers find grazing more profitable than dairying, as being considerably less expensive; but I have known the same farmer at one time graze, and at another keep cows, just as markets altered.

"JAMES ANSDELL,
"Vicar of Shottesham, Norfolk."

"In the mean time, the stock of cows is more than double; and the yield of butter, calves, hogs, and, finally, the fatting of the cows themselves, has produced a very material increase. In this point of view, the enclosure of the hamlet of Hardwick has been greatly beneficial to the community at large.

"W.H. WOODROFFE,
"Resident Curate of Hardwick.
"*Jan.* 19, 1801."

"*Butter.*—About twelve dozen pounds were annually made, previous to the enclosure; there are now one thousand dozen pounds annually made.

"CHARLES GARDNER,
"Rector of Stoke Hammond, Bucks."

Potatoes.

		Suppose 20 the Standard Quantity before Enclosure.
Bedford, ..., return of	1 enclosure,	25
Cambridge, ...	2 ditto,	60
Chester, ...	4 ditto,	32
Cumberland, ...	9 ditto,	76
Derby, ...	13 ditto,	75
Dorset, ...	2 ditto,	29
Durham, ...	7 ditto,	79
Essex, ...	1 ditto,	21
Gloucester, ...	3 ditto,	25
Hunts, ...	1 ditto,	200
Lincoln, ...	8 ditto,	77
Lancaster, ...	4 ditto,	60
Leicester, ...	18 ditto,	119
Northampton, ...	8 ditto,	61
Notts, ...	14 ditto,	36
Norfolk, ...	2 ditto,	23
Northumberland,	9 ditto,	56
Oxford, ...	5 ditto,	25
Rutland, ...	2 ditto,	30
Salop, ...	2 ditto,	42
Somerset, ...	17 ditto,	28
Stafford, ...	6 ditto,	26
Suffolk, ...	6 ditto,	21
Warwick, ...	3 ditto,	38
Wilts, ...	8 ditto,	32
Westmoreland, ...	3 ditto,	36
Worcester, ...	5 ditto,	74
York, ...	63 ditto,	45
		1424
Average,	....	50

" As

APPENDIX. 263

This inquiry will receive considerable light, by adding certain observations detailed by some of the officiating Ministers.

"As potatoes are found a wholesome food, for both hogs and man, and as one acre of them would supply as much food as many acres of wheat, why should not the Legislature enact, 'That every farmer shall have an acre of land yearly producing potatoes, for every definite number of acres he has in all other cropping, under a certain sufficient penalty?'

"Minister of March, Cambridge."

"The decrease of wheat, 50 acres;—the decrease of beans, 220 acres;—the increase of oats, 100 acres;—the increase of barley, 30 acres;—the increase of cheese, 18 tons; proportion, from 2 tons to 20 tons;—the increase of mutton, 4420lb.; proportion, from 0 to 4420lb.;—the increase of beef, 1680lb.; proportion, from 0 to 1680lb.;—the increase of wool, 156 tods; proportion, from 20 tods to 176 tods.

"The Minister of Money Stanton,
"Leicester."

"The popular objection, whether well or ill founded, that by enclosures, arable land is converted to pasture, and the quantity of grain produced in the kingdom is diminished, is no new complaint: it was one of the grievances touched upon by ALEXANDER NOWELL, in a sermon before Queen ELIZABETH, 1562, as appears by an account of the sermon in Caius College, Cambridge, MS. 1183; and I think Bishop LATIMER somewhere makes the same complaint.

"In

"In AMES's Typogr. ed. HERBERT, p. 746, is a pamphlet, temp. EDW. VI. wherein is shewn the decay of England, only by the great multitude of sheep, to the utter decay of householders' keeping, dearth of corn, &c.

" Ib. p. 1083, ' Orders for the Relief and Stay of the present Dearth,' 1586, which were ordered to be executed again on like occasions, 1594, ib. p. 1087.

" ' A Solace for this Hard Season; published by Occasion of the Continuance of the Scarcity of Corn, &c.' 1595, ib. p. 1423.

" ' A Dietary ; being Ordinances for the Preventing of Dearths' (in 1565), ib. p. 1614.

" 'The new and admirable Art of Setting Corn,' &c. 1600, ib. p. 1210.

" RALPH CHURTON,
" Rector of Upper Middleton Cheney, Nottingham.

" *Feb.* 24, 1801."

" Whatever doubts may have arose as to the vegetable, there is no question but the animal diet is enlarged among us, and that in far greater proportion than the vegetable can be supposed to be diminished. There is not so large a quantity of land in tillage after enclosure, as there was before; but whether the produce of wheat, rye, and barley, falls greatly short of what it used to do, is still a question. The animal diet, and other conveniences of life appendant thereto, are certainly greatly increased, in the proportion of one to thirty.

" THOS. WELCH,
" Vicar of Pattishill, Northampton."

" Before the enclosure, the farmers reckon that they lost by the rot, and other causes, about one in ten of their

their sheep annually; but since the enclosure, they assure me they have not lost one in twenty.

" WM. ROSE,
" Rector of Whilton, Northampton."

" The increase of food for man and beast by the enclosure, has been prodigious. Two-thirds of this parish before was barren heath, fox-covers, and common. The best land was laid down, and the inferior is now under what is called the up and down system of husbandry, that is, laying down with seeds for a certain number of years, and then breaking up again.

" THOS. WILKINSON, M. A.
" Great Billing, Northampton."

" To which must be added, the great demand at Nottingham for every produce of grass-land, owing to the greatly increased trade, opulence, and consequent luxury of the inhabitants. By the introduction of artificial grasses, lands that by our forefathers were thought totally unfit for any thing but corn, are so easily converted into sheep-walks, &c. that unless, not only every facility, but every encouragement is given to the plough, grass will continue to encroach upon it, till the consequences are even more alarming than they now are.

" JAMES HERVES,
" Minister of Burton Joyce, &c. Nottingham.

" *Feb.* 2, 1801."

" The decrease of wheat, ... 55
Ditto beans, ... 200
Increase of oats, ... 75
Ditto barley, ... 5

" The

" The increase of cheese is 18 tons, the proportion from two to twenty tons.

" The increase of mutton, 6210 lbs. the proportion from 0, to .... } 6210 lbs.

Ditto beef, 840 lbs. ditto .... 840 lbs.

Ditto wool, 150 tods, the proportion from 20 tods to .... } 170 tods.

" Joseph Cotman,
" Rector of Sharnford, Leicester."

" As we have now no pease field, and no pulse is sown, we have, besides the superior crops of wheat before-mentioned, many times over the quantity of barley and oats we had in the open-field state. The crops upon an average are, oats six quarters per acre, wheat four quarters, barley five quarters; then the superior quantity and quality of herbage, on ground in good heart and well managed, enables to keep larger, much larger flocks of sheep, and of a better sort, and to send many scores of fat wethers, and some fat cows to market, not to mention lambs and wool, an article of good consideration. Cheese too, is an article not to be omitted, when we sum up the advantages of our enclosure. We send out annually, more than 25 ton of cheese at 60*s.* per hundred on an average.

" The rents have not been advanced since the enclosure; they were then trebled without any one's complaining; have been always well paid; and were they now raised 5*s.* or 6*s.* an acre, I verily think every one would agree to it without murmuring. Rents increased in such a proportion, and well and cheerfully paid, will furnish your calculators with work enough to calculate the advantages of our enclosure. No one need be told that the
farmer

farmer can have no other way to procure money to pay rent and very heavy taxes, but by furnishing the markets with the necessaries of life.

" The Minister of Sasscote."

" Barley is very much increased as well as oats. Beans are very much decreased.

" Barley is increased three-fourths; there being sown before the enclosure not more than 40 acres, and now from 150 to 160 acres. Oats are also increased in the same proportion.

" Beans have decreased in as great a proportion. There are also five times the quantity of potatoes; and turnips have increased in a greater proportion.

" N. B. Taking a fair view upon the whole, both before, and since the enclosure, there is more grain since the enclosure brought to market; a greater produce from sheep and young cattle, and considerably more than double the quantity of cheese made in the parish. A great deal of waste lands, &c. before the enclosure, the produce of which was but trifling, is now drained, and with proper cultivation, is become the finest land, and the greatest crops are got therefrom. And since the exoneration from tithes, no person is more respected than our clergyman, which was not formerly the case, and there is not now a dissenter in the place.

" ROBERT TOMLINSON,
" Curate of Orton, Leicester."

" It is allowed by all, that more wheat in bulk and quantity, is grown here now, than was grown before the enclosure. Some think a bushel of it does not yield so much

much flour as the open-field wheat did: these are nice observers; but all agree that any deficiency in quality is abundantly made up in quantity.

" The Minister of Sasscote.

" *Jan. 23d*, 1801."

" Beef has increased in proportion of ten to one;—mutton a hundred to one.

" About half the number of horses kept since the enclosure that there was before.

" Wool increased more than a fifth part;—the produce of butter and cheese double;—the increase of potatoes, ten bushels to one;—decrease of pigs one-half;—one-fifth of the quantity of beans;—ten times the quantity of oats;—twice the quantity of barley;—one-tenth of the quantity of rye.

" Turnips, in the open-field state, none; but now about 100 acres annually.

" Decrease of gorse and fern, 200 acres.

" Minister of Queenborough, Leicester."

" In fact, it appears that the produce of the whole parish is at least doubled, including in value the wheat crop, though the produce of wheat is not much increased, in consequence of the change of system in the agriculture of the parish: formerly only the best lands were sown with wheat after a summer-fallow; now, at least, one-third more in quantity is sown, principally on layers, either dibbled, or drilled But great part of the manure which was formerly applied to the wheat crop is now used for turnips.

" The

" The difference of the quantity of wheat sown, in the aggregate, is very little.

" HENRY MOON,
" Vicar of Chippenham, Cambridge."

" *Rent.*—Rent of the parish (Chippenham) before the enclosure, 1300*l.*; after, and at present, 2000*l.* The farmers were then in no good circumstances (except a rich one, who had his fortune from another source than farming); now all pay their rents well, and make money.

" *Produce*:

	Before the Enclosure.	Since.
" Wheat,	5 coombs.	6 coombs.
Rye,	4 coombs.	none.
Barley,	4 coombs.	$8\frac{1}{2}$ coombs.
Oats,	4 coombs.	10 coombs.

" Before, the parish was all a bed of rubbish and weeds; now, well cultivated in every respect *."

" The great increased difference will consist in artificial grasses, and turnips, to carry stock, more particularly sheep, which will be at least doubled; and all the land much more able to serve any emergency, as it will annually be mending in ability to grow quantity; whereas, by the old method, it was annually and gradually declining, from the quick succession of corn crops.

" D. BERGUER, B. D.
" Rector of Carlton cum Willingham, Cambridge."

---

* Annals, vol. xliii. p. 50.

" *Increased.*

"*Increased.*—Oats, 5000 to 1;—beans, 300 to 1;—rye, little or none grown;—barley, 40 to 1.

"*Diminished.*—Beasts, one-third;—horses, one-third;—sheep, one half;—geese, 100 to 1.

"Sam. Partridge, M. A.
"Vicar of Boston, Lincoln."

	£.	s.
"Barley, 436 acres open field, at 2½ qrs. per acre, 1090 qrs. at 25s. per qr.	1362	10

"*Open Field.*

	£.	s.
"Barley, 380 acres enclosed, at 3½ qrs. per acre, 1330 qrs. at 25s. per qr.	1662	0
Bullocks, 40, bred and sold at 4 years old, at 9*l*.	360	0
Ditto, 20, ditto at 3 ditto, at 6*l*.	120	0
Cows, 69 kept, produced each 6*l*.	414	0
447 stone weight beef, ...	894	0
Sheep, 1200 kept for folding (none fatted), and produced about 200 tods of wool, ...	200	0
	£.1094	0

"*Enclosed.*

	£.	s.
"Bullocks, 54 fed, { 24 wintered, at 7*l*. 168*l*. / 30 summered, at 4*l*. 120*l*. }	288	0
Ditto, 10 bred, and sold at 9*l*.	90	0
Cows, 34 kept; produce each, 6*l*.	204	0
Sheep, 420 fatted, { 300 sold at 2*l* ....; 120 sold at 1*l*. 13s.	600 / 180	0 / 0
160 lamb hogs, sold at 1*l*. 5s.	200	0
1600 shorn; produce, 400 tods wool, ...	400	0
981 stone weight mutton and beef, £.1962		0

"In

APPENDIX.

" In the open field, 73 working horses; the enclosed, 53 working horses.

" *Produce of Canwick:*

	Open Field.	Enclosed.
	£.	£.
" Wheat,	1425	1030
Barley,	1362	1662
Cattle and sheep,	1094	1962
	£.3881	4654
		3881
Total increase on enclosing,		£.773

	Open Field.		Enclosed.	
	Acres.	Qrs.	Acres.	Qrs.
" Wheat,	228	570	150	412
Barley,	436	1090	380	1330
Oats,	48	—	40	—
Pease,	80	—	60	—
Tares,	100	—	—	—
Turnips,	218	—	250	—
Clover seeds,	—	—	593	—
Fallow,	300	—	—	—
	1410		1473	

	Wheat.	Barley.	Animal Food.	Oats.	Pease.	Turnips.	Horses.
	Qrs.	Qrs.	Cwt.	Qrs.	Qrs.	Acres.	No.
Open field,	570	1090	447	160	180	218	73
Enclosed,	412	1330	981	240	210	250	53

" Minister of Canwick, Lincoln."

" Though

"Though there appears, however, to be a sensible diminution in the growth of every species of grain in my parish since the enclosure, it is perhaps not an effect produced by the enclosure, but by the operation of other causes. The great prices which animal food has fetched of late years, perhaps tempted the farmer to convert a greater part of his lands than formerly, to raise the necessaries for the subsistence of fattening cattle, and to apply a less portion of them to the production of bread-corn. It is at least evident, that in some adjoining parishes which are not enclosed, but consist of common, and common fields, the produce of bread-corn of late years has diminished, and the growth of turnips and grass-seeds greatly increased.

" A. SANDERSON,
" Vicar of Cold Aston, Gloucester."

" Fat beasts increased in the proportion of five to one; —sheep increased in the same proportion;—dairy cows decreased in the proportion of four to one;—fat hogs decreased in the proportion of six to one;—fat calves decreased in the proportion of four to one;—poultry decreased in the proportion of one half;—weaned calves decreased in the proportion of four to one;—potatoes increased in the proportion of nearly ten to one.

" PHILIP FISHER,
" Rector of Elton, Huntingdon."

" *Enclosing, in general, in Hunts.*—Mr. POOLEY has seen much of enclosing, and is clearly of opinion, that they have, upon the whole, been the cause of increasing the food of mankind to an almost incalculable degree. Some landlords resist the plough too much, but still the benefit

benefit has been decisive; and he is sure that the advantage to the public, and to the tenant, has been as great as it has been to the landlord. He knows many open lordships in this county, for which he would rather pay a fair rent of 15*s*. or 20*s*. an acre for enclosed, than have them in their present state for nothing, and should make more money. His expression was, " I should drink wine sooner than they can ale*.' "

" *General Observations.*—Mr. HOLMES, from the experience of 30 years, is convinced that the benefit the public, the farmer, and the landlord, receives from enclosures, is immense; that the advantage is not to be calculated by the number of live stock, or the number of acres sown with corn, but from the aggregate of many circumstances. Sheep before died of the rot, and no remedy: they could not drain; the lands were drowned for want of connected cuts to carry off the water. Labour is saved, which was useless and unproductive; six or eight harvest men went a distance to reap half an acre; then another distance more or less to another bit; lost time in examining which way to cut it; walked about listlessly, and lost full half their time†."

Gloucestershire.

" On the subject of enclosures much has already been said; and, as some proof from fact, of the advantages attending the system, on the Cotswolds, the following results are given of a comparison between the present state of the hamlet of Eastington, in the parish of Northleach, and

---

* Annals, xliv. p. 189.   † Annals, xliv.

the

the parish of Aldsworth; and what it was before the enclosure, or in open field.

" The management of the field land in the latter state was " two-shifts;" that is, one crop and fallow, alternately.

Average produce of wheat crop, 6 bushels per acre.
        barley ditto, 10 ditto.
        oats ditto, 10 ditto.

About 60 acres of the fallow field was sown with pease, } 6 bushels per acre.

" Sheep bred, 200, and sold poor the second year at the latter end; then called shearlings: stock of the fields was consequently 400: wool produced from the same after the rate of eight fleeces to the tod.

" Beasts bred, 20 in a season, and sold at different ages, after three years old: full stock in the fields, 80 beasts.

" Quantity of wheat, 200 acres, ... Produce, 150 qrs.
      barley, 200 ditto, ... Ditto, 250 do.
      oats, 200 ditto, ... Ditto, 250 do.
      pease, 60 ditto, ... Ditto, 40 do.

  Land in corn, 660 acres, ... Ditto, 690 qrs.

" Wool of 400 sheep, 50 tod.

" *Present State.*

" Average produce of wheat, 12 bushels per acre.
        barley, 22 ditto.
        oats, 24 ditto.
        pease, 16 ditto.

" Sheep bred annually 500; the same number sold annually fat. Yearly stock kept up 1500. Wool at the rate

rate of five fleeces to the tod. 100 beasts kept on the same, and 60 sold to the butcher.

	Acres.		Qrs.
" Quantity of wheat sown,	300	.... Produce,	450
barley ditto,	300	.... Ditto,	825
oats and pease do.	300	.... Ditto,	825
Land prepared for corn,	900	.... Ditto,	2100

" It is supposed that the oat and pea crops are in such proportion, as that the average produce of both do not exceed the average produce of barley.

" *Comparative View.*

	Before the Enclosure.	After Enclosure.	Improvement.
Wheat,	150 qrs.	450 qrs.	300 qrs.
Barley,	250 do.	825 do.	575 do.
Oats and pease,	290 do.	825 do.	535 do.
	690	2100	1410
Wool,	50 tod,	300 tod,	250 tod,

Sheep, none fed, 500, which estimated at 80 lbs. each, add to the stock of animal food 40,000 lbs. weight.

" Also 60 beasts, estimated at 560 lbs. each, gives 32,600 lbs. of beef in aid of the markets. Rental in favour of the landlord, increased from 500*l.* to 1460*l.* per annum.

" *Alsdworth,*

" *Aldsworth, before Enclosure.*

" Management, two shifts, crop and fallow:

Wheat 200 acres, at 6 bushels per acre,	150 qrs.
Barley 200 ditto, at 10 ditto, ...	250 do.
Oats 200 ditto, at 10 ditto, ...	250 do.
Pease on fallow land called etchings:	
100 ditto, at 6 ditto, ...	70 do.
700 acres,	720 qrs.

" Sheep bred, 200. Full stock, 400. Wool at eight fleeces per tod. Six hundred sheep taken to agistment, at 1*s.* per head.

" Ten beasts bred, and kept till four years old: ten sold yearly, and forty taken to agistment, at 5*s.* per head.

" *After Enclosure.*

Wheat sown,	390 acres,	Produce,	585 qrs.
Barley ditto,	390 ditto,	Ditto,	825 do.
Pease & oats do.	390 ditto,	Ditto,	950 do.
	1170		2360
	700		720 before enclosure.
	470 acres added.		1640 qrs.

" Sheep bred annually, 1800; beasts ditto, 12. Sent to market, several being bought in, 20.

" One thousand eight hundred sheep, at five fleeces per tod, produce 360 tod, which adds 310 tod of wool after the enclosure*."

" Posterity, however, will scarcely believe, that the expenses of enclosing 1000 acres, without taking in the

---

* Corrected Gloucester Report, p. 379.

subse-

subsequent costs of fences and buildings, amounted to 4500*l.* in the year 1795; which was the fact in the parish of Turley. Great as may be the future advantages of an enclosure, this operates as an obstacle to the general adoption of the plan. It is probable, in the instance now referred to, the fee-simple of the land in its waste state, would not have much exceeded in price the actual expenses incurred. With this heavy burden, however, attached to it, the change has been in favour of the landlord, tenant, and public. Land which before was only valued for a few miserable sheep depastured upon it, and often subject to the rot, is now in a state of profitable cultivation, eagerly rented at 30*s.* an acre, and adding 20,000 bushels of corn at least to the stock of the market annually, or some produce equal to it. In a recent enclosure of Staverton and Boddington, the weight of expense, and complaints of delay, have been considerably lightened and removed, being less than 20*s.* per acre, by trusting the management to one Commissioner, instead of three. Independent of expense, an advantage attends this mode in point of time, which much recommends it: a single Commissioner having no one to consult as to the time of meeting, can proceed with the business whenever he pleases, and need not wait the convenience or slow deliberations of others. In the choice of this Commissioner, all parties, in proportion to their degree of interest, should have a voice, and, if possible, be unanimously agreed; and here perhaps lies the great difficulty of the plan. As, however, so much public good depends upon it, any method of accomplishing it is better than none*."

In the report of the examination undertaken by order of the Board in 1800, the result was similar, as will appear by the following table.

---

* Corrected Gloucester Report, p. 91

Effect

APPENDIX.

Effect of Enclosures on the Produce of Human Food.

County.		Place.	Date.	Cattle.	Sheep.	Corn.
1. Bedford		Milton Bryant	1793	7 cows less	630 less	much increased
2.	....	Cople	private			increased
3.	....	Willington	ditto			increased
4.	....	Apsley Guise	1761		lessened	
5.	....	Blunham	1797			increased
6.	....	Sandy	1797			increased
7.	....	Eaton	1795	lessened	increased	increased
8.	....	Bolnehurst	1779			lessened
9.	....	Knotting	1779			lessened
10.	....	Lidlington	1775	cows doubled	much increased	
11.	....	Marston	1797		much increased	lessened
12.	....	Shelton	1794			increased
13.	....	Dunton	1797			increased
14.	....	Risely	—		decreased	increased
15. Hunts	....	Great Catworth	1795	lessened two-thirds	increased	the same
16.	....	Petenhall	1797	more	lessened, but equal in value	increased
17.	....	Ludgershall	1777	increased a little	lessened nine-tenths	less by half

APPENDIX.

County.		Place.	Date.	Cattle.	Sheep.	Corn.
18.	Hunts	Southoe	1797	the same	increased	much increased
19.	....	Diddington	—	the same	—	much increased
20.	....	St. Neots	1770	increased	increased	increased
21.	....	Eynesbury	1797	much raised; from 7s. to 30s. an acre	—	—
22.	....	Kimbolton	1795	more	much more	lessened
23.	....	Warboys	1795	much lessened	lessened	vastly more
24.	....	Winwick	1794	the same	the same	more
25.	....	Ramsey	1796	much lessened	increased	much more*
26.	....	Spaldwick	1777	increased	increased	lessened
27.	....	Laighton Broomsend	1764	—	—	increased
28.	....	Easton	1775	—	increased	increased
29.	....	Little Catworth	1780	—	increased	increased
30.	....	Barham	1780	—	increased	lessened
31.	....	Stonely	1769	—	increased	increased
32.	....	Holywell	1800	—	—	will be much increased
33.	....	King's Ripton	1772	—	increased	equal
34.	....	Ravely	1786	lessened	increased	much increased
35.	....	Little Stukely	1773	—	more	more

* Mr. POOLEY knows many open lordships in this county, for which he would rather pay 15s. to 20s. an acre for enclosed, than hire them now for nothing; and should drink wine, sooner than ale in their present state.

APPENDIX.

	County.	Place.	Date.	Cattle.	Sheep.	Corn.
36.	Hunts	Woolley	1772	much lessened		lessened
37.	....	Alconbury	1791	much lessened	more mutton & wool	increased
38.	Cambridge	March	1793	lessened 1090 to 100	lessened above 500	a vast increase*
39.	....	Wimblington	1792	lessened as ditto	lessened	ditto
40.	....	Chattris	1782 1793 re-gulation	lessened 300	lessened	much increased
41.	....	Milton	1799	lessened	lessened	increased
42.	....	Gramdchester	1799	—	doubled	will increase
43.	....	Whaddon	private	—	—	increased
44.	....	Barrington	1796	lessened	much lessened	lessened by conduct of one person
45.	....	Long Stow	1796	lessened	lessened	increased
46.	....	Abington, P.	1770	greatly lessened	the same	increased
47.	....	Morden Guildon	1799	will be ditto	—	will be increased
48.	....	Conington	1800	—	will not be lessened	—
49.	....	Knapwell	1780	lessened half	lessened half	—
50.	....	Elsworth	1800	—	—	will much increase
51.	....	Chippenham	1791	increased	increased	greatly increased
52.	....	Little Wilbraham	1797	lessened in number	increased	greatly increased

* 3140 acres of common has produced, in seven crops, 163,220*l*.

APPENDIX. 281

	County.	Place.	Date.	Cattle.	Sheep.	Corn.
53.	Cambridge	Great Wilbraham	1797	lessened	—	increased
54.	......	Carleton	1799	—	will increase	great increase
55.	......	Weston Colville	1776	lessened half	much increased	great increase
56.	Norfolk	Terrington	1790	increased	the same	great increase
57.	......	Walpole	1789	—	—	great increase
58.	......	Carleton	1777	increased	lessened half	vast increase
59.	......	Banham	1789	the same	lessened	great increase
60.	......	Winfarthing	1781	the same	lessened	increased
61.	......	Talconeston	1778	—	—	much increased
62.	......	Northwold	1796	lessened half	increased	much increased
63.	......	Hillborough	1769	lessened	lessened	much increased
64.	......	Oxborough	1723	—	—	—
65.	......	Fincham	1772	much lessened	lessened	much increased
66.	......	Barton	1774	—	—	much increased
67.	......	Shouldham	1794	less by 50	the same	much increased
68.	......	Garboisthorpe	1794	—	lessened 300	much increased
69.	......	Marham	1793	much lessened	the same	great increase
70.	......	Ellingham	1798	increased	decreased	great increase
71.	......	Lexham	1795	lessened	increased	great increase
72.	......	Ashill	1785	lessened	—	vast increase
73.	......	Dunham	1794	—	—	increased
74.	......	Lytcham	1758	—	—	increased

APPENDIX.

County.	Place.	Date.	Cattle.	Sheep.	Corn.
75. Norfolk	Stifkey	1793	increased	increased	great increase
76.	Bircham	1740			increase
77.	Heacham	1780	increased	increased	great increase
78.	Ringstead	1781	increased	increased	more than doubled
79.	Sedgford	1795	lessened	increased	much increased
80.	Snettisham	1762	increased	increased	much increased
81.	Dersingham	—	the same	increased	doubled
82.	Brancaster	1755			much increased
83.	Titchwell	1786	trebled	more than doubled	much increased
84.	Thornham	1794	lessened	trebled	much increased
85.	Sharnburn	1770			much increased
86.	Sharrington			the same	increased
87.	Salt-house	1780	increased	lessened	greatly increased
88.	Heveningham	1799	probably will be less	increased	greatly increased
89.	Felthorpe	1779	the same	the same	the same
90.	Drayton	1770 / private	increase	increase	vast increase
91.	Marsham	1799			increase
92.	Sayham	1798	lessened	lessened	immense increase*
93.	Ovington	1793	lessened	lessened	increased

* 26,010*l.* of arable produce, in three years, from the common only, and the poor not injured.

APPENDIX.

County.	Place.	Date.	Cattle.	Sheep.	Corn.
94. Norfolk	Poringland	1799	lessened	lessened	increased
95.	Framingham	1799	—	—	increased
96.	Sprowston	1800	will be the same	lessened	great increase
97.	Plumstead	1800	will be the same	lessened	great increase
98.	Sellhouse	1800	will be increased	lessened	great increase
99.	Cantley	1800	ditto	increase	great increase
100.	Langley	1800	increase 6 times as many	the same	the same*
101.	Shropham	1798	increased	decreased	great increase
102.	Causton	—	the same	the same	great increase
103.	Acle	1797	increased	the same	increased

* In Mr. BURTON's 15 enclosures, 10,800 acres of common have been cultivated, which, beside feeding the horses, produce per annum, at average prices:

Wheat,	£.6000
Barley,	4800
Oats,	4000
Bullocks,	4000
Sheep,	5000
Cows,	1200
Per annum,	£.25,000

And pay as follow:

Tithe,	£.1500
Interest on capital,	800
Labour,	5000
Seed,	2500
Wear and tear,	700
Rates,	1031
Contingencies,	1000
Rent,	7725
Farmer's profit,	4744
	£.25,000

APPENDIX.

County.		Place.	Date.	Cattle.	Sheep.	C....
104.	Norfolk	Bintry	1795	the same	increased	increased
105.	....	Brook	1800			increased
106.	....	Ellow, &c.	1797	much increased	much increased	much increased
107.	....	Woodbastwick	1767	lessened	lessened	increased
108.	....	Upton	1800	will be great increase	increase	increase
109.	....	Stokesby	1722	increase		
110.	....	Hetherset	1798	increased	lessened	much increased
111.	....	Cranworth, &c.	1796	increased	lessened	great increase
112.	....	Wrenningham	1779			great increase
113.	....	Shottesham	1781	much increased	increased	increased
114.	....	Old Buckenham	1790	increased	increased	great increase
115.	....	Hockham	1795	decreased	increased	great increase
116.	....	Bressingham	1799	increase	will lessen	great increase
117.	....	Keninghall	1799	increase	decreased	great increase
118.	....	Wheating	1780	lessened	much lessened	not increased
119.	Suffolk	Coney Weston	1777			great increase
120.	....	Barningham	1796		much lessened	great increase
121.	....	Barnady		great increase	the same	increased
122.	....	Pakefield	1798	increased	the same	increased
123.	....	Wollington	1799	increased	increased	great increase
124.	....	Barton Mills	1794	annihilated	much lessened	great increase
125.	....	Tudenham	1796	the same	lessened	great increase

APPENDIX.

County.	Place.	Date.	Cattle.	Sheep.	Corn.
126. Essex	Parndon	1795	the same	much lessened	increased
127. Middlesex	Enfield	1778	about the same	increased	great increase
128. Surrey	Cobham	1793	the same	the same	great increase
129.	East Horseley	private			great increase
130. Hants	Maidstead	1798	increased	increased	increased
131.	Nately	1792	increased	the same	increased
132.	Basingstoke	1786	much increased	lessened	vast increase
133.	Basing	1796	increased	lessened	doubled
134.	Odiham	1789	increased	greatly lessened	great increase
Total			134	134	134
No minute			42	33	7
			92	101	127
Lessened in			37	40	9
Increased in			39	46	112
The same			15	14	5

No. XIII.

Calculation of Benefit by Enclosing.

TABLE I.

General Heads.	Rent to Landlord.	Nett Profit to Farmer.
	£.	£.
First general head, 1000 acres rich open fields, 6s. per acre,	300	364
Ditto, 10 years after enclosure, 15s. per acre,	750	500
Second general head, 1000 acres open field land, of poorer nature, 4s. per acre,	200	300
Ditto, 10 years after enclosure, 8s. per acre,	400	370
Third general head, 1000 acres rich common pastures, 2s. per acre,	100	240
Ditto, 10 years after enclosure, 15s. per acre,	750	500
Fourth general head, 1000 acres commons, heaths, and moors, 1s. per acre,	50	60
Ditto, 10 years after enclosure, 8s. per acre,	400	370*

* The Advantages and Disadvantages of Enclosing Waste Lands, by a Country Gentleman, p. 18.

TABLE II.

General Heads.	Hand Labour. £.	Horse Labour. £.	General Expense. £.
First general head, unenclosed,	400	367	966
Ditto, enclosed,	100	25	125
Second general head, unenclosed,	400	367	733
Ditto, enclosed,	325	250	455
Third general head, unenclosed,	10	—	120
Ditto, enclosed,	100	25	125
Fourth general head, unenclosed,	10	—	70
Ditto, enclosed,	325	250	455*

TABLE III.

General Heads.	Value of Wool. £.	Value of Provisions. £.	Total Produce. £.
First general head, unenclosed,	50	2350	2400
Ditto, enclosed,	250	1250	1500
Second general head, unenclosed,	50	1950	2000
Ditto, enclosed,	100	1700	1800
Third general head, unenclosed,	100	370	470
Ditto, enclosed,	250	1250	1500
Fourth general head, unenclosed,	90	100	190
Ditto, enclosed,	100	1700	1800*

* The Advantages and Disadvantages of Enclosing Waste Land, by a Country Gentleman, pp. 39, 62.

" From

" From hence it appears, that the kind of enclosure which returns the greatest profits to the land-owner, is that of good, rich, common pastures; and experience, I believe, verifies the calculation, though every one of these general heads, even of bad open-field land, certainly gives him a sufficient premium to proceed.

" On this consideration there can be no dispute, that it is the land-owner's interest to promote enclosures; but I verily believe, the impropriator of tithes reaps the greatest proportional benefits; whilst the small freeholder, from his expenses increasing universally to the smallness of his allotment, undoubtedly receives the least*."

" *General Recapitulation of Profit to the Land-owner and Occupier.*

		£.
First head.	Landlord,	350
	Tenant,	133
		483
Second head.	Landlord,	100
	Tenant,	70
		170
Third head.	Landlord,	550
	Tenant,	260
		810
Fourth head.	Landlord,	250
	Tenant,	310
		560

---

* The Advantages and Disadvantages of Enclosing Waste Lands, by a Country Gentleman, p. 24.

"From this recapitulation it will appear, that the occupiers of land have nothing to fear from enclosing; the profits from every one of these general varieties of it, returning a sufficient premium for the advance of labour and expense, which must fall on it for some years after the commencement, part of which ought undoubtedly to be paid by the land-owner, if the tenant is not assured of a competent term of years to repay him: but I do not propose entering into the proportion which reason and necessity would exact from each, the general conclusion being my only consideration*."

"On the whole, then, I will venture to assert, that, by the system of enclosing, the land-owner will increase the value of his lands; the farmer his profits; labour will be at least as plentiful, and provisions much more so: that, taking them into consideration in a national light, we have nothing to fear from even a General Enclosure Bill, were such a thing practicable, as it neither tends to depopulate nor starve us*."

---

* The Advantages and Disadvantages of Enclosing Waste Lands, by a Country Gentleman, pp. 29, 73.

No. XIV.

Enclosure Acts.

Parliamentary Enclosures.

17 CAR. II. Malvern Chase.
8 ANNE, Ropley.
12 ANNE, Farmington, Gloucester.

Year			Year		
1719	....	2	1740	....	4
1720	....	3	1741	....	3
1721	....	1	1742	....	5
1722	....	2	1743	....	7
1723	....	3	1744	....	1
1724	....	4	1745	....	2
1725	....	3	1746	....	0
1727	....	3	1747	....	5
1728	....	6	1748	....	5
1729	....	6	1749	....	2
1730	....	7	1750	....	5
1731	....	3	1751	....	5
1732	....	5	1752	....	8
1733	....	3	1753	....	4
1734	....	2	1754	....	17
1735	....	4	1755	....	11
1736	....	2	1756	....	21
1737	....	3	1757	....	14
1738	....	4	1758	....	25
1739	....	5	1759	....	34

Carry forward, ... 249

Brought

APPENDIX. 291

	Brought forward,	249
1760		21
1761		20
1762		16
1763		37

1764	63
1765	57
1766	48
1767	33
1768	69
1769	51
1770	63
1771	73
1772	63
1773	63
1774	59

} 941 average, 58

1775	38
1776	55
1777	88
1778	61
1779	66

1780	35
1781	22
1782	17
1783	13
1784	12
1785	22
1786	25
1787	21
1788	34
1789	31
1790	23
1791	34
1792	35
1793	58
1794	73

} 455 average, 30

1795	76
1796	70

} 146

Carry forward, ... 1885

Brought

APPENDIX.

	Brought forward,	1885
1797	....	86
1798	....	52
1799	....	65
1800	....	82
1801	....	49
1802	....	158
1803	....	92
1804	....	52
1805	....	68
		704
		2589

1775	....	53,740 acres in 30 enclosures.
1776	....	75,300 ditto in 48 ditto.
1777	....	91,933 ditto in 70 ditto.
1778	....	31,238 ditto in 51 ditto.
1779	....	61,219 ditto in 51 ditto.
1780	....	50,847 ditto in 32 ditto.
1781	....	21,134 ditto in 19 ditto.
1782	....	14,507 ditto in 13 ditto.
1783	....	28,977 ditto in 13 ditto.
1784	....	15,117 ditto in 13 ditto.
1785	....	21,617 ditto in 18 ditto.
1786	....	23,011 ditto in 20 ditto.
		488,640 378

Not the whole; only those in which the acres are specified.

Average, 1292 acres.

Enclosure

APPENDIX. 293

Enclosure Bills every Ten Years.

				Average.
Ending anno	1735	....	38	4
	1745	....	39	4
	1755	....	61	6
	1765	....	312	31
	1775	....	471	47
	1785	....	469	47
	1796	....	371	37
			1761	
	1806	9 years	706	78

Enclosures by Counties, 1st Queen ANNE to 1797.

	Acts.	Acres.	Acts: Acres not specified.
Bedford, ...	17	30,031	14
Berks, ...	7	6,333	20
Bucks, ...	31	38,457	22
Cambridge, ...	5	8,816	2
Chester, ...	12	10,563	—
Cumberland, ...	7	25,146	11
Derby, ...	63	54,985	11
Dorset, ...	9	13,354	5
Durham, ...	26	64,115	—
Essex, ...	2	1,022	1
Gloucester, ...	39	51,471	35
Hereford, ...	7	3,300	—
Carry forward,	225	307,593	121

Brought

	Acts.	Acres.	Acts: Acres not specified.
Brought forward,	225	307,593	121
Hertford,	6	8,022	3
Hunts,	19	30,750	8
Lancaster,	27	26,801	1
Leicester,	117	161,208	18
Lincoln,	153	368,018	19
Middlesex,	2	3,350	3
Norfolk,	37	70,176	16
Northampton,	97	157,956	30
Northumberland,	30	111,248	—
Nottingham,	60	108,541	19
Oxford,	34	50,736	33
Rutland,	15	22,704	3
Salop,	16	18,920	2
Somerset,	42	44,986	3
Southampton,	20	15,782	15
Stafford,	35	35,646	3
Suffolk,	7	7,501	1
Surrey,	2	437	1
Sussex,	4	1,450	—
Warwick,	38	49,155	31
Westmoreland,	2	2,158	11
Wilts,	18	31,681	36
Worcester,	26	24,184	36
York,	265	338,757	50
Carry forward,	1297	1,997,760	464

Brought

APPENDIX. 295

	Acts.	Acres.	Acts: Acres not specified.
Brought forward,	1297	1,997,760	464

Wales.

Flint,	6	16,990	—
Glamorgan,	1	750	—
Monmouth,	1	780	—
Montgomery,	4	8,626	1
Pembroke,	1	2,450	1
	1310	2,027,356	466
	466		
	1776		

Acres conjectured of the others, ... } 811,108

2,838,464

Acts passed during the First Forty Years of His present MAJESTY.

Bedford,	39	Gloucestershire,	67
Berkshire,	24	Hants,	22
Bucks,	61	Herefordshire,	7
Cambridge,	27	Herts,	13
Chester,	12	Hunts,	36
Cumberland,	20	Lancashire,	33
Derbyshire,	69	Leicestershire,	105
Devonshire,	2	Lincoln,	210
Dorsetshire,	15	Middlesex,	6
Durham,	23	Norfolk,	70
Essex,	5	Northampton,	115

North.

APPENDIX.

Northumberland,	21	Surrey,	5
Notts,	88	Sussex,	7
Oxon,	67	Warwick,	64
Rutland,	17	Westmoreland	13
Salop,	21	Wilts,	57
Somerset,	68	Worcester,	50
Staffordshire,	40	York,	309
Suffolk,	14	Wales,	23
			1845

Returns made to the Requisition of the Honourable the House of Commons.

Bedford,	37	Middlesex,	4
Berks,	12	Norfolk,	54
Bucks,	50	Northampton,	90
Cambridge,	20	Northumberland,	16
Chester,	11	Notts,	68
Cumberland,	15	Oxon,	45
Derby,	47	Rutland,	15
Devon,	1	Salop,	12
Dorsetshire,	13	Somerset,	55
Durham,	21	Staffordshire,	29
Essex,	3	Suffolk,	10
Gloucester,	53	Surrey,	5
Hants,	16	Sussex,	3
Hereford,	4	Warwick,	53
Herts,	13	Westmoreland,	10
Hunts,	28	Wilts,	41
Lancashire,	21	Worcester,	34
Leicester,	85	York,	231
Lincoln,	145	Wales,	14
			1384

[*The*

[*The First Private Bill of Enclosure ever passed.*]

" *An Act for Enclosing Ropley Commons, in the County of Southampton, and for the Improvement of the Old dispark'd Park of Farnham, in the Counties of Surry and Southampton (*8. ANNE. *Private Acts, No.* 20*).*

" Whereas there is a tract of ground, called Ropley Commons, containing by estimation five hundred acres, more or less, parcel of the manors of Bishops Sutton and Ropley, in the county of Southampton, in which the tenants of the same manours have the sole right of commoning, and depasturing their cattle levant and couchant on their respective tenements, parcel of the same manors, exclusive of all others whatsoever. And whereas the said Ropley Commons are at present of small annual value, but capable of improvement, in case the tenants of the same manors might have the liberty of enclosing, ploughing, and sowing the same, and many poor people would be employed in making such improvements, which will tend to the publick good. And whereas the tenants of the said manours have agreed to divide and enclose the said Ropley Commons, and to allot to every tenant of the said manours his due share and proportion, according to their respective interest and right of common therein; and that each and every one of them would accept and take such a proportion and share therein, as shall be set forth and allotted by WILLIAM GODWIN, late of Ovington, in the said county of Southampton, yeoman, RICHARD SEAWARD, late of Bishops Sutton, in the said county, yeoman, and HENRY WHITEAR, of Lanham, in the parish of Old Alresford, in the said county, yeoman, men indifferently elected and chosen by the said tenants, to divide and allot the same, according to the several interests and

rights

rights aforesaid; and that each tenant in manner as directed, should fence and hedge in the share and dividend to him to be so allotted, and keep the fences so to be made in good repair, and for ever enjoy the parts so to be respectively allotted in severalty, and as parts of their respective tenements, in respect or right of which such parcels, allotments and dividends shall be made. And whereas the old dispark'd park of Farnham, in the counties of Surrey and Southampton, part of the Bishoprick of Winchester, is likewise capable of being greatly improved, in case tenants might have a certain interest therein, for their encouragement to make such improvements, which would also be for the publick good. And whereas a house, called the Lawday House, lately standing in such park, was accidentally burnt down and consumed: wherefore for the rebuilding of the same, and for the making such improvements as aforesaid, and for the encouragement of the said tenants therein, JONATHAN Lord Bishop of WINCHESTER, the Warden and Fellows of Winchester Colledge, together with the tenants of the said manours of Bishops Sutton and Ropley, do respectively, and in most humble manner beseech Your Most Excellent MAJESTY, that it may be enacted, and be it enacted by the QUEEN's Most Excellent Majesty, by and with the advice and consent of the Lords Spiritual and Temporal, and Commons in this present Parliament assembled, and by the authority of the same, that the commons called Ropley Commons, parcel of the manours of Bishops Sutton and Ropley, in the county of Southampton, shall on or before the twentieth day of December, which shall be in the year of our LORD one thousand seven hundred and ten, be divided and allotted by the said WILLIAM GODWIN, RICHARD SEAWARD, and HENRY WHITEAR, or the survivors of them, unto and amongst the said several tenants and persons according to their

their respective interests and right of common appertaining to their respective tenements. And that each tenant of the said manours shall hold and enjoy his share and part, so to be allotted, to, and with his respective tenement, as part of the same, and to have as great, and the same interest and estate, in the part so to be allotted, as as he and they respectively now have in the respective tenements, to which, or in respect whereof such allotments are to be made, and fence, hedge in, and enclose the same in such manner and proportion, as the said WILLIAM GODWIN, RICHARD SEAWARD, and HENRY WHITEAR, or the survivors of them, shall at the making such allotments, direct and appoint; and that the aforesaid allotment be in writing, and be inrolled in the courts of the said manours. And be it further enacted by the authority aforesaid, that the said Lord Bishop of WINCHESTER and his successors for the time being, shall and may from time to time, and at all times hereafter, demise, lease, and grant all the said old dispark'd park to any person or persons, for any term of years, not exceeding twenty-one years, from the making thereof, reserving the annual rent of seventy pounds, to be paid half yearly for the same, and to continue payable, during such lease, or demise, to the said Lord Bishop and his successors, Bishops of WINCHESTER; saving to the QUEEN's Most Excellent Majesty, her heirs and successors, and to all other persons and bodys politick their heirs and successors (other than the tenants of the said manours of Bishops Sutton and Ropley, and their heirs, and the said Bishop of WINCHESTER and his successors, and the said Warden and Fellows of Winchester Colledge and their successors) all such estates, rights, and interests, as they, or any or either of them had, or might have had if this Act had not been made."

NO. XV.

No. XV.

Enclosure of Small Commons.

Upon this subject Mr. KENT thus expresses himself in a letter to the President of the Board.

" The enclosing of commons, being so properly and urgently recommended, as the best and most effectual means of providing against any future deficiency of corn, and keeping up a permanent stock adequate to the consumption of the country, the cheapest and most expeditious method of carrying that object into execution, ought of course to be immediately adopted.

" It has long been the wish of all persons interested in commons, to have a general act of parliament passed, under the authority of which they might effect these enclosures at less expense and trouble than now attends those undertakings. Though individuals would be tenacious of property which they had long enjoyed, and doubtful as to the value of what might be offered them as a compensation in exchange, few would make objection as to the value of an allotment of common, as it would be a new addition to their estates. I am therefore of opinion, that the most effectual way to give a spirited stimulation to the object recommended by the Grand Jury of York, would be, to pass a general act of parliament, for the enclosing, allotting, and dividing of commons *only*, not connecting them with common fields. Three parts out of four, of the difficulties attending enclosing

closing commons, would by this means be avoided, and more than half the expenses saved.

"In the ordinary business of an enclosure, there is a Solicitor, a Surveyor, and at least three acting Commissioners employed, and the business is seldom done at less than nine meetings; the first merely to qualify (as it is called) or swear themselves in. The second, to ascertain the boundaries and receive claims. The third, to make their valuation of the parish, and hear objections to the claims. The fourth, to set out roads, and hear objections to boundaries. The fifth, to examine the progress made by the Surveyor. The sixth, to shape out the allotments. The seventh, to hear objections to the allotments. The eighth, to settle the award; and the ninth, to execute it. These meetings are sometimes more, for want of due attention in the claimants, which enhances the expense considerably; and the charges occasioned by a general survey and valuation of the whole parish, are very heavy, and deter proprietors from undertaking enclosures, which would not be the case if the business could be effected in a shorter time, and at a less expense. To bring this about, I would propose, that the number of acting Commissioners should never exceed two, not only on account of saving a third of the expense, but because two men will always meet easier than three, and when met, will be more likely to apply to business than three, and more likely to continue and stay together than three; but as it will sometimes, though not often, happen, that they will not both agree, means must be had to settle any differences in opinion that may arise, which might be done by giving the two Commissioners, or those who appointed them, a power to call in a third man, as an umpire, to take into consideration such matters as they could not agree upon;

but

but not to go further into the business. Or perhaps it might have more weight with the country, if some person, perfectly well qualified for an umpire, was named in every county, by the Board of Agriculture, or approved or elected by the Grand Jury at the Assizes. This person should be respectable in his character, a real judge of land, and one to whom the profit of the business would not be a consideration. The office of a Solicitor, might, I conceive, be entirely done away, as the Surveyor, under the direction of the Commissioners, according to a form that might be settled, might keep an account of the proceedings, which should be ultimately digested into a regular award, and when executed by the Commissioners, registered with the clerk of the peace; and if done agreeably to the provisions in the general act of parliament, should have the effect of law, and be considered as binding to all parties concerned. But the greatest saving, would result from the mode to be established in ascertaining the proportions of common which each proprietor of land and tenements would be entitled to: this should not be done by the expensive method of a survey and valuation of the whole parish, but merely from the assessment to the poor-rate, which should be first regulated at a vestry, subject to such alterations and amendments as the Commissioners, acting upon their oaths, should think themselves justified in making. This would so shorten the transactions, that the whole business of enclosing a common, might be completed as well in three meetings as it is now in nine, and I verily believe as equitably. There might be many Commissioners offered, or proposed, but the two should be chosen by ballot, in which the lord of the manor, and the rector or vicar, might have a double vote, or a greater proportion

tion if necessary: this would tend to do away all appearance of influence, or partiality, which it would be well to remove.

"If a plan of this sort were properly digested, and introduced to parliament, under the credit of the Board of Agriculture, it is to be hoped it would receive the sanction of the Legislature; and would unquestionably be adopted to a very considerable extent, and have a happy effect upon the country, particularly if the clergyman's portion be set out to him in land, suppose one-ninth part, and the remainder of the common declared tithe free."

Mr. CHAMBERLIN, of Cropredy, near Banbury, who has been a Commissioner in various enclosures, is of opinion, that to enclose commons of less than 200 or 300 acres, would not answer the expense, especially if the land is poor.

Even in small commons, consents are numerous, and he thinks the persons interested would not agree without great difficulties, which would require the common mode of proceeding adopted in the parliamentary method.

That agreements even for the smallest commons, could not be procured, nor sittings held to ascertain rights, without the attendance of a lawyer, which would be followed by a heavy expense, too great for small commons to pay.

However small the commons, Commissioners of known ability and integrity must be employed, and these living perhaps at a distance, would create an expense too heavy to answer on a small tract. If persons unused to the business were employed; all would go to confusion, and expenses increase from other causes. Commissioners could not be got.

Distinctions are found between *common land* and *waste land*, though both are pasturage; and these would, in the hands

hands of men not used to the business (while men used to it could not be paid) create difficulties. In common land there are always a certain number of common-rights in the possession of certain persons, arising from the property of land when not alienated from it; but the common-right is sometimes sold from the land, so as to belong to a person who has no land at all. With these commons there are certain days for turning on and taking off, called *breaking* and *haining*.

But on *waste land*, a man with three acres has a right to turn on as many cattle or sheep as another with 100 acres; and no time of turning on or clearing laid down.

Another source of difficulty is, that common pastures are often connected with open arable fields; and then they must both be enclosed together, or the property much cut in pieces by successive operations.

Upon common fields, and pastures of great extent, all expenses now amount, fences included, to 4*l*. or 4*l*. 10*s*. an acre (seven or eight years ago 3*l*. per acre): what, therefore, would not the expense per acre be for small common pastures!

Rights of fuel create difficulties also. At Ensham, five miles beyond Oxford, 1000 acres of heath: the cottagers have the right of cutting bushes and furze, and taking them away on their backs, as fuel to be used in their own houses; but to use no cart, nor take any for sale. Such rights may be found on small commons, and would occasion perplexity.

When one or two farmers near the common, by usage take the food they would want to allot by the *practice* of the right, others, who have right, but live at a distance, would want the *right* to govern the allotments.

These are difficulties which, by experienced Commissioners,

sioners, are got over; but such men could not be paid by small commons.

Sometimes parishes intercommon with no boundaries or limits known, and perhaps could not be ascertained but by a trial at law.

If by employing men unaccustomed to the business, expenses were lessened, appeals to the sessions would be necessary, and the expenses thus incurred might be considerable.

For these reasons, Mr. CHAMBERLIN thinks that no small commons can separately be enclosed: it would be necessary to unite many in one measure, by means of an inspector to be appointed; on which subject he thus expresses himself.

" I think an inspection of all the open fields and commons in each county might lead to the removal of difficulties in the way of enclosures; and to a judgment whether it might be advisable to attempt the enclosure of a parish or common or not, the inspector to report the following particulars:

" The reputed quantity of open-field lands in the parish, and what proportion thereof is arable, and what proportion grass.

" What quantity of common pasture lands stocked at certain times and in certain proportions; and what quantity of common or waste lands commonable at all times, and without stint; and what it is that entitles any person to right of common thereon.

" The situation and distance of the parish or common with respect to the nearest market towns.

" The kind of soil, and state of the roads.

" Who the lord of the manor, and what are his rights, besides those rights which others have in common with him.

" Whether

" Whether the living is a rectory or vicarage, and who the incumbent, who the patron, and in what diocese.

" Whether the proprietors of the open lands and commons are numerous; and to put down the names of some of the principal ones, and the name of the owner of the impropriate glebe and tithes of the living, if not a rectory.

" To learn whether any attempt has been made to get an act to enclose; and if such attempt has been made, to learn for what assigned or probable reason the attempt did not succeed.

" The reasons why many enclosures in contemplation have not been carried into effect.

" Because it would spoil fox-hunting, &c.; or,

" The exorbitant demands of the tithe owners, or of the owners of some other special interests or rights in the lands to be enclosed: when this happens to be the case, I think the Board of Agriculture, or some other committee, should decide.

" The lands to be enclosed small in quantity or low in value, or perhaps both, so as not likely to answer the expenses.

" Proprietors not having money to pay the expenses, and the difficulty and expense of raising it—an easy remedy, I think, by a power in the Commissioners to sell part of the estate sufficient to pay the expenses.

" Quarrels, ill-will, or pique amongst the proprietors.

" The lavish expense of Solicitors; Commissioners residing very distant, and some of them charging for time which they have not attended, and other heavy expenses, I think, have deterred the owners of some open fields from any attempt at all. I think the Solicitor's bill if exorbitant, should be taxed, and that all the Commissioners should on every day of their attendance, sign and date

date the book of minutes of their proceedings, and verify the same on oath if required, or else not be paid.

" The road clause in all modern enclosure acts, brings on very heavy expense in deep countries, where materials are scarce or distant; in some parishes making the new roads have cost above 3000*l.*

" J. C.

" *May* 7, 1800."

No. XVI.

Fences.

Salop.

" I enclosed a small common a few years ago, without the expense of posts and rails. When the line of fence was marked out, a trench was dug of considerable width and depth. Strong bushes of hazle, willow, hawthorn, or whatever could be met with in a neighbouring wood, were planted in this trench. The loose soil was then placed to the roots, then a bank of turf was raised on both sides, rather higher than the soil adjoining the stems. By these means, the roots of the quick are placed in cool and moist soil; the turfs on each side form rather a hollow line, whereby the rain is directed to the plants; whereas, if a bank is made first, and the hedge planted afterwards, the roots have not the same quantity of loose soil to strike in, and what soil they have is dry; so that many of the plants die, or do not thrive. When the fence was so far advanced, young hawthorns, or hollies, or their berries, were put between the stems of the old quick, the tops of which were then cut off, leaving them about a stake high, and these tops made bearding, *i. e.* were stuck on the top of the turf bank, on each side, thickening the present fence, and protecting the future.

" Of between two and three miles of fencing made in this manner, on very high ground, scarcely any plants failed, though the age of them, and the rude manner in which they were transplanted, by being stocked out of old

old wood-land, the distance of carriage, and the frequent interruptions by frost and snow, to their being replanted, were very adverse circumstances. As the value of most coppice wood is daily declining, I look upon this as a valuable appropriation of it, wherever it can be done; one lot of ground is cleared, and another is enclosed*."

Herts.

" In new enclosures, Mr. IRONS of Market-street, banks double quicks and rails, and cleans for eight years, when he engages to deliver up a complete fence, taking his rails away, for 10s. a rod. This is a valuable fact, for it forms a fair estimate of expense in calculations of the profit and loss of new improvements†."

Lincoln.

" Mr. PARKINSON, in his business as a Commissioner in many enclosures, has necessarily had a great opportunity of seeing the result of various modes of planting and securing quick; and when he enclosed his own estate at Asgarby, he pursued a Leicester method, with one fence of a very small trench, planting the quick upon the surface of the field for the sake of moisture; the other side in the same soil he made a double ditch, three feet deep; and the difference in the growth was very great; the former was as good at three years as the other at seven‡."

Northumberland.

" Stone walls are also used for fences in some situations; the usual dimensions are two feet and a half at

---

* Salop, p. 145.
† Hertford Agriculture, p. 44.
‡ Lincoln Report, p. 91.

bottom,

bottom, fifteen or sixteen inches at top, and from four to four feet and a half high: about half way up a row of through-stones are put, at the rate of nine or ten in a rood of seven yards, and on the top a coping of sods, or stones set edgeways; the latter is preferable, as being the more lasting, and presenting a more awful aspect to deter the Highland sheep from attempting to leap them. The expense of making these walls is from 5*s*. 6*d*. to 6*s*. 6*d*. a rood of seven yards, for winning and walling the expense of leading depends on the distance.—Twelve or fourteen cart-loads will do a rood*."

" Gates are made of various forms, but agree nearly in size, being generally eight feet and a half wide, and from four and a half to five feet high, with five strong bars about three inches and a half deep, and a weaker one about an inch square, placed between the two lowest bars. The lighter a gate is, especially the fore part, the better, provided it be sufficiently strong; for this reason the top bar should be considerably stronger than the rest, as it is the most liable to be broken, especially where horses are kept, if not made so high that they cannot easily get their necks over it. The most approved form, is that represented, *Fig.* 1. *Plate* I.

" Hanging gates, so as to have a proper fall or tendency to shut of themselves, being little understood by carpenters, we hope the following directions for effecting that purpose may be acceptable.

" Having set the post perpendicular, let a plumb line A B, be drawn upon it: on this line, at a proper height, place the hook C, so that it may project three inches and a half from the face of the post; and at a convenient distance below this, place the lower hook D, one inch and

---

* Northumberland Report, p. 57.

a half

a half to one side of the perpendicular line, and projecting two inches from the face of the post; then place the top loop or eye two inches from the face of the "hawtree," and the bottom loop three inches and a half: thus hung, the gate will have a tendency to shut in every position. For if the weight of the gate be represented by the line C D, *Fig.* 2, *Plate* I. this, by the resolution of forces, is resolvable into the other two, C E, and D E, the former representing that part of the weight which presses in a perpendicular position; and the latter, that part of the weight which presses in a horizontal direction, and gives the gate a tendency to shut*."

"Walter Trevelyan, Esq. of Nether Wilton, shewed us a new mode of raising fences :—he erects an earth mound *(Fig.* 3, *Plate* I.) seven feet wide at bottom A B, four feet wide at top C D, and five feet high; on the middle of the top he plants a row of quicks Q, and on each side at two feet distance, puts in willow stakes W W, an inch in diameter, and one and a half or two feet long, sloping outwards, which take root and form a live fence, for the preservation of the quicks in the middle. These stakes are at first bound together by a kind of eddering; at the time we saw them they had been only two years done, of course no judgment could be formed, for some years to come, whether it possessed superior advantage to the mode above described: it appeared to us an experiment yet undetermined. In some situations, we are inclined to believe, it may be very useful, especially in cold, soft, marshy soils: whether it will be superior in all, we still entertain some doubts; but are persuaded, that a full trial will be given, by the spirited

---

* Northumberland Report, p. 58.

improver who is making the experiment. The expense is 2s 6d. per rood of seven yards*."

"The fences most generally used for new enclosures, are earth-mounds; at the base of which, and on the edge of the ditch out of which they are raised, are planted the quicks, generally upon a turned sod six inches high; which we think too low, as we always find the quicks grow much better when planted three sods high, with the thickness of two surface sods laid under their roots. This in most cases doubles, and in thin soils trebles, the surface soil, and forms a thick bed of the best earth for the roots of the quicks to grow in, as will be more clearly seen in the annexed sketch of such a fence, *Fig.* 1, Plate II. where A B, is the ditch, four feet and a half wide at top; B C D the mounds; the base B D, six feet wide; and height C D, four feet. Q, the quicks planted upon three turned sods, at least fifteen inches high, with surface sods and soil twelve inches thick, under and behind their roots. The expense of making this kind of fence, is 1s. 4d. per rood of seven yards, exclusive of quicks and railings.

"The quicks should never be planted nearer each other than nine inches, and upon good land a foot. Quicks four or five years old, with strong clean stems, are always to be preferred to those that are younger and smaller.

"It is a custom, in some parts, to clip young quicks every year; this makes the fence look neat and snug, but it checks their growth, and keeps them always weak in the stem, and, when they grow old, open at bottom; while those that are left to nature, get strong stems and side branches, which by interweaving one with another,

---

* Northumberland Report, p. 57.

make a thick and impenetrable hedge, and if cut at proper intervals (of nine or ten years), will always maintain its superiority, over those that have been clipped from their first planting. In point of profit, and of labour saved, there is no comparison; and for beauty, we prefer nature, and think a luxuriant hawthorn in full bloom, or laden with its ripened fruit, is a more pleasing, enlivening, and gratifying object, than the stiff formal sameness produced by the shears of a gardener*."

Hereford.

" But perhaps it would be a material improvement in this very useful practice, if the plants were permitted to remain in the nursery in rows distant one yard from each other, until they become of a size which would make an immediate fence, and require no protection. The enormous expense of posts and rails would thus be saved, and the plants would thrive, with at least as much certainty, as if they had been set at a younger age†."

Norfolk.

" In these several Norfolk enclosures, the fences consist of a ditch four feet wide, and three deep, the quick laid into the bank, and a dead bush hedge made at the top.—Expenses:

	s.	d.
Digging, banking, and planting, ...	1	3
Bushes, a load 20s. does near 300 rods, ...	1	3
Quick, ...	0	6
	3	0‡"

---

* Northumberland Report, p. 56.
† Hereford Agriculture, p. 40.
‡ Norfolk Report, p. 185.

" Mr.

" Mr. REEVE, of Wighton, in forming new fences, gives a complete summer-fallow to the lines where the quicks are to be set, and dresses the land with a good compost: and instead of leaving the bank in a sharp angle at top, he flattens it, to retain the moisture*."

Gloucestershire.

" The dimensions of the Cotswold fence wall is twenty-six inches at the base; eighteen inches at the coping; and four feet and a half high, exclusive of a coping of flat stones, where these are to be had. Sometimes, a " coomb" of stones set edgeways, is used as a finish to the top.

" The line of the intended fence being drawn, and the foundation cut out, quarries are dug by the side of it, the stones are wheeled in barrows, and the wall built by a gauge, by masons. If the wall be set upon the soil, the turf is liable to rot partially, and throw down the fence.

" The cost of a wall thus made, and of these dimensions, is 8*l*. to 10*l*. a furlong, or about 10*d*. a yard. A penny a yard is the common price for walling; the raising and wheeling 8*d*. to 10*d*. a yard†."

York.

" The prevailing hedge wood is white-thorn. Formerly it was in this, as in other places, gathered in the woods and rough grounds. But at present, and for some years past, " garden quick-wood" has been pretty generally, though not yet universally planted.

" But although the white-thorn is the common hedge wood of the district, and in ordinary situations may be the most eligible, I have seen crabtree used in cold soils,

---

* Norfolk Report, p. 185. † Marshall's Gloucester, p. 24.

as well as in bleak situations, with great success. In an instance where crabtree and white-thorn were planted alternately, by way of experiment, the crabtree plants have outgrown those of the thorn in a striking manner. In six years they have acquired stems as thick as the wrist, with tops sufficient as a fence against ordinary stock.

" Upon the Wolds I have observed the elder, a plant which braves the bleakest situation, made use of as a hedge wood, but never saw it planted with sufficient judgment to answer the intended purpose. Nevertheless, in the abundance and luxuriance of this plant upon the most exposed parts of the Wolds, it is evident that, with proper management, it might be made at least a skreen to better hedge woods.

" The holly I have seen raised (in the practice of a man who has paid great attention to the business of hedge planting, and in this particular with great success) with an unusual degree of rapidity and certainty.

" The secrecy of the art lies in the time of transplanting: a holly transplanted at Midsummer scarcely receives a check from the removal; a fact this which few planters are aware of. Thousands of hollies are every year destroyed by removing them in the winter months*."

" The same judicious planter has, in dividing upland enclosures, planted hedges without any ditch whatever. His practice has been, to plough a slip of ground on each side of the intended line of the fence, the preceding spring; and having previously dunged it, to plant it with potatoes. During summer the land is repeatedly cleaned with the hoe; in autumn, the potatoes being removed, the entire slip is gathered into a ridge with the plough; and the ensuing spring the quick is planted nursery-ways

---

* Marshall's York, p. 202.

in a trench run along the middle of the ridge. The success of this method has proved equal to what might be expected from management so obviously judicious*."

" In perusing the different County Reports, the whole of the Surveyors concur in opinions as to the utility of enclosures; but it is mentioned by several of them, in terms of regret, that the obstacles thrown in the way of this valuable improvement, by ignorance and obstinacy, are great and manifold. In some cases they speak in terms of the highest panegyric of the utility, cheapness, and durability of certain fences, such as quicks, beeches, crabs, &c. when they are planted upon the soils to which they are respectively the best adapted; while in others they mention, in pointed terms, the perishable nature and transitory value of many of the fences employed; the annual expense required to keep certain descriptions of them in repair (the dead hedges and palings), and the great extent of valuable ground that is occupied by the others; especially the enclosures made by double ditches with a bank between them and a hedge on each side, and of the common hedge and ditch, and hedge and bank, which, at the same time that they occupy a considerable space of ground, are very seldom good fences; in some instances covering thrice, and in others four times, the space that a fence of a different kind would do, if properly kept. Great contrariety of opinion also prevails in regard to making trees a part of the enclosure, either in hedge-rows or belts of planting: from such diversity and opposition of sentiment, it is difficult to form any fixed or certain opinion upon the subject†."

---

* Marshall's York, p. 205.
† Board of Agriculture Communications, p. 5.

" In

" In all upland situations, the beech hedge, and hedge with a belt of planting, deserve a preference, as they unite in the highest degree the important requisites of shelter, ornament, and enclosure. The beech, under proper management, attains a great size, even upon the poorest soils, and soon forms a useful fence, in situations where thorns and other kinds of hedge plants would either perish or remain in a dwarfish state; with this additional material advantage, that by keeping its leaves during the winter, it affords shelter to the stock and pasture at the most inclement season, and when it is most wanted*."

Scotland.

" If I mistake not, you have recommended hedges to be planted against the common dry stone walls: Sir GEORGE SUTTIE has rather improved on this thought; he planted his hedges after the common method here, in the face of the ditch, but instead of putting a paling, or post and rail, on the top of the bank, he placed a wall of two feet and a half high. His local situation induced him to build with lime; and in places where that commodity is tolerably reasonable, it is the best method, as the satisfaction they afford by requiring no repairs, and the duration of them, more than repays the expense; but where the price of lime is high, they may be built without any cement, and answer the purpose very well, if the work is properly executed.

" I† have now experienced the benefit of those fences for some years, so that I can with great confidence venture to recommend them; indeed their superiority over

---

* Board of Agriculture Communications, p. 7.
† W. Erskine, Esq. Tower of Alloa, Clackmannanshire.

all others is so manifest to every one who has seen them, that they are daily becoming more and more common in this country.

"When a new fence is proposed to be made, the surface of the ground of the breadth of the ditch, and likewise for two feet more, should be pared off, in order to prevent, as much as possible, the weeds and grass from hurting the growth of the young thorns.

"The ditch should be five feet broad, two feet and a half deep, and one foot broad at the bottom; leave one foot for an edging or scarcement, then dig the earth one spit of a spade for about one foot, and put about three inches of good earth below the thorn, which should be laid nearly horizontal, but the point rather inclining upwards, in order to let the rain drip the roots; then add a foot of good earth above it; leave three or four inches of a scarcement before another thorn is planted; it must not be directly over the lower one, but about nine inches or a foot to one side of it, then throw a foot of good earth on the thorn, and trample it well down, and level the top of the bank for about three feet and a half, in order for the base of the wall to rest on. The base of the wall should be about nine or ten inches (but must not exceed one foot) from the thorn. The wall to be about two feet thick at the bottom, and one foot at the top; the cope to be a single stone laid flat, then covered with two sods of turf, the grass of the undermost to be next the wall, and the other sod must have the grass side uppermost; the sods should be of some thickness, in order to retain moisture, so that they may adhere together, and not be easily displaced by the wind. The height of the wall to be two feet and a half, exclusive of the sods, which together should be from four to six inches, by which means the wall would be near to three feet altogether.

"I would

"I would willingly add the cost of these fences, but as the rate of wages, and the quantity of work performed for them, differ so widely in one place from another, I can only offer some data to enable people in different places to form some conjectures about them.

"I have them done, every thing included (the walls built with lime), from $10\frac{1}{2}d.$ to $13d.$ per ell (which is equal to 37 inches 2 parts), according to the ease and difficulty of working of the quarry, and the distance of it from the place where the fence is erected. The lime costs about $6d.$ per boll (the boll is equal to 4 bushels, 0872,667 parts). I use from 15 to 16 bolls of lime to the rood of 36 square ells, Scotch measure; there are upwards of 43 Scotch ells, or 44 English yards, in length in a rood of a wall two feet and a half high.

"Sometimes, where there are plenty of what is here called land stones, such as flints, &c. on the ground that is to be enclosed, I use them; it then requires from 30 to 35 bolls of lime to the rood.

"The thorns are to be bought from any nurseryman, who commonly raises them from the seed, and sells them from $5s.$ to $10s.$ per thousand, according to their age, reckoning six score to the hundred.

"I generally have the ditches, as well as quarrying the stones, loading them, and building the wall, done by the great, and commonly pay for making the ditch, laying the thorns, and preparing the top of the bank for the wall, from $7d.$ to $8d.$ for six ells running measure.

"The wages of day labourers here are from $8d.$ to $10d.$ per day, commonly $9d.$ The stones are quarried from $8s.$ to $12s.$ per rood, according to the softness or hardness of the quarry.

"The quarriers wages are from $12d.$ to $16d.$ per day. I give the mason from $11s.$ to $12s.$ per rood for building.

The

The wages of such kind of masons are from 14*d*. to 16*d*. per day. About 50 carts (the weight that the cart carries from 7 to 9 cwt.) will build a rood. Carriage of ditto, about half a mile distance, about 8*s*. 4*d*. per rood (2*d*. per cart). The hire of these carts are from 1*s*. 6*d*. to 2*s*. per day; the man generally drives two carts, sometimes a man and boy drive five carts*."

" That quickset hedges are more useful and profitable, that they are more ornamental, cannot be denied, and they are generally allowed to afford more shelter; but the length of time, the constant attention, and continual expense of defending them until they bear even a resemblance of a fence, induces many people in those places where the materials are easily procured, to prefer the dry stone walls; for though the first cost is considerable, yet, as the farmer reaps the immediate benefit of the fence (which is undoubtedly the most secure one), they are thought on the whole to be the least expensive; besides, the cattle in exposed situations, and especially in those northern parts, are so impatient of confinement at the commencement of the long, cold, wet nights, that no hedges I have ever yet seen in any part of this island are sufficient to keep them in*."

---

* Annals, xiii. p. 483.

No. XVII.

Expenses of Enclosures.

Apsley Guise, 1761—1053 Acres.

Act,	£.324	15	9
Survey 1206 acres, at 1s. 2½d.	72	9	0
Map,	84	0	0
Five Commissioners, at 10s. a day,	105	0	0
Commissioners' expenses,	55	6	2
Rector's fence,	46	3	6
Clerk,	23	2	0
Labour and petty charges, 13s. 3d. per acre,	65	1	7
	£.691	18	0

Marston, 1797—1999 Acres.

Law,	£.400	0	0
Commissioners,	422	0	0
Survey,	409	0	0
Clerk, award, &c.	288	0	0
Sundries,	37	0	0
Roads,	729	0	0
	£.2286	0	0

Dunton

Dunton, 1797—2200 *Acres.*

Law,	£.584	0	0
Survey,	403	0	0
Commissioners,	357	0	0
Roads and drains,	459	0	0
	£.1803	0	0

Great Catworth, 1795—2033 *Acres New :* 136 *Old.*

Expenses: 36*s.* on pound rent new,	£.3019	11	9
7*s.* 6*d.* ditto on old,	51	0	$8\frac{1}{2}$
	£.3070	12	$5\frac{1}{2}$

Petenhall, 1797—*Between* 800 *and* 900 *Acres.*

Expense about five pounds per acre; being opposed.

Southoe, 1797—1150 *Acres.*

Expense forty-five shillings an acre besides fences.

St. Neots, 1770—1390 *Acres.*

Expense nine hundred and eighty-six pounds, including every thing; fourteen shillings and threepence an acre.

Kimbolton, 1795—958 *Acres* 747 *New:* 210 *Old.*

Expense: 50*s.* in the pound on new,	£.1867	18	$11\frac{1}{2}$
5*s* on old,	59	1	3
	£.1927	0	$2\frac{1}{2}$

Spaldwick,

APPENDIX.

Spaldwick, 1777—1450 *Acres*.

Law (two acts),	£.766
Survey,	226
Drainage,	388
Public fencing,	427
Five Commissioners,	636
Surcharge fencing,	16
	£.2462

Easton, 1775—667 *Acres*.

Law,	£.420
Survey,	143
Commissioners,	267
Public fencing,	214
Drains and bridges,	276
	£.1323

200*l.* charged to old enclosures.

Little Catworth, 1780—757 *Acres*.

Law,	£.474
Survey,	134
Public fencing,	202
Commissioners,	180
Sundries,	24
	£.1015

Barham, 1780—672 *Acres*.

Law,	£.332
Survey,	79
Clover seed,	94
Public fences,	90
Commissioners,	146
	£.742

Bozeat,

Bozeat, 1798—2268 Acres.

Law,	£.305
Survey,	341
Commissioners,	315
Clerk, award, &c.	152
Public fences,	259
Roads and drains,	900
Sundries,	128
Clover seed,	427
	£.2827

Stoneley, 1769—1000 Acres.

Solicitor,	£.205
Survey,	117
Commissioners,	87
Clerk and award,	55
Expenses,	67
Sundries,	35
	£.566

Alconbury, 1791—1846 Acres.

About four thousand pounds.

March, 1793—3440 Acres.

About twenty shillings an acre, roads included: two thousand six hundred pounds of it land sold for.

Wimblington, 1792—800 Acres.

Act, Commissioners, survey, roads, &c. about	£.1200
Drains, banks, mills, &c.	2000
	£.3200

Terrington,

Terrington, 1790—868 *Acres.*

Sea banks, &c.	£.12,821
Sluice,	309
Act, Solicitor, &c.	759
Commissioners,	514
Survey,	200
Sundries,	2367
	£.16,970

Long Stow, 1796—1000 *Acres.*

Total, including fences, 1500*l.*

Elsworth, 1800—3659 *Acres.*

Put out to the country Solicitor at 10*s.* an acre for every thing except fences, roads, and drains, which are under distinct Commissioners, and estimated at 3*l.* per acre resident. The Commissioners are settled in the act to have 150*l.* each for time and expenses.

Little Wilbraham, 1797—1800 *Acres.*

Solicitor,	£.802	0	1
Surveyor and board,	361	6	6¼
Drainage,	578	10	2
Public fences,	812	9	0
Engineer,	95	15	10
Roads,	150	0	0
Commissioners: Dugmore, £.126 0 0 ⎫			
Watford, 163 13 0 ⎬	486	13	0
Stone, ... 200 0 0 ⎭			
Contingencies,	50	0	0
	£.3336	14	7½

Great

Great Wilbraham, 1797—2400 *Acres, whole Parish.*

Solicitor,	£.816	16	2
Surveyor,	390	2	10
Ditto board,	82	1	0
Drainage,	318	8	0½
Public fences,	554	8	0
Engineer,	95	15	10
Roads,	200	0	0
Commissioners,	486	13	0
Contingencies,	50	0	0
	£.2994	4	10½

Barningham, 1796—580 *Acres.*

One thousand eight hundred and sixty pounds, exclusive of fences, except of poor's allotment.

Carleton, 1777—1200 *Acres.*

About two thousand five hundred pounds the whole.

Banham, 1789—1000 *Acres.*

Above two thousand pounds; much road to make.

Winfarthing, 1781—600 *Acres.*

Something under two thousand pounds.

Northwold, 1796—4100 *Acres.*

Four thousand two hundred pounds, roads included.

Marham, 1793—3500 *Acres.*

Two thousand eight hundred and seventy pounds.

Lexham, Dunham, 1795—3000 *Acres in the Parishes.*

In all two thousand two hundred pounds.

Little Dunham, 1794—1800 *Acres in the Parish.*
One thousand two hundred and sixty pounds.

Stiffkey, 1793—4600 *Acres.*
Twelve shillings an acre, exclusive of fences; done by owners or tenants.

Heacham, 1780—3329 *Acres.*
One thousand one hundred and seventy-four pounds.

Snettisham, 1762—5000 *Acres in the Parish.*
Two thousand two hundred pounds.

Thornham, 1794—2100 *Acres.*
Twelve shillings and sixpence an acre.

Salt-house, 1780—2700 *Acres.*
About one thousand five hundred pounds.

Sayham, 1799—1000 *Acres.*
Three thousand six hundred pounds, land sold for, except five hundred pounds; roads seven hundred pounds.

Acle, 1797.
Four pounds an acre.

Bintry, 1795—600 *Acres.*
One thousand nine hundred pounds.

Barnaby, 1799—750 *Acres.*
Three thousand five hundred pounds, drains and mill included.

Hetherset, 1798—700 *Acres.*
Two thousand seven hundred pounds.

Shottesham,

Shottesham, 1781—314 Acres.

Law and act,	£.218	10	0
Roads,	105	0	0
Commissioners,	69	0	0
Ditto expenses,	18	13	4
Fences,	43	0	0
Survey,	42	0	0
	£.600	19	2½

and yet opposed in parliament.

Old Buckenham, 1790—900 Acres.

One thousand five hundred pounds, roads included.

Barton Mills, 1796—800 Acres.

Two thousand five hundred pounds, besides fences.

Parndon, 1795—150 Acres.

Four hundred pounds.

Cobham, 1793—1500 Acres.

Two thousand seven hundred pounds; of which, one thousand two hundred pounds for roads.

Basingstoke, 1786—3690 Acres.

Commissioners (six),	£.701	7	0
Solicitor,	554	19	8
Referees,	25	15	4
Valuation of common rights,	22	1	0
Interest of money,	35	11	1
Survey,	550	10	9
Drains, &c.	145	0	0
Law charges,	180	0	0
Incidents,	82	17	7
	£.2298	3	3

Average.

Average of the Preceding.

Act,	£.497	5	8
Survey,	259	12	1
Commissioners,	344	17	1
Fences, &c. &c.	550	7	6
Acres,	1612	0	0

Expenses of Tirley, alias Trinley Enclosure, in the County of Gloucester.

[Communicated by Sir Geo. O. Paul, Bart.]

The Act for enclosing the whole parish passed in 1795; and the award, signed April 1, 1798, was enrolled at the Office of the Clerk of the Peace in Gloucester, April 20, 1799. The parish contains 1891 acres, of which there were,

	Acres.	Acres.	Fruit, valued at per Ann.		
Old Enclosures.					
Arable,	131.087				
Meadow and pasture,	734.434		£.	s.	d.
		865.521	127	2	1
Common Field.					
Arable,	118.155		5	12	0
Intermixed meadow and pasture,	172.556		18	6	3¼
Common meadow, open from hay-harvest to Candlemas*,	178.852		£.151	1	4¼
		469.563			
Ham, a common,	167.718				
Forty-green, ditto†,	1.196				
Corse-lawn, ditto,	387.435				
		556.349			
		1891.433			

* These subject to inundation of the Severn; not likely to become arable.

† Subject to inundation, &c. &c.

The

The Earl of Coventry was impropriator and owner of the great tithes in part of the parish, and the Vicar was entitled to the great tithes in the remaining part, and to the whole of the small tithes within the said parish.

The enclosure was universal; land was allotted in lieu of tithes, and the roads were set out under the direction of the Commissioners of Enclosure; they were more than four miles in extent, and, for the *most* part, forty feet wide.

Expense of enclosure,	£.3149	16	9
Roads, including a salary of 10*l.* per ann. to Surveyor, while they were made,	1354	2	5¼
Total,	4503	19	2¼
Of which:			
Commissioners,	716	1	7
Survey,	361	0	0
Solicitor,	850	0	0
	£.1927	1	7

Expenses of Aure Enclosure.

[Communicated by Sir Geo. O. Paul, Bart.]

This enclosure concerned only one part of the parish, viz. the tithing of Aure, which tithing consisted of,

	Acres.
Common waste land, fed upon by sheep, &c.	63
Common meadow, thrown up every year, from the end of hay-harvest to the following Candlemas,	34
Common arable,	260
Intermixed lands,	150
Old enclosed lands,	700
	1207

The

The tithe estate was not affected by the enclosure, nor were the roads of the tithing.

Of the common waste land, 22 acres were sold by public auction, in five different lots, in order to defray the expenses of the Act, for 1336*l*.

Payments.

	£.	s.	d.
EDWARD BARWELL, Esq. Clerk of the House of Commons, upon passing the Act, ...	177	0	8
Messrs. WILTONS, the Solicitors of the Act,	423	14	7
Mr. STONE, Commissioner,	160	13	0
Mr. DAVIS, ditto,	179	13	0
Mr. CADLE, ditto,	119	14	0
Mr. CLARK, Surveyor of the land,	187	15	6
To labourers, for information, attendance, &c.	25	13	0
Mr. WADE, for attending the Committees of the Commons and Lords,	21	0	0
To servants, messengers, &c.	11	3	9
To the Engrossing Clerk,	3	3	0
To erecting three bridges, and making a road at the entrance of the old common,	26	9	6
Total, £.	1336	0	0

Mr. DAVIS, of Longleat, a Commissioner of great reputation, thus writes to the President of the Board:

"My ideas may be, in some degree, singular, but they are the result of near forty years' practice; and I will venture to say, a practice more extensive than has ever fallen to the lot of any man of my age, having acted as Clerk, Surveyor, Commissioner, and Solicitor in enclosures, from the year 1763.

"In the first place, as the general opinion is *now*, though

though it has not been the *general* opinion till lately, that enclosures are beneficial to the public, the question is naturally asked, Why, then, are not all waste lands enclosed? The answer is—because of the expense. It is then asked, How can this expense be lessened? The answer has hitherto been—by lessening the parliamentary expenses, which are usually about 200*l.* besides the expense of attendance of a Solicitor, and his necessary witnesses, in London, which is frequently as much more (I have myself been detained in town six weeks on an Enclosure Bill; and another time, more than five). This was what was attempted to be got rid of by Sir JOHN SINCLAIR's Bill; but was opposed by all those whose interest it was that fees should not be abolished.

" But we are now told (if the newspapers tell truth), by authority of a Committee of the House of Commons, that the expenses of an enclosure are not occasioned by the parliamentary expense, but by the extravagant charges of Commissioners in the country.—Did this assertion come from anonymous authority, it would not deserve an answer; but coming from the high authority it does, or is said to do, it seems to be too serious a charge to be made without contradiction. I do, for one, most solemnly contradict it; and do assert, that, in most enclosures, the expense of all the three Commissioners is very little more than the expense of obtaining the Act of Parliament, and frequently not so much. We are told, that Commissioners charge two guineas a day, besides their expenses—and so they ought, though they seldom do.—The period of judgment to conduct an enclosure, and activity to ride 20 or 30 miles to a meeting, is but of a few years' duration.

" I have been concerned in sixteen enclosures at one time, and I never cleared 300*l.* in a year in my life;
while

while many attornies have gained five times the sum at home, in their offices. When *we* grow old, we get out of request, and are, indeed, unable to bear the fatigue. Our business cannot be done by deputy: a lawyer's can, even to a late period of life; because his knowledge is supposed to increase with his years, while our's is supposed to decrease.

" If any attempt be made to decrease the allowance to Commissioners, no man of real business will be a Commissioner.

" We are told, that *two* Commissioners do all the work, and *all three* charge for it.—It is no such thing; at least, I never knew one instance of it.

" I mentioned, in a letter on the subject to Sir JOHN SINCLAIR, some time since, that I was certain the fees of the House would never be got over; and recommended, rather to propose to lay them on Enclosure Bills, *ad valorem;* but suffering all *under a certain yearly value,* to go *without fees.* This would bring in a number of small commons, which never will be enclosed separately, if the present fees continue; and if two are put together, an additional charge is now made, unless they adjoin, or are contiguous. To this proposal I added another, which would be of very great service, viz. that there ought to be a standing Committee of both Houses to attend to Enclosure Bills, for many good reasons, besides saving delay. One instruction to these Committees might be, to examine and sign the Solicitor's bill of charges. I might also have added, that the notices on the church door might be sworn to before two magistrates in the country; but I am not certain that the allegations should be proved in the country, unless the whole business was done there; because, in that case, Committees could ask no questions.

" I am

"I am certain, if these plans of passing Enclosure Bills could be adopted, much good would arise to the parties concerned; and I will venture to prophecy, that if more is attempted, the business will fall to the ground, or probably be left in a worse state than it is now. I have heard it said, that divisions of common *fields* are not to be included in the regulations to be made respecting enclosures, but only *common pastures*, or what are commonly called *wastes* (though improperly). This would not do. Where there are common fields, there are usually also commons, though not always *vice versâ*. An enclosure of the latter alone, is impracticable; because the cattle feed the common fields at one period of the year, and the commons at another: and an enclosure of the latter would ruin the former. Besides, the enclosure of common fields is *always* a great advantage to *all parties*—that of commons, only *to a part;* for they are always fed by *somebody*, but common fields must be managed by *all* parties, at a certain loss *to all*.

"If it were practicable, it would be a very wise regulation, that the old Statute, exempting waste lands broken up, from tithes for seven years, could be extended *to all commons*, but still retaining the usual *vicarial* tithes. That Statute is now so ambiguous, as to be of very little use."

No. XVIII.
Corn.

THE papers that have been at various periods laid upon the table of the House of Commons, relative to the import and export of corn, prove the fact with sufficient clearness. It is conceived, that a selection from these will be interesting to the inquisitive reader of this Report. Additions are made to them from other respectable authorities.

An Account of the Quantity of Corn and Grain of all sorts, and of Rice*, imported into Great Britain, from the Year 1800 to 1806, both inclusive; distinguishing Ireland from Foreign Parts, and shewing the amount of Bounty paid in each Year.

YEAR 1800.

Corn.				Meal.					
Ireland.		Foreign Parts.		Species.	Ireland.			Foreign Parts.		
Q.	B.	Q.	B.		Cwt.	qrs.	lbs.	Cwt.	qrs.	lbs.
78	4	130,897	5	Barley	—	—	—	—	—	—
—	—	15,796	5	Beans	—	—	—	—	—	—
—	—	8436	1	Indian corn	—	—	—	—	—	—
640	—	542,602	7	Oats	—	—	—	—	—	—
2	2	26,794	2	Pease	—	—	—	—	—	—
—	—	138,713	—	Rye	—	—	—	—	—	—
251	—	1,174,403	2	Wheat	—	—	—	—	—	—
—	—	—	—	Indian meal	—	—	—	—	—	—
—	—	—	—	Oatmeal	2782	3	1	6	3	6
—	—	—	—	Rye meal	—	—	—	22,025	1	27
—	—	—	—	Wheat flour	2163	3	21	312,367	2	4
971	6	2,037,643	6	Total	4946	2	22	334,399	3	9

* Rice imported, 315,649 cwt. 1 qr. 23 lbs.
Bounty paid on corn and rice imported, 44,836*l*. 13*s*. 0½*d*.

YEAR 1801.

Corn.				Species.	Meal.					
Ireland.		Foreign Parts.			Ireland.			Foreign Parts.		
Q.	B.	Q.	B.		Cwt.	qrs.	lbs.	Cwt.	qrs.	lbs.
—	—	113,966	4	Barley	—	—	—	—	—	—
—	—	16,246	3	Beans	—	—	—	—	—	—
—	—	44,472	5	Indian corn	—	—	—	—	—	—
366	—	582,628	5	Oats	—	—	—	—	—	—
—	4	44,217	5	Pease	—	—	—	—	—	—
—	—	99,847	5	Rye	—	—	—	—	—	—
—	—	1,186,236	7	Wheat	—	—	—	—	—	—
—	—	—		Indian meal	—	—	—	113,141	—	21
—	—	—		Oatmeal ..	13	3	—	63	—	24
—	—	—		Rye meal..	—	—	—	177,494	1	2
—	—	—		Wheat flour	1833	3	14	833,016	1	21
366	4	2,087,616	2	Total ..	1847	2	14	1,123,715	—	12

Rice imported, 310,608 cwt. 3 qrs. 21 lbs.
Bounty paid on corn and rice imported, 1,420,355*l*. 1*s*. 1½*d*.

YEAR 1802.

Corn.				Species.	Meal.					
Ireland.		Foreign Parts.			Ireland.			Foreign Parts.		
Q.	B.	Q.	B.		Cwt.	qrs.	lbs.	Cwt.	qrs.	lbs.
7116	4	8135	3	Barley	—	—	—	—	—	—
1654	4	4138	2	Beans	—	—	—	—	—	—
—	—	736	7	Indian corn	—	—	—	—	—	—
275,882	6	241,053	—	Oats	—	—	—	—	—	—
139	1	10,532	1	Pease	—	—	—	—	—	—
282	—	14,889	2	Rye	—	—	—	—	—	—
86,938	4	470,698	2	Wheat	—	—	—	—	—	—
—	—	—		Indian meal	—	—	—	15,513	2	—
—	—	—		Oatmeal ..	105,039	3	14	—	—	—
—	—	—		Rye meal..	—	—	—	1162	1	14
—	—	—		Wheat flour	79,031	3	3	236,061	3	12
372,013	3	750,183	1	Total ..	184,071	2	17	252,737	2	26

Rice imported, 432,300 cwt. 3 qrs. 13 lbs.
Bounty paid on corn and rice imported, 715,323*l*. 16*s*. 4*d*.

APPENDIX.

YEAR 1803.

Corn.				Species.	Meal.				
Ireland.		Foreign Parts.			Ireland.			Foreign Parts.	
Q.	B.	Q.	B.		Cwt.	qrs.	lbs.	Cwt.	qrs. lbs.
12,924	3	1103	1	Barley	—	—	—	—	— —
1652	4	85	2	Beans	—	—	—	—	— —
—	—	669	6	Indian corn	—	—	—	—	— —
231,142	4	254,573	—	Oats	—	—	—	—	— —
665	1	23,326	5	Pease	—	—	—	—	— —
752	4	3347	4	Rye	—	—	—	—	— —
48,230	3	224,052	7	Wheat	—	—	—	—	— —
—	—	—	—	Indian meal	—	—	—	145	3 16
—	—	—	—	Oatmeal ..	55,694	3	19	13	3 21
—	—	—	—	Rye meal ..	—	—	—	—	— —
—	—	—	—	Wheat flour	45,638	—	3	309,409	1 14
295,367	3	507,158	1	Total ..	101,332	3	22	309,569	— 23

Rice imported, 113,999 cwt. 1 qr. 10 lbs.

Bounty paid on corn and rice imported, 43,977*l*. 9*s*. 10*d*.

YEAR 1804.

Corn.				Species.	Meal.				
Ireland.		Foreign Parts.			Ireland.			Foreign Parts.	
Q.	B.	Q.	B.		Cwt.	qrs.	lbs.	Cwt.	qrs. lbs.
2523	3	9071	5	Barley	—	—	—	—	— —
3060	—	8868	1	Beans	—	—	—	—	— —
—	—	242	1	Indian corn	—	—	—	—	— —
198,975	7	500,151	5	Oats	—	—	—	—	— —
1077	7	18,570	1	Pease	—	—	—	—	— —
206	—	2437	7	Rye	—	—	—	—	— —
65,918	6	386,166	3	Wheat	—	—	—	—	— —
—	—	—	—	Indian meal	—	—	—	8	2 9
—	—	—	—	Oatmeal ..	64,845	2	9	1	— 22
—	—	—	—	Wheat flour	14,635	2	5	17,059	2 8
271,761	7	925,507	7	Total ..	79,481	—	14	17,069	1 11

Rice imported, 60,401 cwt. 3 qrs. 20 lbs.

Bounty paid on corn and rice imported, 4791*l*. 3*s*. 11½*d*.

YEAR 1805.

Corn.				Species.	Meal.					
Ireland.		Foreign Parts.			Ireland.			Foreign Parts.		
Q.	B.	Q.	B.		Cwt.	qrs.	lbs.	Cwt.	qrs.	lbs.
15,656	3	27,644	3	Barley	—	—	—	—	—	—
2009	4	8727	—	Beans	—	—	—	—	—	—
—	—	15	7	Indian corn	—	—	—	—	—	—
187,092	7	274,156	2	Oats	—	—	—	—	—	—
1685	7	8531	6	Pease	—	—	—	—	—	—
235	—	24,031	6	Rye	—	—	—	—	—	—
79,467	5	820,388	5	Wheat	—	—	—	—	—	—
—	—	—	—	Indian meal	—	—	—	26	3	12
—	—	—	—	Oatmeal ..	26,968	3	12	—	—	—
—	—	—	—	Wheat flour	18,884	—	25	54,539	1	8
286,147	2	1,163,495	5	Total ..	45,853	—	9	54,566	—	20

Rice imported, 78,925 cwt. 1 qrs. 16 lbs.
Bounty paid on corn and rice imported, 24,799*l*. 8*d*.

YEAR 1806.

Corn.				Species.	Meal.					
Ireland.		Foreign Parts.			Ireland.			Foreign Parts.		
Q.	B.	Q.	B.		Cwt.	qrs.	lbs.	Cwt.	qrs.	lbs.
3327	4	2058	1	Barley ..	—	—	—	—	—	—
2361	—	1045	3	Beans	—	—	—	—	—	—
—	—	108	2	Indian corn	—	—	—	—	—	—
326,813	6	183,428	5	Oats	—	—	—	—	—	—
1388	4	126	—	Pease	—	—	—	—	—	—
330	—	499	5	Rye	—	—	—	—	—	—
91,343	4	132,007	6	Wheat	—	—	—	—	—	—
—	—	—	—	Indian meal	—	—	—	20	2	9
—	—	—	—	Oatmeal ..	47,555	2	21	2	—	14
—	—	—	—	Rye meal ..	—	—	—	2	—	—
—	—	—	—	Wheat flour	38,264	3	26	248,431	3	14
425,564	2	319,273	6	Total ..	85,820	2	19	248,456	2	9

Rice imported, 147,276 cwt. 3 qr. 1 lb.
Bounty paid on corn and rice imported—*Nil.*

Inspector-General's Office,
Custom-House, London,
8d April, 1807.

APPENDIX.

An Account of the Value of all the Corn and Flour Imported, according to the Quantities stated in the preceding Table, and the Prices of the respective Years.

YEAR 1800.

Species.	Quantity.		At per Quarter.		Value.		
	Q.	B.	s.	d.	£.	s.	d.
Barley	130,976	1	60	0	392,928	7	6
Beans	15,796	5	69	3	54,696	1	8
Oats	543,212	7	39	10	1,031,959	14	5
Pease	26,796	4	67	5	90,326	0	8
Rye	138,713	—	76	11	533,467	1	7
Wheat	1,384,345*	—	113	7	7,841,925	19	7
Total	2,249,870	1			9,995,303	5	5

YEAR 1801.

Species.	Quantity.		At per Quarter.		Value.		
	Q.	B.	s.	d.	£.	s.	d.
Barley	113,966	4	67	9	386,061	1	4
Beans	16,216	3	62	8	50,904	14	6
Oats	582,994	5	36	6	1,063,965	3	9
Pease	44,218	1	67	8	149,604	6	3
Rye	99,847	5	79	9	403,559	1	7
Wheat	1,464,518	3	118	3	8,658,964	17	4
Total	2,321,791	5			10,713,059	4	9

* The flour included, at 3 cwt. to the quarter of wheat.

YEAR 1802.

Species.	Quantity.		At per Quarter.		Value.		
	Q.	B.	s.	d.	£.	s.	d.
Barley	15,251	7	33	1	25,229	3	8
Beans	5792	6	36	4	10,523	9	8
Oats	516,935	6	20	7	532,013	2	10
Pease	10,671	2	39	6	21,075	15	0
Rye	15,171	2	43	3	32,807	16	7
Wheat	662,668	—	67	5	2,233,743	7	8
Total	1,226,490	7			2,855,392	15	3

YEAR 1803.

Species.	Quantity.		At per Quarter.		Value.		
	Q.	B.	s.	d.	£.	s.	d.
Barley	14,027	4	24	10	17,417	9	6
Beans	1737	6	34	8	3012	2	0
Oats	485,715	4	21	3	516,072	11	4
Pease	23,991	6	38	6	49,634	1	6
Rye	4100	0	36	11	7567	18	0
Wheat	390,632	3	56	6	1,103,536	9	0
Total	920,204	7			1,697,290	11	4

YEAR 1804.

Species.	Quantity.		At per Quarter.		Value.		
	Q.	B.	s.	d.	£.	s.	d.
Barley	11,595	0	30	4	15,785	15	0
Beans	11,928	1	38	7	23,011	6	10
Oats	699,127	4	23	9	830,213	18	3
Pease	19,648	0	40	10	40,114	13	4
Rye	2643	7	37	1	4902	3	10
Wheat	642,650	1	60	1	1,930,628	1	8
Total	1,387,592	5			2,844,655	18	11

APPENDIX.

YEAR 1805.

Species.	Quantity.		At per Quarter.		Value.		
	Q.	B.	s.	d.	£.	s.	d.
Barley	43,300	6	44	8	96,704	19	6
Beans	10,736	4	47	5	25,454	9	0
Oats	461,249	1	28	0	645,798	15	6
Pease	10,217	5	48	4	24,702	11	8
Rye	24,266	6	54	4	65,922	13	2
Wheat	924,330	6	87	10	4,059,352	10	0
Total	1,474,101	4			4,917,935	18	10

YEAR 1806.

Species.	Quantity.		At per Quarter.		Value.		
	Q.	B.	s.	d.	£.	s.	d.
Barley	5385	5	38	6	10,367	6	3
Beans	3406	3	43	9	7451	8	9
Oats	510,242	3	25	8	654,811	8	10
Pease	1514	4	43	6	3294	0	9
Rye	829	5	47	4	1963	3	10
Wheat	1,506,986	—	79	0	5,952,594	14	0
Total	2,028,364	4			6,630,482	2	5

RECAPITULATION.

Years.	Qrs.	Bush.	£.	s.	d.
1800	2,249,870	1	9,995,303	5	5
1801	2,321,791	5	10,713,059	4	9
1802	1,226,490	7	2,855,392	15	5
1803	920,204	7	1,697,290	11	4
1804	1,387,592	5	2,844,655	18	11
1805	1,474,101	4	4,917,935	18	10
1806	2,028,364	4	6,630,482	2	5
Grand Totals	11,608,416	1	39,654,119	17	1

RECAPITULATION SINCE THE SCARCITY.

Years.	Qrs.	Bush.	£.	s.	d.
1802	1,226,490	7	2,855,392	15	5
1803	920,204	7	1,697,290	11	4
1804	1,387,592	5	2,844,655	18	11
1805	1,474,101	4	4,917,935	18	10
1806	2,028,364	4	6,630,482	2	5
Totals	7,036,754	3	18,945,757	6	11
Average of these five years	1,407,350	7	3,789,151	9	$4\frac{1}{2}$

N. B. Exclusive of rye meal, oatmeal, Indian corn, and rice, The re-export of rice is large, and therefore not included.

APPENDIX.

The following Account is extracted from the Meal Weighers' Books at the Mansion-House, the Act having taken place the 1st of August, 1796.

Wheat and Flour Average for the Years 1801, 1802, 1803, 1804, 1805, 1806.

	Wheat.	Average.	Flour.	Average.
	s.	d.	s.	d.
From 1st August 1800, to 1st August 1801, ..	117	6¼	112	6¼
1st August 1801, to 1st August 1802, ..	71	8½	64	5¼
1st August 1802, to 1st August 1803, ..	60	1¾	51	4¼
1st August 1803, to 1st August 1804, ..	54	4¾	49	0¼
1st August 1804, to 1st August 1805, ..	87	1¼	82	11¼
1st August 1805, to 1st August 1806, ..	73	3½	70	2

Price of Rice.

		Average.	
		s.	d.
In 1801, 56s. 39s. 24s. 6d. 37s. 6d. 23s. 6d. 29s. 35s.	—	34	11
1802, 44s. 30s. 38s. 31s. 38s. 35s. 42s.	—	36	6
1803, 42s. 30s. 38s. 34s.	—	36	0
1804, 35s. 26s. 22s. 31s. 6d. 34s. 41s. 49s.	—	34	0
1805, 46s. 28s. 33s. 37s. 35s. 41s. 45s.	—	37	6
1806, 36s. 27s. 23s. 29s. 24s. 6d. 30s. 35s. 33s.	—	33	11

The above prices were exclusive of duty, which was about 6s. 8d. per cwt.

Import.

Useful Tables for various Periods.

Import.

	1793.		1794.		1795.
Wheat, qrs.	420,350	....	324,637	....	287,930
Flour, cwt.	213,667	....	11,429	....	90,521
Barley, qrs.	147,169	....	128,568	....	18,070
Oats, qrs.	699,459	....	846,022	....	441,088
Oatmeal, bushels,	29,000	....	21,317	....	24,250
Price of the year of wheat, ...	£.2 8 2		£.2 11 4		£.3 14 3

	1796.		1797.		1798.
Wheat, qrs.	820,381	....	456,903	....	395,407
Flour, cwt.	205,866	....	17,026	....	4,598
Barley, qrs.	40,033	....	64,197	....	116,485
Oats, qrs.	740,348	....	563,743	....	722,035
Oatmeal, bushels,	76,717	....	57,045	....	65,321
Rice, cwt.	—	....	118,241	....	203,447
Price of wheat,	£.3 17 2		£.2 13 0		£.2 10 4

Prices, and Import.

Years.		Wheat. Per Bush. s.	d.	Barley. Per Bush. s.	d.		Import of Wheat. Qrs.
1771	....	5	10¼	3	2	....	2,509
1772	....	6	4	3	2	....	23,134
1773	....	6	4½	3	6½	....	50,312
1774	....	6	7	3	6¾	....	269,235
1775	....	6	0½	3	3	....	544,640
1776	....	4	9¼	2	6¼	....	20,148
1777	....	5	8_4	2	6¾	....	233,069
1778	....	5	3	2	10	....	106,394
1779	....	4	2½	2	5¾	....	4,611
1780	....	4	5¾	2	1½	....	3,041
1781	....	5	7	2	1¾	....	159,766
1782	....	5	11¾	2	9¾	....	79,778
Average,		5	6	2	9½	Total,	1,496,637

APPENDIX.

Years.	Wheat. Per Bush.		Barley. Per Bush.			Import of Wheat.
	s.	d.	s.	d.		Qrs.
1783	6	7	3	9½	....	505,161
1784	6	1	3	6	....	173,398
1785	5	2¼	3	0	....	94,631
1786	4	10¼	3	0¼	....	50,587
1787	5	1¼	2	10	....	50,467
1788	5	8	2	8	....	123,242
1789	6	4¼	2	10	....	93,374
1790	6	7¼	3	2¼	....	216,948
1791	5	10½	3	2¼	....	459,494
1792	5	3½	3	4	....	22,140
1793	6	0½	3	11¼	....	482,766
1794	6	5	4	1	....	327,244
Average,	5	10	3	3¼	Total,	2,599,460
1795	9	3	4	8	....	287,893
1796	9	6¼	4	6	....	818,811
1797	6	7	3	5	....	454,882
1798	6	2¼	3	7	....	394,447
1799	8	5	4	5½	....	472,991
Average,	7	11	4	1	Total,	2,733,968

"It appears from SMITH's Corn Tables*, that, from the year 1697 to 1765, the whole quantity of wheat exported exceeded the quantity imported by 14,048,994 quarters; and that during the last nineteen years of that period, from the year 1746 to 1765, the quantity exported exceeded the quantity imported by 6,649,609 quarters, or, on an average, by about 350,000 quarters, amounting,

---

* Vide Tracts on Corn Trade, pp. 130, and 136.

at

at 32s. per quarter, to about 560,000l. per annum; and the whole export of grain produced in the same period, on an average, 651,000l. per annum. Soon after the year 1765, we began to lose our exportation trade; and from 1771 to 1791, the import of wheat exceeded the export by 793,917 quarters*, and the sum paid for grain imported during this period, was 5,901,969l. or at the rate of 295,000l. per annum. From the beginning of the year 1791, to the 10th of October in the present year, a period of less than half the time, the import of wheat has exceeded the export by 3,894,594 quarters.

	Imported.	Exported. British.	Exported. Foreign.	Total Export.
1791	430,798 1	31,008 2	17,265 7	48,274 1
1792	20,201 2	224,190 4	26,791 5	250,982 1
1793	429,350 4	12,239 2	32,626 1	44,865 3
1794	324,637 2	24,640 4	91,632 0	116,272 4
1795	287,930 3	—	677 0	677 0
1796	820,381 4	92 6	584 3	677 1
1797	456,903 5	7,921 7	15,153 7	23,075 6
1798	395,407 5	775 0	21,363 0	22,138 0
1799	445,047 5	10,103 6	6,855 7	16,959 5
Three quarters, ending Oct. 10, 1800,	817,859 7	London, about		10,000
				533,919†
	4,428,513			
Deduct, exported,	533,919			
	3,894,594			

* Vide Custom-house Accounts.
† A Temperate Discussion of the Causes which have led to the High Price of Bread, p. 4.

" Within

APPENDIX.

" Within twelve months, from September 26, 1799, to September 27, 1800, there were imported into Great Britain no less than

  1,261,932 quarters of wheat and flour,
   67,988 ditto of barley,
   479,320 ditto of oats,
   300,693 cwt. of rice*."

An Account of all the Bounties paid on the Importation of Corn and Rice, in the Years ending the 10th of October, 1801, and 1802, respectively, distinguishing each Quarter.

	£.	s.	d.
Quarter ending 5th January, 1801,	44,836	13	0¼
5th April,	30,429	11	9
5th July,	41,205	16	9
10th October,	416,815	17	11¾
Year ending 10th October, 1801, £.533,287	19	6¼
Quarter ending 5th January, 1802,	931,839	17	9½
5th April,	270,018	3	9¼
5th July,	321,737	12	11¼
10th October,	109,991	14	10¼
Year ending 10th October, 1802, £.1,633,587	9	4¼

---

* Annals, vol. xxxvi. p. 167.

Import

Import of Corn from October 1, 1800, *to October* 1, 1801, *and the Acres of Land necessary to raise the same.*

	Quarters.	Quarters.	Acres.
Barley,		175,323, at 4 qrs. an acre,	43,830
Beans,		18,680, at 4 qrs. an acre,	4,670
Oats,		685,457, at 5 qrs. an acre,	137,091
Pease,		48,729, at 3 qrs. an acre,	16,243
Rye,	56,022 }		
Rye-meal, 163,055 cwt.	65,222 }	221,244, at 3 qrs. an acre,	40,414
Wheat,	1,266,833 }		
Ditto flour, 787,242 cwt.	306,896 }	1,573,729, at 2½ qrs. an acre,	629,490
		Acres,	871,738

Indian corn, ... 41,240
Ditto meal, ... 108,777 cwt.
Rice, ... 260,383 cwt.

Average Prices of Corn, from October 1800, *to October* 1801.

1800.	Wheat.		Barley.		Oats.		Beans.	
	s.	*d.*	*s.*	*d.*	*s.*	*d.*	*s.*	*d.*
October,	13	3	7	5	4	3	7	11
November,	15	0	8	4	4	9	8	7
December,	16	4	9	4	5	2	9	4
1801.								
January,	17	2	10	1	5	5	9	9
February,	17	8	10	5	5	7	10	1
March,	19	3	11	0	5	9	10	0
April,	18	11	11	0	5	8	9	6
May,	16	3	9	7	4	11	8	3
June,	16	1	9	0	4	7	7	10
July,	16	10	8	10	4	8	7	8
August,	15	2	7	6	4	5	6	11
September,	11	1	6	3	3	8	6	4
	16	1	9	0	4	10	8	6

Wheat,

	Quarters.		s.	d.	£.
Wheat,	1,573,729,	at	16	1	10,124,322
Barley,	175,323,	at	9	0	631,162
Oats,	685,457,	at	4	10	1,325,216
Beans,	18,680,	at	8	6	62,312
Pease,	48,729,	at	9	4	22,740
Rye,	121,244,	at	12	3	74,261
	2,623,162				£.12,240,013

Bounties, ... £.1,690,000

" This was the amount of the consumption (as nearly as we can calculate) of foreign corn, which, in a good year, we raise at home; rice and Indian corn (which we cannot raise) being, for that reason, excluded.

" Probably we shall not be far from the truth (it is, however, a mere guess, for there are no documents whereon to found an estimate of any accuracy), if we calculate the average price of potatoes, during the same period, at 12s. a sack, at which price the above import amounts to 20,400,000 sacks; and at the average produce of 100 sacks an acre, it would have required 204,000 acres to produce enough, at the price of the year, to have saved the whole of this importation.

" Or to calculate on a different ground, 48 bushels of potatoes form the average consumption per head, per annum, in Ireland, in a common year; and in the usual ample allowance, in which pigs and poultry come in for no small share.

" Forty-eight bushels of potatoes are, therefore, equal to eight of wheat;—in barley, to nine (nine bushels a head being the consumption of that grain in bread);—in oats, to twenty-five (the consumption in oatmeal);—in rye, to eight;—in pease and beans (suppose), to fifteen;

wheat

—wheat and rye are six for one;—barley we will call six to one;—oats, two to one;—pease and beans, three to one.

	Quarters.		Quarters.	
Wheat,	1,573,729,	equal to	9,442,374	of potatoes.
Barley,	175,323,	equal to	1,051,938	of ditto.
Oats,	685,457,	equal to	1,370,914	of ditto.
Beans,	18,680,	equal to	56,040	of ditto.
Pease,	48,729,	epual to	146,187	of ditto.
Rye,	121,244,	equal to	727,464	of ditto.
	2,623,162		12,794,917	

" Equal to 102,359,336 bushels of potatoes, or 34,119,778 of sacks; and at 100 sacks per acre, 341,197 acres, which, at the largest allowance admissible, is the quantity of land under this root, which would have precluded the necessity of any import. Hence, to view this interesting subject in another light, 341,197 labourers' families, to have had each an acre of potatoes, or 682,394 to have had each half an acre, would have excluded all importation.

" It appears plainly from this statement, that one very effective method of preventing scarcities, is the policy of permitting cottagers to have potatoe-gardens; by this means, a very considerable portion of the people is taken from the consumption of those articles of corn most liable to fail in bad seasons, and, consequently, of providing effectually against the return of such*."

" Should this increase of population be general throughout the kingdom, the Minister of Stavely humbly suggests

---

* Annals, vol. xxxviii.

suggests the necessity of bringing into cultivation the extensive wastes, forests, and common lands, still unenclosed; being convinced, that the soil of these kingdoms (laid out in moderate, not in overgrown farms) is far more than adequate for the sustenance of its inhabitants, however numerous; at once, under Providence, removing every fear of future scarcity, and the unpleasant idea of an industrious people craving a scanty pittance of bread (the staff of life) from America, and from every other nation around them.

" The Minister of Stavely, Derby."

" It has been already observed, that this country, which, within the last fifty years, had a highly valuable export trade in corn*, is become, in an alarming degree, dependent on foreign states for its subsistence, and now pays to other countries, on an average, for grain, a much larger sum than she formerly received from them. On an average of years, viz. 1748 to 1768, both years inclusive, the annual exportation of grain was—wheat, 313,238 quarters; barley, 48,658 quarters; malt, 203,919 quarters; oats, 17,233 quarters; oatmeal, 2494 quarters; rye, 39,057 quarters: the annual average value of which at that period was:

---

* " The greatest exportation during the century was in 1750, viz. wheat, 947,602 quarters; barley, 224,500 quarters; malt, 380,754 quarters; oats, 10,554 quarters; oatmeal, 4268 quarters; rye, 99,049 quarters."

Wheat,

	Quarters.	s.	d.	£.	s.	d.
Wheat,	313,288, at	31	8	496,039	6	8
Barley,	48,658, at	18	3	44,400	8	6
Malt,	203,919, at	12	0	122,351	8	0
Oats,	17,233, at	16	0	13,786	8	0
Oatmeal,	2,494, at	27	4	3,408	9	4
Rye,	39,057, at	21	1	41,172	11	9
				£.721,158	12	3

" The average importation of twenty years, from 1781 to the 10th of October, 1800, both inclusive, was—wheat and flour, 334,587 quarters; barley, 62,094 quarters; oats, 498,425 quarters; rye, 34,447 quarters; pease, 12,074 quarters; beans, 23,487 quarters; rice, 161,751 cwt.:—the annual average value of which was:

Wheat,	£.2	14	3
Barley,	1	8	10
Oats,	1	0	2
Rye,	1	16	8
Pease,	1	14	9
Beans,	1	14	9

" The average exportation for twenty years, viz. from 1781, to 10th of October, 1800, both inclusive, was—wheat and flour, 50,965 quarters; barley, 29,456 quarters; oats, 12,256 quarters; oatmeal, 2789 bolls*; rye, 6488 quarters; pease, 4189 quarters; beans, 9362 quarters; malt, 50,715 quarters; rice, 91,519 cwt.

" The rapid progress of that greatly increasing evil, a dependence on other countries for subsistence, strongly

---

* A boll, 140 lb.

appears

appears from the average importations of the last fifteen years, viz.

Average of Five Years, ending	Wheat.	Wheaten Flour.	Barley.	Oats.	Oatmeal.	Rye.	Rye Meal.	Pease.	Beans.
	Qrs.	Cwt.	Qrs.	Qrs.	Bolls*.	Qrs.	Cwt.	Qrs.	Qrs.
1790	107,978	35,093	31,883	484,657	56,944	9,443	—	1,799	24,857
1795	298,583	87,630	94,693	734,945	94,471	32,195	7519	17,193	37,393
1800	617,935	120,800	60,855	584,765	48,914	67,029	6047	19,746	16,706

" There is a decrease on the average importation of oats for the last five years, in consequence of the export of that article from Ireland and the Baltic, having been prohibited during an essential part of that period. We did not regularly import any considerable quantity of oats, or oatmeal, previous to 1763; but the importation latterly has been still greater, in proportion, than that of wheat, viz. from 600,000 to upwards of a million of quarters annually, including oatmeal.

" The following average exportations from Great Britain, for the same fifteen years, mark how the export of British corn has declined. The greater part of that small exportation was sent to our own dependencies.

Average of Five Years, ending	Wheat.	Wheaten Flour.	Barley.	Oats.	Oatmeal.	Rye.	Pe	Beans.	Malt.
	Qrs	Cwt.	Qrs.	Qrs.	Qrs.	Qrs.	Qrs.	Qrs.	Qrs.
1790	64,602	42,557	67,694	14,948	0.85	17,370	6764	10,794	102,611
1795	58,415	25,547	6,863	12,031	731	3,495	3719	7,702	14,449
1800	3,778	18,900	7,029	11,232	990		24 2093	8,063	8,550

* A boll, 140 lb.

" The

"The last fifteen years include two remarkably bad harvests, and so did the period from 1748 to 1768; and the years 1757 and 1767 were years of such scarcity, that it was necessary to take extraordinary steps, and the country seemed almost as much alarmed as in the years 1796 and 1800*."

Imported into Great Britain.

	Wheat.		Wheat Flour.			Oats.		Oatmeal.		Barley.		Rye.	
	Qrs.	*Bush.*	*Cwt.*	*Qrs.*	*lb.*	*Qrs.*	*Bush.*	*Bolls.*	*lb.*	*Qrs.*	*Bush.*	*Qrs.*	*Bush.*
1794	208,018	7	11,129	0	23	845,483	2	21,317	54	125,765	7	20,900	0
1795	287,893	1	90,447	1	22	440,245	2	24,250	41	17,952	5	11,471	0
1796	818,814	1	204,405	3	0	740,348	1	76,716	10	39,963	1	160,486	1
1797	454,882	7	14,906	3	11	563,743	4	57,043	114	64,197	2	8,257	6
1798	394,447	1	3,182	3	21	721,547	5	65,321	55	116,278	7	6,819	2
1799	472,991	4	60,413	1	20	492,423	6	43,307	121	19,536	3	22,044	4

```
                                              Qrs.      Bush.
Wheat,        -    -    -    -    -    -    2,637,047    5
Flour, at 2 bushsls per cwt.    -    -         96,121    0
                                            ─────────────────
                                          6)2,733,168    5
Average,      -    -    -    -    -    -      455,528    0
Average import of 1796, 1797, 1798, & 1799,   535,283    0†
```

"Average importations of the last fifteen years, viz. importation of wheat,
Average of 5 years, ending 1789, ... 86,172 quarters,
Ditto   of 5 years, ending 1794, ... 257,695
Ditto   of 5 years, ending 1799, ... 485,805
besides large quantities of wheaten flour (almost the whole of the wheat which comes from America is in the shape

---

* Lord SHEFFIELD's Remarks on the Deficiency of Grain, Part III. pp. 133, 134, 135, 137, 138. 1801.
† Question of Scarcity, 1800, p. 93.

APPENDIX.

of flour); and if the present year had been included, the increase would have appeared much greater, as, from the 4th of January to the 10th of October, 1800, the amount is 950,867 quarters of wheat and flour*."

"*Import of Wheat, from* 1781, *into England.*

		Quarters.	Bush.
1781	......	159,766	7
1782	......	79,778	6
1783	......	505,161	2
1784	......	173,398	0
1785	......	94,631	1
1786	......	50,587	5
1787	......	50,467	1
1788	......	123,242	7
1789	......	93,347	3
1790	......	216,948	0
1791	......	459,494	5
1792	......	22,140	3
1793	......	482,766	6
		2,511,730	6
Average,	......	193,210	0†"

* Lord SHEFFIELD's Remarks on the Deficiency of Grain, Part II. p. 58. 1800.
† Question of Scarcity, 1800, p. 92.

356 APPENDIX.

No. I.

An Account *of the Quantities of Barley, Oats, Oatmeal, Rye, Wheat, and Wheat Flour, Imported into England from the Year 1697 to 1780, distinguishing each Year; also shewing the Annual Average Price of Wheat in the same period.*

Years.	Barley.		Oats.		Oatmeal.		Rye.		Wheat and Wheat Flour.		Average Price of Wheat per Quarter of 8 Bush.		
	Qrs.	Bush.	Qrs.	Bush.	Qrs.	Bush.	Qrs.	Bush.	Qrs.	Bush.	£.	s.	d.
1697	—	—	—	—	1	4	—	—	400	—	2	13	4*
1698	150	—	520	—	—	—	3622	2	845	3	3	0	8 8/9*
1699	—	—	1280	4	—	5	350	4	486	6	2	16	10 6/9*
1700	—	—	234	4	—	5	—	—	4	6	1	15	6 6/9
1701	—	—	20	4	—	—	—	—	1	1	1	12	6 7/9
1702	—	—	1	—	—	—	—	—	—	—	1	5	5 7/9
1703	3	—	—	—	2	4	—	—	50	—	1	12	2 7/9
1704	—	—	—	—	—	—	—	—	1	6	2	1	0
1705	—	—	—	—	—	—	—	—	—	—	1	6	8
1706	—	—	98	4	480	4	—	—	77	1	1	3	1 8/9
1707	—	—	12	—	—	—	—	—	—	—	1	5	4
1708	—	—	70	4	—	—	—	—	86	4	1	16	10 6/9

* The three last of the seven dear years after the Revolution; the average price of the seven was 2*l*. 17*s*.

Years.	Barley.		Oats.		Oatmeal.		Rye.		Wheat and Wheat Flour.		Average Price of Wheat per Quarter of 8 Bush.		
	Qrs.	Bush.	Qrs.	Bush.	Qrs.	Bush.	Qrs.	Bush.	Qrs.	Bush.	£.	s.	d.
1709	606	—	1	—	—	—	—	—	1552	3	3	9	9 3/8*
1710	408	—	139	3	113	3	—	2	400	—	3	9	4*
1711	—	—	—	—	—	—	—	—	—	—	2	8	0
1712	—	—	—	—	—	—	—	—	—	—	2	1	2 2/9
1713	—	—	—	—	—	—	—	—	—	—	2	5	4
1714	—	—	21	—	—	—	—	—	15	7	2	4	8 8/9
1715	—	—	—	—	—	—	—	—	—	4	1	18	2 6/9
1716	—	—	—		—	—	—	—	—	—	2	2	8
1717	—	—	62	—	—	—	—	—	—	—	2	0	2 6/9
1718	—	—	21	2	—	—	—	—	—	—	1	14	6 2/9
1719	—	—	300	—	—	—	—	—	20	1	1	11	1 3/9
1720	252	—	2	—	—	—	—	—	—	—	1	12	10 6/9
1721	445	—	—	—	—	—	—	—	—	—	1	13	4
1722	—	—	—	—	—	—	—	—	—	—	1	12	0
1723	—	—	112	2	—	—	—	—	—	—	1	10	9 7/9
1724	—	—	61,630	3	—	—	—	—	148	2	1	12	10 6/9
1725	—	—	2152	4	—	—	—	4	12	2	2	3	1 3/9
1726	—	—	20	—	—	—	—	—	—	—	2	1	10 6/9
1727	100	—	15	6	—	—	—	—	—	—	1	17	4
1728	11,745	—	70,070	1	—	—	42,205	6	74,574	2	2	8	5 1/9

* The two dear years of Queen Anne; the average prices, 3*l.* 9*s.* 7*d.*

APPENDIX.

Years.	Barley.		Oats.		Oatmeal.		Rye.		Wheat and Wheat Flour.		Average Price of Wheat per Quarter of 8 Bush.		
	Qrs.	Bush.	Qrs.	Bush.	Qrs.	Bush.	Qrs.	Bush.	Qrs.	Bush.	£.	s.	d.
1729	17,201	6	184,071	4	21	3	132,045	7	40,315	2	2	1	7 5/6
1730	386	1	95,149	7	—	—	—	—	75	7	1	12	5 3/6
1731	3503	—	15,892	1	—	—	—	—	4	0	1	9	2 2/6
1732	—	—	12,044	—	—	—	—	—	—	—	1	3	8 4/6
1733	2	3	9	—	—	—	—	—	7	4	1	4	2 2/6
1734	1	—	9	—	—	—	—	—	6	5	1	14	6 2/6
1735	—	—	6439	5	—	—	—	—	9	1	1	18	2 6/6
1736	—	—	267	—	—	—	—	—	16	5	1	15	10 2/6
1737	—	7	7	3	—	—	—	—	32	4	1	13	9 3/6
1738	—	3	21	—	—	—	—	—	2	5	1	11	6 6/6
1739	—	2	32	3	—	—	—	—	22	7	1	14	2 2/6
1740	1	—	1333	7	—	—	1090	—	5468	5	2	5	0 4/6
1741	15,132	—	84,821	—	—	—	11,012	4	7540	2	2	1	5 7/6
1742	—	—	25	6	—	—	—	—	—	7	1	10	2 6/6
1743	—	—	12	6	—	—	—	—	2	5	1	2	0 8/6
1744	—	—	67	1	—	—	—	—	2	—	1	2	0 8/6
1745	—	—	5	—	—	—	—	—	5	6	1	4	5 8/6
1746	—	—	—	—	—	—	—	—	—	—	1	14	8
1747	—	—	—	—	—	—	—	—	—	—	1	10	11 5/6
1748	14	4	—	—	—	—	—	—	385	—	1	12	10 6/6

APPENDIX. 359

Years.	Barley.		Oats.		Oatmeal.		Rye.		Wheat and Wheat Flour.		Average Price of Wheat per Quarter of 8 Bush.		
	Qrs.	Bush.	Qrs.	Bush.	Qrs.	Bush.	Qrs.	Bush.	Qrs.	Bush.	£.	s.	d.
1749	40	—	—	—	—	—	—	—	382	—	1	12	10 6/7
1750	—	—	20	3	—	—	—	—	279	5	1	8	10 6/7
1751	—	—	2291	1	—	—	—	—	3	—	1	14	2 6/7
1752	—	2	250	—	10	—	—	—	—	—	1	17	2 2/7
1753	—	—	33	3	2	4	—	—	—	—	1	19	8 4/7
1754	—	—	52,421	7	—	—	—	—	201	—	1	10	9 7/7
1755	—	—	1591	2	292	—	—	—	—	—	1	10	0 8/7
1756	4	6	41,390	—	5280	4	1695	—	5	—	2	0	2 6/7
1757	5779	1	7460	2	298	3	7861	7	130,343	2	2	13	4
1758	9752	2	12,276	2	1563	7	—	—	19,039	7	2	2	5 3/7
1759	42	4	321	4	13	2	—	—	82	1	1	15	4 3/7
1760	—	—	—	—	3	6	—	—	—	—	1	12	5 3/7
1761	—	—	21	—	—	—	—	—	—	—	1	6	10 6/7
1762	942	3	16,570	1	829	6	—	—	56	2	1	14	8
1763	3227	7	217,637	5	836	5	—	—	8	1	1	16	2 6/7
1764	5110	2	122.477	3	11,892	3	—	—	1	1	2	1	6 6/7
1765	3597	—	82,205	4	541	6	—	—	89,642	5	2	8	0
1766	2620	6	209,782	3	—	—	140	—	9387	—	2	3	1 3/7
1767	64,895	3	209,388	4	—	—	65,498	3	444,029	—	3	4	6
1768	11,483	2	121,871	4	3142	4	57,073	2	272,307	6	3	0	6

APPENDIX.

Years.	Barley.		Oats.		Oatmeal.		Rye.		Wheat and Wheat Flour.		Average Price of Wheat per Quarter of 8 Bush.		
	Qrs.	Bush.	Qrs.	Bush.	Qrs.	Bush.	Qrs.	Bush.	Qrs.	Bush.	£.	s.	d.
1769	219	7	73,966	3	1409	4	22	3	2903	1	2	5	8
1770	28	1	109,189	—	13	5	—	—	15	2	2	9	0
1771	162	7	198,066	7	5	4	2179	4	2509	1	2	5	8½
1772	2103	4	70,527	5	15	—	4798	6	23,134	2	2	9	5¼
1773	51,221	3	232,907	6	1458	1	9253	1	50,312	—	2	9	10½
1774	155,147	7	312,503	4	404	7	41,427	—	269,235	4	2	11	0½
1775	126,332	4	280,870	7	2956	4	33,573	5	544,640	6	2	7	8¼
1776	8019	5	372,197	6	1509	5	3414	6	20,148	3	1	18	5½
1777	7981	—	366,020	5	134	4	18,454	1	233,069	4	2	5	0½
1778	42,514	—	199,667	6	12	2	9327	—	106,394	—	2	2	4¼
1779	7084	—	331,858	1	669	—	1693	—	—	—	1	14	6½

No. II.

An Account of the Quantities of Barley, Oats, Oatmeal, Rye, Wheat, and Flour, Exported from England, between the Years 1697 and 1780, distinguishing each Year.

Years.	Barley. Qrs.	Bush.	Malt. Qrs.	Bush.	Oats. Qrs.	Bush.	Oatmeal. Qrs.	Bush.	Rye. Qrs.	Bush.	Wheat and Wheat Flour. Qrs.	Bush.
1697	32,855	—	51,811	5	3751	4	295	3	2596	4	14,698	6
1698	30,984	6	44,526	6	2246	7	151	7	1275	2	6857	1
1699	75	—	1511	3	38	5	301	6	405	—	557	2
1700	25,896	5	37,571	4	3154	2	391	1	27,231	—	49,056	5
1701	21,953	2	50,447	1	2858	—	285	5	43,917	—	98,328	7
1702	16,280	1	71,856	6	1132	5	89	4	51,710	2	90,230	4
1703	71,523	7	123,291	2	1340	2	159	2	58,438	4	106,615	4
1704	30,729	4	102,873	7	718	6	219	7	29,284	7	90,313	5
1705	21,386	6	137,396	2	1116	4	100	4	24,059	4	96,185	1
1706	10,221	3	141,034	4	464	1	62	2	49,892	2	188,332	3
1707	4771	3	111,153	1	708	3	103	7	34,032	—	174,155	1
1708	29,937	6	97,783	3	512	3	67	6	4720	3	83,406	3
1709	40,512	6	139,934	4	5619	2	37	5	166,512	5	69,437	7
1710	5744	5	79,538	—	347	6	125	1	12,215	6	14,426	—
1711	8412	6	139,975	7	862	—	321	4	37,957	4	76,949	—

APPENDIX.

Years.	Barley.		Malt.		Oats.		Oatmeal.		Rye.		Wheat and Wheat Flour.	
	Qrs.	Bush.	Qrs.	Bush.	Qrs.	Bush.	Qrs.	Bush.	Qrs.	Bush.	Qrs.	Bush.
1712	19,838	5	191,624	5	4050	1	303	5	17,735	3	135,157	6
1713	52,542	7	217,975	7	21,576	2	1376	2	38,625	7	176,227	1
1714	18,579	5	220,574	7	12,476	4	129	—	20,455	—	174,821	2
1715	5080	1	103,365	1	6193	7	303	5	31,161	2	166,490	2
1716	14,857	—	226,617	—	6190	3	719	6	40,123	1	74,642	7
1717	18,435	7	251,083	1	4316	7	404	1	23,031	6	22,953	—
1718	71,139	7	303,133	3	6151	4	868	5	49,416	6	71,800	6
1719	9649	3	357,499	1	8921	—	219	3	45,502	2	127,762	2
1720	5505	6	253,509	6	19,893	—	3471	4	49,241	3	83,084	4
1721	11,608	3	338,942	6	2589	4	577	7	69,697	5	81,632	2
1722	37,528	8	366,728	2	1798	2	324	4	42,579	—	178,880	6
1723	45,789	—	305,063	5	2804	7	541	5	12,737	6	157,719	1
1724	10,298	5	241,895	—	3565	3	516	4	23,441	4	245,864	6
1725	13,782	6	294,025	2	6815	6	1447	4	20,539	5	204,413	6
1726	20,017	1	335,925	5	4610	—	1412	6	18,835	2	142,183	3
1727	8688	4	241,428	4	3193	3	2204	7	9169	3	30,315	3
1728	198	2	195,340	6	1584	4	1383	2	13	5	3817	—
1729	4650	4	130,743	7	3512	4	2541	—	1460	3	18,993	3
1730	14,982	3	179,446	2	3534	1	4479	2	12,394	4	93,970	7
1731	13,562	2	177,699	4	4663	6	1808	1	21,089	7	130,025	2

APPENDIX. 363

Year	Barley.		Malt.		Oats.		Oatmeal.		Rye.		Wheat and Wheat Flour.	
	Qrs.	Bush.	Qrs.	Bush.	Qrs.	Bush.	Qrs.	Bush.	Qrs.	Bush.	Qrs.	Bush.
1732	13,874	6	161,075	4	2012	—	1274	7	15,535	5	202,058	4
1733	37,598	—	203,115	—	3587	6	1487	4	28,155	1	427,199	4
1734	70,224	5	223,124	—	2722	2	3038	6	10,735	—	498,196	4
1735	57,520	3	219,781	7	2105	5	1920	6	1329	4	153,343	5
1736	6860	1	192,602	4	2190	—	1196	5	1220	5	118,170	—
1737	22,669	5	103,718	2	3582	2	1921	4	7849	3	461,502	—
1738	70,689	6	188,607	7	2429	7	1777	3	36,159	1	580,596	4
1739	54,447	1	191,876	6	8714	3	1116	3	29,791	2	279,542	4
1740	24,036	6	145,527	5	5279	2	2571	7	8979	4	54,390	4
1741	6,614	1	123,357	6	3736	7	1106	6	7622	1	45,416	7
1742	11,482	4	189,525	7	4526	1	1380	2	63,272	2	293,259	6
1743	34,995	1	219,217	5	8490	—	1882	3	88,272	7	371,431	3
1744	20,990	—	219,862	4	3949	3	1657	6	74,169	1	231,984	5
1745	95,878	7	219,354	6	13,643	5	9770	3	83,966	2	324,839	5
1746	158,719	3	282,024	6	17,927	—	20,203	—	45,782	3	130,646	2
1747	103,140	2	361,289	3	12,010	2	2122	4	92,718	3	266,906	7
1748	73,857	—	349,363	—	15,813	1	3768	4	103,891	4	543,387	5
1749	52,621	3	355,469	5	12,605	7	1281	2	106,312	4	629,049	—
1750	224,500	7	330,754	2	10,554	2	4283	4	99,049	3	947,602	1
1751	32,698	—	256,547	4	8459	1	2476	2	71,048	4	661,416	4

APPENDIX.

Years.	Barley.		Malt.		Oats.		Oatmeal.		Rye.		Wheat and Wheat Flour.	
	Qrs.	Bush.	Qrs.	Bush.	Qrs.	Bush.	Qrs.	Bush.	Qrs.	Bush.	Qrs.	Bush.
1752	106,331	3	287,578	6	9666	3	1590	1	57,847	2	432,886	1
1753	67,049	—	274,424	7	11,107	2	7012	1	24,835	7	299,608	7
1754	47,776	3	321,995	—	20,228	1	2330	2	42,915	1	361,172	—
1755	32,836	—	341,568	6	7799	5	1112	2	43,441	7	235,684	4
1756	26,938	5	236,925	6	8499	5	2310	4	29,963	7	101,936	—
1757	7094	7	56,164	2	12,117	—	4417	6	907	1	11,226	4
1758	691	—	10,728	1	7932	4	1831	4	—	—	10,737	4
1759	22,862	4	166,079	—	6566	5	3134	6	41,480	2	226,426	—
1760	34,592	4	224,195	—	12,299	5	2388	4	52,766	4	390,977	7
1761	97,897	1	279,051	5	14,683	—	2839	6	57,571	1	429,016	—
1762	130,873	3	254,429	5	145,025	7	1368	4	28,410	2	294,500	7
1763	38,391	1	165,494	6	10,844	1	1664	4	12,933	7	242,614	4
1764	9218	6	223,220	5	8436	5	1101	—	27,690	1	396,537	5
1765	19,361	5	208,235	3	9633	5	2047	6	12,083	7	167,030	—
1766	3979	6	106,489	—	9424	7	2386	—	6845	4	165,953	1
1767	7	1	18,647	3	9432	2	1716	5	53	2	5071	—
1768	1674	5	4833	5	10,784	1	1328	—	150	—	7433	1
1769	1348	2	36,105	3	11,753	1	1030	6	21	—	49,892	1
1770	3862	7	162,697	5	15,528	5	4201	4	642	1	75,400	5
1771	1080	1	30,086	2	18,833	3	4530	5	—	—	10,089	—

APPENDIX. 365

Years.	Barley.		Malt.		Oats.		Oatmeal.		Rye.		Wheat and Wheat Flour.	
	Qrs.	Bush.	Qrs.	Bush.	Qrs.	Bush.	Qrs.	Bush.	Qrs.	Bush.	Qrs.	Bush.
1772	2123	6	11,665	1	20,878	5	2663	—	—	—	6958	6
1773	1764	6	680	—	17,152	7	1518	2	—	—	7636	6
1774	1233	2	1182	7	15,402	6	883	2	1433	3	15,171	5
1775	2280	4	43,173	1	22,384	2	208	6	2470	5	28,348	3
1776	5955	7	123,148	5	21,642	2	294	—	10,368	4	174,950	4
1777	3164	3	129,348	3	14,271	2	2603	2	719	—	79,120	4
1778	1042	7	99,777	2	12,449	6	8360	6	1688	6	124,698	—
1779	4948	—	74,286	7	11,291	2	2474	5	3162	—	203,189	—

No. III.

Foreign Corn Exported between the Years 1697 and 1799, both inclusive.

Years.	Barley.		Oats.		Oatmeal.		Rye.		Wheat and Wheat Flour.	
	Qrs.	Bush.	Qrs.	Bush.	Qrs.	Bush.	Qrs.	Bush.	Qrs.	Bush.
1771	—	—	—	—	—	—	—	—	—	—
1772	—	—	—	—	—	—	—	—	—	—
1773	—	—	—	—	—	—	—	—	—	—
1774	—	—	25	—	—	—	826	2	756	6
1775	5940	6	3,552	5	220	2	251	4	62,649	3
1776	2159	5	8418	4	276	2	630	1	32,764	3
1777	479	4	12,506	7	—	—	226	6	5913	5
1778	1393	—	7834	5	208	1	17	—	13,076	6
1779	2583	2	634	7	29	—	37	4	9576	5

No. IV.

An Account of the Quantities of Corn and Grain of all Sorts, distinguishing each, Imported into and Exported from Great Britain, from the Year 1780 to the Year 1799, both inclusive, distinguishing each Year, and the British from the Foreign Corn Exported.

Foreign Corn Imported.

Years.	Barley.		Beans.		Oats.		Oatmeal.		Pease.		Rye.		Rye Meal.			Wheat.		Wheat Flour.			Average Price of Wheat per Quarter of 8 Bushels.			Indian.		Rice.		
	Q.	B.	Q.	B.	Q.	B.	Bolls.	lbs.	Q.	B.	Q.	B.	Cwt.	qrs.	lbs.	Q.	B.	Cwt.	qrs.	lbs.	£.	s.	d.	Q.	B.	Cwt.	qrs.	lbs.
1780	352	0	7406	4	196,643	7	612	7	17,716	0	—	—	—	—	—	1662	4	9030	0	0	1	15	8¼	—	—	7796	2	4
1781	56	2	8244	7	108,682	6	367	2	14,507	6	10,743	1	—	—	—	143,772	3	64,772	2	0	2	3	11¼	—	—	42,889	0	11
1782	13,180	5	3730	3	37,301	3	542	0	4951	3	—	—	—	—	—	76,745	5	15,798	2	0	2	7	9	—	—	2724	1	7
1783	145,561	7	29,964	1	228,386	7	3252	0	2418	4	81,326	4	—	—	—	582,616	4	81,495	2	11	2	12	2¾	—	—	52,603	3	13
1784	78,536	5	28,673	7	257,945	1	36,090	56	18,466	1	24,778	7	—	—	—	211,438	3	15,328	2	9	2	9	3½	—	—	124,564	2	27
1785	67,392	5	9355	6	319,362	4	179,786	112	7457	6	28,761	3	—	—	—	97,611	7	36,245	1	2	2	1	3½	—	—	168,016	3	6
1786	65,453	7	34,013	4	449,242	3	104,746	56	1697	2	3643	2	—	—	—	47,963	7	10,624	0	19	1	19	2	—	—	156,177	0	11
1787	41,636	6	40,752	1	467,162	1	145,694	56	2330	2	7048	1	—	—	—	57,368	4	10,069	2	24	2	0	6	—	—	179,326	0	8
1788	11,479	2	9820	3	381,105	4	100,623	84	1187	7	—	—	—	—	—	142,046	4	26,671	3	14	2	4	11	—	—	227,911	1	23
1789	11,127	7	162	1	421,780	4	19,880	0	229	1	14,844	6	—	—	—	92,397	7	60,773	3	17	2	10	11¼	—	—	160,227	0	17
1790	29,719	1	39,541	5	703,995	4	103,778	0	3551	7	21,683	3	—	—	—	200,114	1	67,329	2	12	2	11	10½	10,546	3	235,176	2	11
1791	61,134	3	12,743	2	758,248	4	104,956	36	1982	6	56,377	6	—	—	—	430,798	1	114,775	3	4	2	7	0¼	1248	5	226,928	0	4
1792	118,526	4	38,451	7	934,907	1	92,831	113	4801	5	13,026	7	—	—	—	20,201	2	7756	3	6	2	2	9	5677	5	234,025	1	23
1793	147,169	2	29,720	8	699,459	0	29,000	122	18,553	4	55,593	7	—	—	—	429,350	4	218,667	3	20	2	8	2¾	2	0	193,679	2	27
1794	128,568	3	90,248	3	846,022	6	21,317	54	40,368	5	24,472	5	—	—	—	324,637	2	11,429	0	23	2	11	4¾	1600	4	86,576	2	2
1795	18,070	5	15,807	5	441,088	2	24,250	41	20,262	6	11,507	0	37,595	1	26	287,930	3	90,521	2	22	3	14	3¼	20,586	3	145,500	2	13
1796	40,033	4	35,206	3	740,348	1	76,717	10	32,710	7	160,583	1	11,611	1	13	820,381	4	205,866	0	5	3	17	2½	29,294	0	407,047	3	1
1797	64,197	6	17,393	7	563,743	4	57,045	47	17,818	2	8257	6	—	—	—	456,903	5	17,026	1	12	2	13	0¼	107	7	118,241	1	11
1798	116,485	3	12,327	4	722,035	1	65,321	55	21,683	0	6924	6	—	—	—	395,407	5	4598	0	11	2	10	4¼	21	0	208,447	0	12
1799	19,537	7	4800	3	495,090	4	43,308	21	8750	4	22,050	6	—	—	—	445,047	5	63,481	3	8	3	7	3	2	0	93,570	0	22

368 APPENDIX.

No. V.
Foreign Corn Exported.

Years	Barley.			Beans.			Oats.			Oatmeal.		Pease.			Rye.			RyeMeal		Indian.			Wheat.			Wheat Flour.			Rice.		
	Q.	B.		Q.	B.		Q.	B.		Bolls.	lbs.	Q.	B.		Q.	B.		Cwt.		Q.	B.		Q.	B.		Cwt.	qrs.	lbs.	Cwt.	qrs.	lbs.
1780	2407	1		2357	7		8965	5		449	0	3131	4		150	0		—		—	—		7067	2		20,935	3	16	885	0	22
1781	—			216	0		18,542	2		119	6	290	0		9	0		—		—	—		1726	0		16,338	2	0	21,606	2	10
1782	—			225	7		7381	5		40	3	860	3		3048	4		—		—	—		1089	5		10,566	2	0	6030	2	9
1783	2965	3		27	2		2404	5		—		118	3		910	6		—		—	—		15,769	4		7,039	2	26	26,821	3	26
1784	2797	4		613	3		1569	5		3254	56	2696	4		647	6		—		—	—		10,424	4		9,466	1	26	119,328	1	23
1785	1463	0		283	7		3481	3		1105	28	140	4		1268	5		—		—	—		6255	4		347	0	0	126,783	2	27
1786	1492	6		434	3		1952	5		696	0	318	2		—			—		—	—		9938	4		3907	3	2	125,242	1	14
1787	2123	0		893	0		2844	7		310	56	63	0		—			—		1	—		335	1		381	2	17	139,614	3	16
1788	390	3		1630	4		1204	1		622	56	473	4		2718	0		—		—	—		11,442	2		1671	3	17	161,137	1	7
1789	360	0		4890	7		2053	6		28	112	—			—			—		—	—		10,019	5		12,403	0	13	160,261	3	12
1790	55	0		1259	3		1428	0		229	84	—			—			—		1246	4		741	5		12,482	2	18	152,551	2	25
1791	—			1043	0		1005	6		198	112	1196	3		1185	0		—		—	—		17,265	7		11,934	1	7	144,546	1	16
1792	774	5		846	2		10,300	3		438	28	237	2		1542	6		—		—	—		26,791	4		11,101	1	14	174,959	0	7
1793	172	5		48	5		2429	1		—		217	2		498	6		—		1448	2		32,626	4		40,322	3	21	96,172	2	4
1794	775	0		—			692	0		—		—			1418	7		—		465	0		91,632	0		24,023	3	3	79,336	3	16
1795	—			375	0		1529	0		—		—			100	0		—		2664	3		677	3		4225	0	0	25,809	0	6
1796	2736	2		225	4		1563	6		95	117	72	4		100	0		487		6418	6		584	0		1566	0	7	76,691	2	27
1797	25	0		—			—			—		50	0		680	2		—		579	0		15,153	7		10,537	3	0	69,730	2	1
1798	1579	4		1545	7		6120	0		—		—			—			—		500	0		21,363	4		4110	0	0	73,532	2	1
1799	656	3		227	2		4799	0		—		72	2		—			—		—	—		5355	7		10,017	1	0	44,626	1	19

APPENDIX.

No. VI.
British Corn Exported.

Years	Barley.		Beans.		Malt.		Oats.		Oatmeal.		Pease.		Rye.		Wheat.		Wheat Flour.	
	Q.	B.	Q.	B.	Q.	B.	Q.	B.	Q.	B.	Q.	B.	Q.	B.	Q.	B.	Q.	B.
1780	52,349	1	14,478	0	138,692	3	11,932	0	5738	5	8163	4	1673	3	64,067	3	151,658	6
1781	36,225	5	15,802	2	113,110	5	8531	2	17,922	4	2863	6	2550	5	2376	7	94,916	4
1782	41,737	1	14,290	7	86,615	6	10,903	7	4676	3	5472	0	3993	7	7049	5	133,412	3
1783	6167	2	10,236	1	45,918	6	8179	6	1412	5	2701	1	431	4	6321	7	28,319	5
1784	21,416	0	7826	3	45,415	3	8895	2	2884	5	2884	2	5821	2	58,510	5	41,474	0
1785	75,638	0	6288	1	95,362	5	17,554	7	4846	2	6986	4	12,516	2	65,366	7	60,964	3
1786	18,411	4	10,360	3	85,422	2	13,838	6	3939	5	5678	4	5467	2	128,384	1	66,161	3
1787	25,036	3	10,504	5	111,626	4	12,044	2	3452	3	6581	0	12,683	3	75,365	0	44,763	3
1788	65,229	7	8958	3	149,567	2	12,364	1	952	1	5118	5	31,219	7	49,769	1	24,538	1
1789	210,950	3	15,017	6	134,375	0	24,933	1	5801	0	9261	6	37,432	5	73,189	5	52,672	1
1790	18,846	6	9132	5	32,063	6	11,560	1	1279	2	7184	1	47	4	1307	0	24,632	7
1791	2394	3	7223	7	39,195	6	14,594	4	715	7	5439	5	2343	0	31,008	2	18,373	7
1792	26,744	3	10,810	0	20,020	5	13,610	2	529	0	4432	6	14,608	2	224,190	4	46,123	4
1793	1341	0	9722	4	1933	2	13,807	6	795	0	4344	3	13	2	12,239	2	20,482	6
1794	2048	7	7519	5	6472	4	12,695	7	1048	1	3063	0	500	7	24,640	4	27,922	3
1795	1788	6	3235	3	4627	1	5419	5	569	0	1315	0	15	0	—		14,835	4
1796	4433	7	8237	1	5928	7	8543	5	773	5	2112	3	72	5	92	6	20,610	2
1797	5194	4	8250	7	7869	6	17,304	1	1095	4	2752	2	8	3	7921	7	21,883	2
1798	1276	1	14,546	1	12,219	5	17,480	3	1436	6	3365	2	—		775	0	31,911	4
1799	24,244	5	9281	1	16,485	1	12,833	6	1647	2	2237	3	40	0	10,103	6	17,097	6

No. VII.

An Account of the Quantities of Wheat, Flour, Oats, Oatmeal, Barley, and Rye, Imported into Great Britain in the Year 1796, distinguishing the Countries from whence, and the Ports into which, Imported.

Imported from	Wheat.		Wheat Flour.			Oats.		Oatmeal.		Barley.		Rye.	
	Qrs.	Bush.	Cwt.	qrs.	lbs.	Qrs.	Bush.	Bolls.	lbs.	Qrs.	Bush.	Qrs.	Bush.
Denmark	17,184	1	—	—	—	7408	2	—	—	206	3	45	—
Russia	102,126	1	702	3	7	13,560	3	—	—	2954	4	30,273	2
Sweden	18,174	5	—	—	—	10,337	—	—	—	6906	6	19,036	4
Poland	126,790	6	—	—	—	1564	5	—	—	4960	4	39,408	7
Prussia	296,180	4	—	—	6	25,678	7	—	—	11,454	7	35,789	6
Germany	192,902	3	14,858	2	14	288,393	7	—	—	10,871	7	42,675	5
Holland	7939	4	25	—	11	112,196	6	6	56	1316	—	662	6
France	—	—	1107	1	—	—	—	—	—	—	—	—	—
Portugal	401	7	—	—	14	—	—	—	—	—	—	—	—
Spain	706	—	12,143	3	7	—	—	—	—	—	—	—	—
Gibraltar	3247	7	2321	—	—	—	—	—	—	—	—	—	—
Italy	18,178	6	—	—	—	—	—	—	—	—	—	—	—
Ireland	—	—	10	3	8	280,416	1	76,705	24	1172	2	—	—
Isle of Man	—	4	—	3	20	16	2	—	—	60	—	—	—
Guernsey and Jersey	—	—	431	2	—	8	4	5	70	—	—	160	—
States of America	2697	2	143,833	—	15	5	—	—	—	60	—	—	—
Africa	30,843	5	4	—	—	—	—	—	—	—	—	—	—
	817,373	7	175,429	—	18	740,084	6	76,717	16	39,963	1	159,956	6
Prize	3007	5	30,436	3	15	263	3	—	—	56	7	626	3
Total	820,381	4	205,866	—	5	740,348	1	76,717	10	40,020	—	160,583	1

APPENDIX. 371

Imported into	Wheat.		Wheat Flour.			Oats.		Oatmeal.		Barley.		Rye.	
	Qrs.	Bush.	Cwt.	qrs.	lbs.	Qrs.	Bush.	Bolls.	lbs.	Qrs.	Bush.	Qrs.	Bush.
Beaumaris	—	—	—	—	—	—	—	—	—	—	—	21	—
Berwick	158	3	—	—	—	1363	1	—	—	—	—	1926	2
Boston	—	—	—	—	—	—	—	—	—	—	—	—	—
Bristol	2032	5	8343	1	24	10,093	4	243	53	—	—	—	—
Chester	—	—	—	—	—	1610	4	—	—	—	—	—	—
Chichester	—	—	—	—	—	3168	5	—	—	—	—	—	—
Colchester	1514	6	—	—	—	—	—	—	—	—	—	—	—
Cowes	30	—	—	—	—	1014	5	—	—	—	—	—	—
Dartmouth	—	—	—	—	—	50	—	—	—	—	—	—	—
Dover	7468	4	32	—	12	83	—	—	—	—	—	16	—
Exeter	54	—	194	1	21	607	—	—	—	—	—	—	—
Falmouth	806	2	9141	—	3	—	—	—	—	—	—	—	—
Gloucester	—	—	—	—	—	943	6	—	—	—	—	—	—
Hull	32,423	2	—	—	—	4253	—	—	—	551	—	7418	5
Ipswich	832	—	—	—	—	250	—	—	—	699	—	280	—
Lancaster	—	3	—	—	—	—	—	23,872	23	—	—	—	—
Liverpool	144,091	—	16,653	1	13	178,486	5	—	—	9495	5	12,872	1
Lyme	475	—	—	—	—	662	3	—	—	—	—	—	—
Lynn Regis	18,059	6	—	—	—	7887	3	—	—	966	—	2816	1
Newcastle	21,581	7	—	—	—	1036	4	—	—	—	—	91,054	7
Newhaven	578	1	—	—	—	—	—	33	64	—	—	—	—
Penzance	—	—	2375	2	23	—	—	6	56	56	7	97	—
Plymouth	8466	2	—	—	—	1491	1	—	—	—	—	408	2
Poole	2903	4	—	—	—	—	—	—	—	—	—	—	—
Carry forward,	241,525	5	36,940	—	18	203,006	1	24,155	76	11,768	4	116,920	—

APPENDIX.

Imported into	Wheat.		Wheat Flour.			Oats.		Oatmeal.		Barley.		Rye.	
	Qrs.	Bush.	Cwt.	qrs.	lbs.	Qrs.	Bush.	Bolls.	lbs.	Qrs.	Bush.	Qrs.	Bush.
Brought forward,	241,525	5	86,940	—	18	203,006	1	24,155	76	11,768	4	116,920	—
Portsmouth	12,120	6	19,930	3	21	2470	1	—	—	3	3	—	—
Preston	—	—	—	—	—	1030	3	—	—	615	4	—	4
Rochester	123	—	—	—	—	—	—	—	—	—	—	109	—
Sandwich	629	3	—	—	—	711	—	—	—	—	—	—	—
Scarborough	333	5	2090	1	14	—	—	—	—	—	—	62	4
Southampton	1293	—	—	—	—	12,137	7	—	—	60	—	—	—
Southwold	—	—	—	—	—	370	—	—	—	—	—	—	—
Sunderland	1171	—	—	—	—	—	—	—	—	577	—	1657	4
Swansea	—	—	1423	1	4	27	4	—	—	—	—	—	—
Wells	1064	2	—	—	—	7484	—	—	—	—	—	—	—
Weymouth	—	—	—	—	—	—	—	—	—	—	—	—	—
Whitby	1291	2	—	—	—	—	—	—	—	—	—	162	3
Whitehaven	17	4	—	9	3	7277	3	8	100	81	—	205	—
Wisbeach	2096	3	—	—	16	—	—	—	—	—	—	—	—
Yarmouth	25,395	7	—	—	—	941	7	—	84	—	—	10,108	4
London	178,395	5	145,222	1	—	408,723	5	1	84	24,663	—	29,984	2
Scotland	54,924	2	249	—	17	86,168	1	52,551	30	2231	5	1373	4
Total	820,381	4	205,866	—	—	5,740,348	1	76,717	10	40,020	—	160,583	4

APPENDIX.

Account of the Number of Black or Neat Cattle, and Sheep, annually brought for Sale to Smithfield-Market, from the Year 1732 to 1806, both inclusive.

Years.	Cattle.	Sheep.
1732	76,210	514,700
1733	80,169	555,050
1734	78,810	566,910
1735	83,894	590,970
1736	87,606	587,420
1737	89,862	607,330
1738	87,010	589,470
1739	86,787	568,980
1740	84,810	501,020
1741	77,714	536,180
1742	79,601	503,260
1743	76,475	468,120
1744	76,648	490,620
1745	74,188	563,990
1746	71,582	620,790
1747	71,150	621,180
1748	67,681	610,060
1749	72,706	624,220
1750	70,765	656,340
1751	69,589	631,890
1752	73,708	642,100
1753	75,250	648,440
1754	70,437	631,350
1755	74,290	647,100
1756	77,257	624,710
1757	82,612	574,960
1758	84,252	550,930

APPENDIX.

Years.	Cattle.	Sheep.
1759	86,439	582,260
1760	88,594	622,210
1761	82,514	666,010
1762	102,831	772,160
1763	80,851	653,110
1764	75,168	556,360
1765	81,630	537,000
1766	75,534	574,790
1767	77,324	574,050
1768	79,660	626,170
1769	82,131	642,910
1770	86,890	649,090
1771	93,573	631,860
1772	89,503	609,540
1773	90,133	609,740
1774	90,419	585,290
1775	93,581	623,950
1776	98,872	671,700
1777	93,714	714,870
1778	97,360	658,540
1779	97,352	676,540
1780	102,383	706,850
1781	102,543	743,330
1782	101,176	728,970
1783	101,840	701,610
1784	98,143	616,110
1785	99,057	641,470
1786	92,270	665,910
1787	94,946	668,570
1788	92,829	679,100
1789	93,269	693,700
1790	103,708	729,660
1791	99,838	729,800

Years.	Cattle.	Sheep.
1792	107,263	752,569
1793	116,488	729,810
1794	109,064	717,990
1795	131,090	745,640
1796	117,152	758,840
1797	108,377	693,510
1798	107,470	753,010
1799	122,986	834,400
1800	125,043	842,210
1801	134,556	760,560
1802	126,389	743,470
1803	115,884	776,090
1804	113,993	912,390
1805	130,069	916,560
1806	124,392	859,870

It is to be observed also, that the size and weight, both of cattle and sheep, have probably increased at least one-fourth since 1732; according to which rate, the consumption of meat per pound, has augmented, besides the addition in point of number.

The increase every ten years, since 1732, is as follows:

	Sheep.	Cattle.
Consumption in 1794,	109,064	717,990
Increase, compared with the consumption in 1784—ten years,	10,921	101,880
Ditto in 1774—twenty years,	18,645	132,700
Ditto in 1764—thirty years,	33,896	161,630
Ditto in 1754—forty years,	34,774	86,640
Ditto in 1744—fifty years,	32,416	227,370
Ditto in 1732—sixty-two years	32,854	203,290

Conse-

Consequently the total increase, in sixty-two years, amounts to the enormous number of 32,854 head of cattle, and 203,290 sheep, for the metropolis alone*.

Human Food from Grass-Land: a Lordship in Cambridgeshire.

Acres.		Profit.	Increase.
3000.	Say 1000 beasts cost 14*l.* each; weight in 30 stone, out 56 stone; increase 26 stone; sold for 21*l.*	£. 7000	lb. 364,000
	3000 sheep; weight in 16 lb. a quarter, out 20 lb.; increase 16 stone	1200	48,000
	Wool of ditto, at 3½ to a tod; say 856 tods, at 1*l.* 1*s.* or 9*d.* a pound	900	..
	Average profit, 3*l.* 8*d.* per acre.		
	Average animal food, 137 lb. per acre.		
	7000 acres to keep 24,500 sheep in summer.		
	In winter 5000		
	29,500		
	Of which,		
	20,000 shearlings will increase 20 lb. each	10,000	400,000
	4500 lamb-hogs, 12 lb. each	1350	54,000
	5000 winter stock, 6 lb. each	750	30,000
	29,500		
	200 store beasts, increase 10 stone each	700	28,000
	And the 24,500 summer stock will clip 3¼ to a tod, or 7000 tods of wool, at 1*l.* 1*s.*	7350	—
		29,250	924,000

---

* General Enclosure, p. 11.

Average,

10,000. Average, 2*l.* 18*s.* 6*d.* per acre.
Average of animal food, 92 lb. per acre.
Average rent per annum of said 10,000 acres, 18*s.* 6*d.* an acre, viz.

  Of the 3000 acres, 1*l.* 2*s.*
  Of the 7000 ditto, 17*s.*

18*s.* 6*d.* an acre rent, producing 92 lb. of food, is in the proportion of 5 lb. of meat for every shilling of rent*.

---

* Annals, Vol. XXXVIII.

No. XIX.

General Enclosure.

"The whole extent of these commons, I apprehend, does not comprehend more than 20,000 acres. The soil of a few of them consists of a poor cold loam; of others, of a wet stiff clay; but the principal part abound in gravel and sand. They are in general covered with furze, and fern, interspersed with patches of grass; and feed some lean cattle and poor half-starved sheep. If they were in a state of severalty, under proper systems of management, they might undoubtedly be made of great value. Enclosures would do much; industry and due attention to the natural produce, and what has been cultivated on similar soils in other places, would do more. Nature is a wise counsellor, and those who follow her advice, can, with the aid of art and observation, do wonders in agriculture.

" I shall here take the liberty of suggesting to the Honourable Board of Agriculture, the propriety of recommending to the Legislature a plan for a General Act of Enclosure, founded on the principles of Mr. GILBERT's Act for incorporating parishes for the support of the poor, so far as that Act relates to the calling a meeting, and determining by a majority of two-thirds in number and value of the occupiers, whether their common shall be divided; and if determined in the affirmative, then to proceed by appointing Commissioners, and expediting the business, as in cases where separate acts of parliament have been obtained*."

" At present, the expense of obtaining a separate Act, and of the proceedings of the Commissioners, is so large, as to deter many from such an undertaking. Where commons are small, they will probably long continue in their present unprofitable state, as it generally happens that some obstinate or selfish proprietor objects to an equitable and fair distribution, if there is not authority to enforce it.

" Were a General Enclosure Bill obtained, many thousand acres of naturally good land, would soon be changed from their present neglected and unprofitable state, to find employment and food for the people, of which we do not raise sufficient at this time for our consumption The bill should extend not only to wastes, but include common fields, common meadows, and an allotment or recompense to the claim of common right, during a certain part of the year; to a considerable quantity of rich meadows upon the Severn, the Avon, &c.†"

" There are many good and rich commons in Kendall, and the adjoining parishes, well worth enclosing; but the expense of obtaining the acts of parliament, and the Commissioners' charges in fixing the different allotments, prevent the owners from applying to parliament.

" H. ROBINSON,
" Minister of Kendall, Westmoreland."

" Could a General Enclosure Bill be devised, the writer

---

* Kent Report, p. 122. † EDW. HARRIES, Esq. of Shropshire.

has

has no doubt but that a general increase of produce would soon be experienced. In this dale we have several thousand acres of common pasture over-run with rushes, heath, and brushwood, that would be immediately enclosed, and consequently improved, by the exertions of the land-owners, and their tenants.—Though particular enclosures may have failed in these beneficial effects, it is to be attributed rather to the serious expenses of procuring a bill, and the unprincipled opposition of a few interested individuals, than the general bad policy of the measure.

" Jeff. Wood,
" Curate of Aysgarth, York

" *January* 31, 1801."

" In the best parts of this Riding, few open or common fields now remain, nearly the whole having long been enclosed; the moors and mountainous parts still remain in their original state; but such is the spirit of improvement, that were the many obstacles removed that oppose enclosures, no waste lands would long remain neglected, that were capable of cultivation: and even under all the present difficulties, several enclosures, under acts of parliament, have taken place. But since this Report was first drawn up, an almost total stop has been put to all improvements, and not more than one or two acts for enclosure in this Riding have been passed in 1797, 1798, and 1799*."

" At present, a notice of a petition to parliament, for the appropriation of unstinted commons, implies the watch-word havock!—he is the best fellow who gets the

---

* North Riding, York Report, p. 90.

most

most plunder. And until some general law of enclosure be established, this uncivilized mode of procedure must necessarily continue.

"The multiplication of statutes has ever been spoken of as an evil; and although public acts may in general be meant, private bills may properly be included. There needs no apology, therefore, for venturing to recommend one act of parliament which would preclude the passing of a thousand.

"Bills of enclosure must occupy much of the attendance of parliament, and divert their attention from matters of public importance. Besides, private interest, although it may not be able to exert its influence in parliament at large, it may be difficult to shut out entirely from its committees: but who can lower the dignity of parliament more than private interest being permitted, in any way, to warp its determinations?

"That a general bill of enclosure might be framed to answer the purpose of an equitable appropriation of commonable lands, in a much higher degree than has been, or perhaps ever can be obtained by separate bills, appears to my mind indisputable; and why such a measure has not long ago been adopted, would be difficult for any man out of parliament to conceive.

"It would be improper in me to dictate to parliament, and might be wrong to offer my sentiments too freely in this place, but having ventured to censure the present mode of enclosure by act of parliament, it is incumbent on me to convey some idea of what I conceive would be an improvement,

"In every township, four distinct interests claim a right of sharing in its commonable lands: namely, lands, houses, tithes, and the lordship. The two former have a benefit in commons in their open state; but the benefit of of the other two arises solely out of the enclosure*. Hence it follows, that it is the consent and approbation of the two former interests which ought to be obtained previous to a change from the open to the enclosed state; for the two latter may be supposed to be always ready to receive proposals for an enclosure.

"It has already been seen, that when the tithe and lordship are able to draw over to them a third interest, they can gain the desired point. But the evil effect of enclosures thus conducted has also been seen. Therefore, in fixing a general rule for the quantity of appropriation requisite to an enclosure, the other interests are more particularly to be attended to.

"Were the lands and the houses equally situated with respect to the commons to be enclosed, a majority of each might be sufficient. But this not being the case in any township, a larger proportion seems necessary. Three-fourths might in many cases be too small; but as enclosures are, in all human probability, beneficial to the public, it might be impolitic to fix it higher.

"Thus it appears to me, that in framing a general law of enclosure, three-fourths in value of the land, and three-fourths in number of houses, with the consent of the lord of the soil, ought to be considered as the requisite quantity of approbation.

"The quantity of right of the several interests, and of the individuals of each interest, has been already discussed: and although the present sketch may not afford sufficient matter for the completion of the general law proposed, I am clearly convinced that, without any ex-

---

* The tithe of wool, lambs, and milk, only excepted; articles of small value, compared with the tithe produce of lands in a state of cultivation.

traordinary exertion of study or application, such a law might be formed.

"Unstinted commons would constitute the principal object of the bill; but stinted commons, common fields, common meadows and every class of special matter respecting enclosures, might be included and provided for.

"Authorized and guided by a general law of this nature, the business of enclosure would be safe and easy. Every man, before he set out, would know with certainty his proportional share; and the act would empower the several interests to make choice of Commissioners to secure to them their respective rights.

"Numberless enclosures remain yet to be made; and it were much to be regretted, that the attention of parliament should be so unprofitably employed; and that the property of individuals should be subjected to so much hazard, as it is to be feared they will be, while common lands are continued to be appropriated by separate bills, without any established principles of enclosure*."

"Mr. FORSTER, a gentleman very intelligent in husbandry, at Royston, lamented the great inconvenience of open fields, pleading strenuously for a general enclosure. He cannot sow turnips in the open fields, without leave from the parish flock-master, and pays 1s. 6d. an acre to the shepherd for not eating the crop, as there are scarcely any sheep kept but on the parochial flock farms; and on their chalky lands they are bound by the common course, to fallow land to which much ploughing is injurious to a very great degree, making that lighter, which is too light already. Most of their straw they are at present forced to send to inns, to take the dung, whereas, if the lands

---

* Marshall's York, vol. i, p. 100.

were enclosed, it would be more profitable for the farmers to have stock of their own*."

" The preceding cases are sufficient to shew that enclosing has gone on as well in Hertfordshire, as we have any reason to expect in a county so generally enclosed of old time. There remains, however, much to be done in the northern part of the county; and there are smaller scattered common fields in many other parts, with extensive commons also in the western district. Many of them are too small to pay the expense of a distinct act of enclosure, but all would be properly cultivated under the sanction of a general act*."

---

* Hertford Agriculture, p. 48.

County Reports.

The means of effecting a General Enclosure of all the open fields and commons in the kingdom, is a subject highly deserving the attention of the Board; and very fortunately for the future attainment of so great an object, the Reports abound with numerous calls from every part of the kingdom, on the Legislature, to take so important a matter into their deliberation. Nor ought it to escape notice, that every one of these Reports that touch upon this business, recommend the same measure; and coming not always as the opinion simply of the respective Surveyors, but collected from the most intelligent persons there met with, it deserves no inconsiderable attention. The measure is a General Act, that shall render separate applications to Parliament for every parish unnecessary. The expense attending Bills of this sort, whether contested or not, are very great, and in some cases enormous; arising from the question being evidenced, debated, and decided in the capital, under the unavoidable delays which business of greater consequence, and other circumstances, will necessarily occasion.

By giving this power to some judicature already established, like the court of Quarter Sessions, or to a jury of the vicinage, summoned by the Sheriff; a great part of such expense and delay might be saved; the smallest commons would become objects of improvement as well as the largest; and the proprietors of all would be much less ready to oppose such propositions, when they had no longer reason to dread such heavy expenses as sometimes render

render their views of reimbursement, uncertain and remote.

The intelligence with which the County Reports to the Board of Agriculture abound, upon this very important subject, is various and interesting; and so uniform in every part of the kingdom, that there seems but one voice to condemn the common and open-field system, to represent the unquestionable benefits of several and distinct property, and to call upon the Board to make the most energetic efforts to procure a General Act, that shall prevent the necessity of any future application to the Legislature.

Dorset.

Very valuable tracts of common land, of horse and cow-leas, which yield now 7*s.* or 8*s.* an acre, would, if divided, become worth 18*s.* or 20*s.* To effect such divisions, something is wanting less expensive than an Act of Parliament, which often defeats the improvement by the heavy charge incurred; seldom less than 300*l.* or 400*l.* besides the risk of not succeeding.

Bedford.

A well digested General Bill, for the Enclosure of common fields, commons and waste lands, would wonderfully operate towards the success of Enclosures.

Carmarthen.

The great impediment is the difficulty of obtaining separate Acts of Parliament for every Enclosure: to remove this difficulty, would be one of the most popular and beneficial undertakings in which the Board could engage.

Intelligent

Intelligent persons think that an Act should be passed to empower the Custos of each county, with the Magistrates assembled in Sessions, to appoint Commissioners. It is generally believed in this county, that such an Act would be the means of enclosing every acre of waste land in South Wales (capable of cultivation) in a very few years.

Cumberland.

Enclosures would be a source of great improvement, could it be done at a moderate expense: the charge of obtaining an Act of Parliment, and the various additions made thereto by the practitioners of the law, are in some cases three or four times more than all the other expenses put together. Surely this might be avoided by a General Act.

Durham.

Some general law or process of light expense, for the division of unenclosed lands, is a frequent and fervent wish among the proprietors, and the most intelligent farmers of this county.

Hunts.

A well-digested General Bill for the Enclosure of common fields, commons and waste lands, would wonderfully operate towards the success of Enclosure.

Lancaster.

Great is the want of a General Enclosure Bill, to facilitate the troublesome business of enclosing, and render it more expeditious and less expensive.

There are many thousand acres capable of being cultivated, and made into either arable, pasture, or meadow land, of a very good quality, provided these wastes were enclosed, divided and improved; and, to effect this, there is neither want of inclination nor spirit among the inhabitants. But there is a want of a General Enclosure Bill to facilitate that troublesome business, and render it more expeditious and less expensive.

Middlesex.

The expense, inconvenience, and difficulty of obtaining separate Acts of Parliament, are found to be so burthensome, as to prevent Enclosing. The unanimous opinion among all who have paid attention to it is, that one General Act should empower the enclosure and division, without separate application.

Norfolk.

Enclosing found to be of such immense consequence, that every obstruction much wanted to be removed. One general Act of Parliament, under which any parish that would agree in itself, should be able to effect it. The great expense of separate bills operate as a powerful discouragement: for, in the course of obtaining the Bill, the evidence must go up to town, and attend a Committee of the Commons; afterwards be sworn at the Bar of the Lords, and attend their Committee also. And as these attendances are often at intervals considerably distant from each other, the evidence must, all this time, either be supported in town, at a great expense, or make three or four journies; and as this sort of evidence is generally given by professional men, whose time is valuable,

these

APPENDIX. 389

these delays are very inconvenient, and frequently operate so powerful upon the minds of the people, that many an Enclosure is passed over, which would otherwise be effected. This in a great measure will account for so many of our commons and common fields having remained so long in their present state.

Rutland.

Highly to be lamented, that an Act of Parliament should be made so expensive, as the advantages of Enclosing are so great to the national interests.

Pembroke.

The great trouble and enormous expense attending the present mode of applying to parliament for enclosure and draining bills, is known to be a very great hinderance to the improvement of waste lands. People of small fortune dread the expense of these applications so much, that they will rather permit their interest in waste lands, to lie dormant, than subject themselves to an expense they are unable to bear. To remedy this evil would be a most popular and beneficial undertaking. A General Act should empower the Custos of each county, with the Magistrates in Sessions, to appoint Commissioners to divide and enclose.

Westmoreland.

A General Enclosure Bill for the whole kingdom greatly wanted.

Northampton.

Northampton.

The great obstacle to Enclosure, is the difficulty and expense of procuring distinct Acts of Parliament.

Somerset.

It is a subject of regret and astonishment, that so few means have been devised by the Legislature, either to facilitate or extend its progress. How much is to be done this way, a General Enclosure Act, unfettered by tedious and expensive formalities, would speedily manifest. Such an Act might, without hazard of injury, be entrusted to a given number of Justices at the Quarter Sessions, to dispense its powers, and controul its execution.

Worcester.

More would certainly take place, were it not for the expense which attends the procuring of Acts of Parliament for that purpose.

York—North Riding.

The principal obstacle to the improvement of the moors, is the great expense of obtaining Acts of Parliament for the Enclosure. One open field of only 250 acres was made a few years since, and the expense of obtaining the Act alone, without any opposition, cost the proprietors 370*l.*

York—West Riding.

The expense of particular Acts impedes this great work.

APPENDIX. 391

It would be of great utility that a General Bill was passed for that purpose, as is already the case in Scotland, leaving it to the Judge Ordinary of the bounds, to put it in execution, when application for that purpose was made by any of the proprietors.

" On account of which difficulties, and its general benefits, surely it ought to be taken up as a national concern, and be freed from the great expense of soliciting and obtaining separate Acts of Parliament, by passing a General Bill, to empower a certain proportion of owners, according to the rental of their estates, to agree and enter upon enclosing, draining, and improving the common waste lands in the parish or parishes of, &c. &c. after having given regular notice of such resolution at the General Quarter Sessions, and having the same properly registered by the Clerk of the Peace. In which Act, each district containing lands to be enclosed, should be limited to not more than three parishes, and a due portion of land to be allotted to the poor in each parish, in lieu of ancient usage; the rest to be ordered and provided according to the tenor of particular Acts, or as the wisdom of parliament shall think fit. An indulgence of this kind was granted a few years since, in a general bill, for the better maintenance of the poor*."

" Was a General Bill for the Enclosure of Waste Lands, under proper restrictions, to be passed, the undertaking would be less formidable, as to expense, and be more readily put into practice by every class of owners and tenants. Many an idler would then be employed, and numbers of useful hands be diverted from a hazardous

---

* Remarks on the Expedience and Utility of Enclosing Waste Land, p. 4.

clandes-

clandestine traffic, to a certain comfortable subsistence. Extensive wastes would be duly apportioned into proper sized farms; farm-houses and cottages be erected; and national wealth and strength would consequently increase*."

---

* Remarks on the Expedience and Utility of Enclosing Waste Lands, p. 9.

THE END.

RENEWALS 458-4574
DATE DUE